The Cambridge Introduction to
Postmodernism

The Cambridge Introduction to Postmodernism surveys the full spectrum of postmodern culture – high and low, avant-garde and popular, famous and obscure – across a range of fields, from architecture and visual art to fiction, poetry, and drama. It deftly maps postmodernism's successive historical phases, from its emergence in the sixties to its waning in the first decades of the twenty-first century. Weaving together multiple strands of postmodernism – people and places from Andy Warhol, Jefferson Airplane, and magical realism to Jean-François Lyotard, Laurie Anderson, and cyberpunk – this book creates a rich picture of a complex cultural phenomenon that continues to exert an influence over our present "postpostmodern" situation. Comprehensive and accessible, this *Introduction* is indispensable for scholars, students, and general readers interested in late-twentieth-century culture.

Brian McHale is Arts and Humanities Distinguished Professor of English at the Ohio State University. He is the author of *Postmodernist Fiction, Constructing Postmodernism,* and *The Obligation Toward the Difficult Whole.* His articles have appeared in such journals as *Diacritics, Genre, Modern Language Quarterly, Narrative, New Literary History, Poetics Today, Style,* and *Twentieth-Century Literature.* He is currently coediting with Len Platt *The Cambridge History of Postmodern Literature.*

The Cambridge Introduction to
Postmodernism

BRIAN MCHALE

Ohio State University

CAMBRIDGE
UNIVERSITY PRESS

CAMBRIDGE
UNIVERSITY PRESS

University Printing House, Cambridge CB2 8BS, United Kingdom

One Liberty Plaza, 20th Floor, New York, NY 10006, USA

477 Williamstown Road, Port Melbourne, VIC 3207, Australia

4843/24, 2nd Floor, Ansari Road, Daryaganj, Delhi - 110002, India

79 Anson Road, #06-04/06, Singapore 079906

Cambridge University Press is part of the University of Cambridge.

It furthers the University's mission by disseminating knowledge in the pursuit of education, learning and research at the highest international levels of excellence.

www.cambridge.org
Information on this title: www.cambridge.org/9781107605510

© Brian McHale 2015

First published 2015

A catalogue record for this publication is available from the British Library

Library of Congress Cataloging in Publication data
McHale, Brian.
The Cambridge introduction to postmodernism / Brian McHale, Ohio State University.
    pages   cm
Includes bibliographical references and index.
1. Postmodernism (Literature)   2. Postmodernism (Aesthetics)   3. Post-postmodernism (Literature)   I. Title.
PN98.P67M38   2015
809'.9113–dc23   2015005130

ISBN 978-1-107-60551-0 Paperback

For Esther, fellow traveler

Contents

Figures

Acknowledgments

Where to begin? I'd better start with Ray Ryan of Cambridge University Press, who commissioned this book and whose patience I have sorely tried. At the outset I told him that writing this book would be quick and easy for me. I was wrong; it wasn't. Sorry, Ray.

After Ray, the deluge. First, abundant thanks to my interlocutors in the faculty modernist group, founded and hosted by Steve Kern, especially the regulars: Murray Beja, Kate Elkins, Ellen Jones, Jesse Matz, Bill Palmer, Jim Phelan, and Jessica Prinz. Most of them are my colleagues at Ohio State University. Others at Ohio State who have been generous with their feedback are John Hellman and Robyn Warhol. Farther afield, people who have invited me to present drafts of some of this material, who have vetted parts of the book, or who referred me to material that I would otherwise have overlooked include Louise Bethlehem, Amy Elias, Ellen G. Friedman, Mosik Gilad, Chaim Ginggold, Tami Hager, Luc Herman, John Hoppenthaler, Hu Quansheng, Kit Hume, Ty Miller, Clem Robyns, Mooky Ron, Shang Biwu, Anat Zanger, and Yael Zarhy-Levo. Thanks, too, to Roland Pease, formerly of Zoland Press, who helped me track down the Jean-Michel Basquiat image that I discuss in Chapter 3, and to Mike Bierschenk who helped prepare a useable image file. Bran Nicol, apart from being a generous reader of the whole manuscript, also called my attention to one particularly embarrassing blunder in time for me to correct it. Deepest gratitude all around.

I benefitted from a Faculty Professional Leave from Ohio State University in winter and spring of 2011, which allowed me to devote my full energies to developing this project.

Special thanks to our friends Amalia and Stanley Slater, who generously invited us to share a house in Puerto Rico for a couple of weeks in the winter of 2013, making it possible for me to write my way out of a particular impasse in this book. Not to mention the afternoons on the beach.

A tip of the hat to our daughters Lily and Alma and their dogs, Levon (after Mr. Helm) and Miss Moneypenny (after you-know-who). Levon, in particular, was a great help, because no matter how badly the writing has gone that day, a dog still needs walking.

Finally, no end of thanks to Esther Gottlieb, who put up with more than everyone else combined. Mood-swings, loss of self-confidence, failure of nerve, episodes of writer's block, spasms of megalomania – the whole spectrum. I literally can't thank her enough.

I have pilfered ideas, phrases, full sentences, and even a few intact paragraphs from my own publications, especially my essays "What Was Postmodernism?," *Electronic Book Review* (December 2007), http://www.electronicbookreview .com/thread/fictionspresent/tense; "1966 Nervous Breakdown, or, When Did Postmodernism Begin?," *Modern Language Quarterly* 69, 3 (September 2008); "Break, Period, Interregnum," in *Postmodernism, Then,* edited by Jason Gladstone and Daniel Worden, a special issue of *Twentieth-Century Literature* 57, 3–4 (Fall/Winter 2012); and "Postmodernism and Experiment," in *The Routledge Companion to Experimental Literature*, edited by Joe Bray, Alison Gibbons, and Brian McHale (Routledge, 2012). My thanks to the editors and publishers – Joe Tabbi of *ebr*, Duke University Press (publisher of *Modern Language Quarterly*), the editors of *Twentieth-Century Literature*, and Routledge – for their permission to reuse this material. I couldn't think of better ways to say what I had to say.

What Was Postmodernism?

1. Changing Tenses

> ... you've arrived too late, we are already beyond postmodernism, it's dead, dead and gone, don't you know, it's been buried, where have you been ... (Federman, 2001, 245; my ellipses)

What was postmodernism? It's the purpose of this book to answer that question as concretely and circumstantially as possible, but for now, just to get us started, a colorless and somewhat noncommittal answer will serve. Let's say, then, that postmodernism was the dominant cultural tendency (it might be safer to say *a* dominant tendency) during the second half of the twentieth century in the advanced industrial societies of the West, spreading eventually to other regions of the globe.

When future cultural historians look back on our era – provided that human beings even *have* a long-term future on this planet – it's not inevitable that they will identify late twentieth-century culture as "postmodern." Perhaps they will call it "Cold War culture," to capture the tension and turmoil that the global standoff of the period 1947–91 transmitted to contemporary cultural expression, or perhaps they will call it "neoliberal culture," to reflect the new global economic order that emerged in the seventies (see Chapter 3). Neither of these periodizing terms exactly corresponds to the temporal scope of "postmodern culture," however, which seems to predate neoliberalism and to persist beyond the collapse of the Soviet Union and the end of the Cold War in 1989–91 (see Chapter 4). Maybe future historians will make do with the rather drab and inexpressive "Postwar," or maybe they will follow Fredric Jameson, for whom postmodernism is "the cultural logic of late capitalism" (Jameson, 1991), and call it "late-capitalist culture."

Who and what were they, these postmoderns? It is tempting just to compile a list, and many have done so, the eclectic catalogue itself being a characteristically postmodern form. "Eclecticism," writes the philosopher Jean-François Lyotard mordantly, "is the degree zero of contemporary general culture: you listen to reggae; you watch a western; you eat McDonald's at midday and local cuisine at night; you wear Paris perfume in Tokyo and dress retro in Hong Kong; knowledge is the stuff of TV game shows" (Lyotard, 1993, 8).

Thus, Jameson (1991, 1–2) lists Andy Warhol and pop art; photorealist and "Neo-Expressionist" painting; the composers John Cage, Philip Glass, and Terry Riley; punk and New Wave music; the filmmaker Jean-Luc Godard and other cinema and video experimentalists (but also certain commercial movies, the ones that pastiche earlier cinematic styles); the writers William S. Burroughs, Thomas Pynchon, and Ishmael Reed; the French New Novelists (*nouveaux romanciers*) and their successors; the new kinds of literary criticism grouped under the category of "Theory" (see Chapter 3); and the postmodern architecture that derives from the theory and practice of Robert Venturi. Todd Gitlin, who is darkly skeptical of such lists ("as if culture were a garage sale"), nevertheless mentions, among many other things, "Disneyland, Las Vegas, suburban strips, shopping malls, mirror-glass building façades . . . the Kronos Quartet, Frederick Barthelme, MTV, 'Miami Vice,' David Letterman, Laurie Anderson, Anselm Kiefer, Paul Auster, the Pompidou Center, the Hyatt Regency" (Gitlin, 1988, 35, quoted in Frow, 1997, 27–8).

Most of the figures on these two lists appear in this book. So do many others. Writers who appear here include Kathy Acker, J. G. Ballard, John Barth, Christine Brooke-Rose, Italo Calvino, Angela Carter, Robert Coover, Don DeLillo, Philip K. Dick, Umberto Eco, William Gibson, Allen Ginsberg, Sarah Kane, Tony Kushner, Cormac McCarthy, James Merrill, Toni Morrison, Haruki Murakami, Gloria Naylor, Georges Perec, Richard Powers, Salman Rushdie, W. G. Sebald, Zadie Smith, Art Spiegelman, Ron Sukenick, David Foster Wallace, Marina Warner, Colson Whitehead, John Edgar Wideman, and "Araki Yasusada." Also making appearances are the pop musicians Bob Dylan, The Beatles, The Velvet Underground, Jefferson Airplane, David Bowie, Patti Smith, and R.E.M.; the avant-garde composers and performers Laurie Anderson, David Del Tredici and John Zorn; the architects Frank Gehry, Charles Moore, and Aldo Rossi; the theorists Jean Baudrillard, Francis Fukyama, Donna Haraway, George Landow, Larry McCaffery, and Michel Serres; the visual artists Matthew Barney, Jean-Michel Basquiat, Nan Goldin, William Kentridge, Alexis Rockman, David Salle, Sarah Sze, Camilo José Vergara, and Robert Yarber; and the film directors Kathryn Bigelow, Derek Jarman, Aki Kaurismäki, David Lynch, and Wim Wenders.

Among the schools, movements, and genres featured in this book are surfiction, metafiction, magical realism, the OuLiPo, Avant-Pop, cyberpunk science fiction in print and on the screen, graphic narrative, hypertext fiction, L=A=N=G=U=A=G=E writing, the Young British Artists (YBAs), the SoHo scene, Afrofuturism, Conceptual Writing, and Flarf. Some of these figures and tendencies are "postmodernist" in the fullest sense, while others, less fully postmodernist, nevertheless belong to the postmodern era, contributing to the dense weave of postmodern culture. If you connected up all these figures, as in a connect-the-dots puzzle, would a picture of the era's culture emerge? It is the hope of this book that it will.

> . . . now that postmodernism is dead, writers don't know how to replace it, the disappearance of postmodernism was devastating for the writers, but it was not surprising, it was expected to happen for some time, the last gasp happened the day Samuel Beckett changed tense and joined the angels, I can give you an exact date if you want to, postmodernism died because Godot never came . . . . (Federman, 2001, 245; first ellipsis is mine, second one is Federman's)

The term "postmodernism," which for a while – let's say, from the mid-seventies to the mid-nineties, at least – seemed indispensable for identifying contemporary culture, today seems increasingly irrelevant. For the sake of argument, let's assume along with Raymond Federman, from whom I have been quoting, that postmodernism itself, like Samuel Beckett, has "changed tense." The date on which Beckett himself "changed tense and joined the angels" – December 22, 1989, little more than a month after the fall of the Berlin Wall – seems too early, but never mind. Once, not so long ago, it seemed urgent to ask the question in the present tense, as the architecture critic Charles Jencks was still doing in 1986: *What Is Post-Modernism?* But by 1990, when John Frow first asked his version of the question, the tense had already changed: "What Was Postmodernism?"

It's a trick question. It has been asked before, about modernism, not postmodernism. The comparative literature scholar, Harry Levin, asked in 1960, "What Was Modernism?" Levin looks backward from the perspective of 1960 to the accomplishments of modernist writing around 1922, the year when Joyce's *Ulysses*, Eliot's *The Waste Land*, and Rilke's *Sonnets to Orpheus* were all published. Nineteen twenty-two was the year of Brecht's first play and the year that Proust died, leaving behind the manuscripts of the remaining unpublished volumes of his huge novel, *In Search of Lost Time*. Nineteen twenty-two, in other words, was something like the high-water mark of literary modernism. In characterizing the modernism of 1922, Levin signals that modernism belongs to history; it is no longer "now," no longer contemporary. He *periodizes* modernism, turning it into one period among others in the historical sequence. For Levin, writing in 1960, modernism has changed tense. Notable here is the forty-year time lag between modernism's peak moment and this moment of retrospective periodization: modernism can "appear" as a period only forty years after the fact, around 1960.

Now fast-forward thirty years to John Frow's essay, "What Was Postmodernism?" (1990, republished 1997). For Frow, the changed tense indicates not that postmodernism is "dead and gone," over and done with, but that it continues to obey the modernist logic of innovation and obsolescence. Postmodernism, in his view, is "precisely a moment of the modern" (1997, 36). Modernism is driven by the imperative to innovate, and every innovation is rendered obsolete by the next one, so that modernism is constantly distancing itself from its own most recent manifestation, which then "slides into the past" (1997, 31). Eventually, this relentless logic of *superceding oneself* requires that modernism itself becomes obsolete, necessitating a successor – a *post*modernism.

If postmodernism is modernism's successor, made necessary by the very logic of modernism, then how does it differentiate itself from its predecessor? Since modernism's determining feature, according to Frow, is its form of temporality – its ever-renewing newness and "nextness" – then postmodernism can only differentiate itself by adopting a *different* temporality from modernism's (1997, 36). One option might be to adopt a temporality of *stasis* in contradistinction to modernism's dynamism – either in the form of a static neoclassicism (a version favored by Charles Jencks in his various accounts of postmodern architecture; see Chapter 1), or in the form of apocalypse and the end of history (see Chapter 5 and "Ruins"). Alternatively, postmodernism might attempt to outstrip modernism by adopting an even more frantic pace of innovation and obsolescence, speeding up the cycle until it approached the seasonal rhythm of fashion (Frow, 1997, 38).

There is evidence of *all* of these temporalities in postmodernist practice: stasis, apocalypse, speed. However, there is also compelling evidence of yet another alternative, that of multiple and uneven times, or nonsynchronicity (Frow, 1997, 9, 42). Despite being each other's contemporaries in the everyday sense, not everyone who lived during the postmodern decades were fully postmoderns; some were, but others were moderns or premoderns, or some combination of these. Modernisms, postmodernisms, premodernisms, perhaps para-modernisms all coexisted. This approach sharply contradicts certain formidable theorists of postmodernism, including Jencks, but especially Jameson, who holds the view that postmodernism is a sort of blanket *condition*, that it constitutes a really "big tent," extending right across the whole culture, covering all genres and media, all disciplines of thought, all forms of practice and behavior. However, this seems not to have been the case; rather, the culture of the late twentieth century appears in hindsight to have been *unevenly* postmodern.

The logic of "uneven development" implies that just as the world's regions are in some respects out of synch with each other, so too are different cultural domains even within the same region. Not every domain "postmodernizes" itself, and even the ones that do, don't all do it at the same time or in the same way. Some fields postmodernize sooner, others later, after a lag, others not at all. There is no a priori reason to assume that "postmodernism" means the same thing from one domain to the next, that it is one and the same everywhere. This is because, even if it is driven by the (presumably uniform) "cultural logic" of a historical moment or economic system, cultural change is *also* driven by the internal dynamics of specific fields, differing from field to field. Pursuing this unevenly distributed postmodernism, the present book ranges freely across many fields of post-modern culture – including the visual arts, architecture, film, and television, music, popular culture, digital media, and "theory." It remains grounded, however, in imaginative literature, where my expertise is strongest, and where (arguably) the distinctiveness of postmodernism is most readily demonstrated and grasped. Its center of gravity is the Anglophone world, but it will also look further afield to forms of postmodern cultural expression elsewhere.

> It was sad to see postmodernism disappear before we could explain it, I kind of liked postmodernism, I was happy in the postmodern condition, as happy if not happier than in the previous condition, I don't remember what that was called but I was glad to get out of it, and now here we are again faced with a dilemma, what shall we call this new thing towards which we are going, this new thing I haven't seen yet . . . .
> (Federman, 2011, 245; my ellipsis)

The term and concept "postmodernism" began to lose traction around the beginning of the new millennium – which doesn't imply that until then it was accepted without question; far from it. Everything pertaining to postmodernism – its scope, its provenance, its onset, its seriousness and value, its politics, its very existence – had been a matter of fierce controversy throughout the three or four decades during which the term flourished. Ironically, perhaps the only consensus that has ever been reached about postmodernism has to do with its *end*: postmodernism, it is generally agreed, is now "over." This means that we are now, perhaps for the first time, in a position to *periodize* post-modernism in something like the way that Harry Levin and others were able to periodize modernism around the year 1960. Jeffrey Nealon reminds us that Fredric Jameson's seminal essay "Periodizing the 60s" dates from the year 1984,

> suggest[ing] that only from after the end of an epoch can one begin to size the era up historically or begin to "periodize" it . . . . It is precisely from the boundary of a historical period, from inside its continuing end or closure, that one might hold out some retroactive or retrospective hope of naming what happened there. (Nealon, 2010, 10)

That is the hope of this book: that now finally, some thirty years later, we are distant enough from the peak years of postmodernism to undertake a retrospective synthesis of that era and its products – something like a comprehensive introduction to postmodernism.

2. Coming Attractions

The Cambridge Introduction to Postmodernism is structured around a fundamental distinction between historical *breaks* and *continuities* – between subperiods and period-straddling developments. This distinction, or something like it, is basic to all periodization, indeed to all historical reflection (see Jameson, 2002, 24, 33). On the one hand, to identify a period is to posit one or more historical discontinuities, breaks from what came before and from what comes after. On the other hand, not only does the integrity of a period depend on continuities right across the period, but no period is airtight or freestanding, and continuities can always be identified with periods that precede and follow, and even with periods quite distant in time. These basic conditions of all periodization are acutely heightened in the case of postmodernism, where the dialectic of break and continuity is inscribed in the term itself: *post*modernism, that is, a break from the modernism of the preceding era, but also post*modernism*, that is, somehow continuous with modernism after all – more-modernism, Modernism 2.0.

Reflecting this dialectic of break and continuity, each of the *Introduction*'s main chapters comprises two parts, one of them addressing a particular historical *moment, phase*, or *episode* in the development of postmodernism, emphasizing its differences from what came before and after, the other addressing a particular *continuity* across this phase, connecting it with prior and subsequent phases, and even with historically more distant eras.

Chapter 1, "Before Postmodernism," addresses postmodernism's precursors, both distant and more immediate. The four main chapters each key on one of the four successive phases that I discern in postmodernism. Chapter 2,

"Big Bang, 1966," explores the onset phase, which I date from the mid-sixties. Postmodernism's major or "peak" phase, 1973–89, is the subject of Chapter 3. Next follows an "interregnum" or "in-between" phase of uncertainty and reorientation, roughly coinciding with the nineties, the subject of Chapter 4. I conclude with a coda that addresses the immediate aftermath of postmodernism, a phase dating from about 2001.

Juxtaposed with each of these subperiods, or moments of break, is a period-straddling development of longer duration. Each of these developments comes into its own in the particular moment with which it is juxtaposed, or otherwise reflects or typifies that moment. Thus, postmodernism's onset in the mid-sixties is juxtaposed with a survey of late-twentieth-century versions and remediations of Lewis Carroll's *Alice* books, which undergo a surprising revival and reorientation around the year 1966, and then persist as a presence in postmodern culture right down to the present. The phase of "peak" postmodernism in the seventies and eighties is coupled with an account of the changing fortunes of Shakespeare's *The Tempest*, which by the end of the eighties would become something like a hallmark or yardstick of literary and cinematic postmodernism. Coupled with the "interregnum" phase will be the perennial figure of the angel, which achieves an unprecedented degree of cultural penetration and ubiquity in the nineties. Finally, paired with the aftermath phase will be the imagery of ruins, a venerable motif newly reimagined and reinterpreted in the post–September 11 era.

Chapter 1

Before Postmodernism

1. Postmodernism and Its Precursors

What was new about postmodernism? How new was it? In the days when postmodernism was still controversial, one frequently heard objections along the lines of, "Postmodernism – it's all been done before" or "It all derives from [fill in the blank]." A favorite candidate for filling in that blank was Friedrich Nietzsche, the late-nineteenth-century German philosopher whose radical skepticism certainly informed the poststructuralist theories of Michel Foucault, Gilles Deleuze, and many others from the sixties on (McGowan, 1987, 70–88). But the hypothesis of a Nietzschean origin, or any other philosophical origin for that matter, rests on the assumption that postmodernism is essentially a philosophical tendency, identifiable with what would come to be called "Theory." This assumption is at odds with my own sense of postmodernism as essentially an aesthetic and cultural tendency, of which the emergence of Theory is just one indicator among others (see Chapter 3).

As for the objection that "it's all been done before," here the objectors were abetted by the *retro* orientation of some varieties of postmodernism, manifested in the recycling, rewriting, pastiching, or parodying of historical styles, genres, or even specific texts (see "Alice" and "Prospero's Books"). Further corroboration could be found in postmodern architecture's revival of certain features of classical style, typically with an ironic twist. Classical architecture's "universal grammar and syntax" of columns, arches, domes, and decoration (Jencks, 1984, 147) was a conspicuous feature of such characteristic postmodern buildings as Michael Graves's Portland Public Services Building (1980–82), James Stirling's Neue Staatsgalerie in Stuttgart (1977–84) and Charles Moore's Piazza d'Italia in New Orleans (1976–79) (see "Ruins"). But ironic neoclassicism was only one strain of postmodern architecture, "one style among several: not the sole approach but the most public one" (Jencks, 1984, 164), and it played little role outside architecture.

A favorite case in point, among those who contended that it has all been done before, was Lawrence Sterne's novel *The Life and Opinions of Tristram Shandy, Gentleman* (1759–67). Metafiction (reflection on the text's fictional status), critifiction (writing about novel writing *in* a novel), breaking through the "fourth wall" to address the reader, fragmentation and lack of closure, encyclopedic scope, unstable irony, manipulation of the material resources of the printed book (typography and spacing, diagrams, blank, black and marbled pages) – it's all here in this eighteenth-century novel, 200 years before anybody ever called anything *postmodernist*. What's new in postmodernism if Sterne already did it all? Doesn't postmodernism just *repeat Tristram Shandy*, and other books like it (Rabelais's *Gargantua and Pantagruel*, Cervantes's *Don Quixote*, Swift's *A Tale of a Tub*, etc.)?

Yes, but.

Viktor Shklovsky once provocatively claimed that *Tristram Shandy* was "the most typical novel in world literature" (Shklovsky, 1990 [1929], 170), but of course the point of his provocation was that it is *not* typical at all, from the point of view of canonical literary history. Perhaps it *ought* to be regarded as "most typical" because of the way it exposes the conventions and devices of the novel genre, laying them bare for our inspection, but in fact it stands well off to one side of the literary-historical mainstream – marginal, eccentric, a special case. Try this thought experiment: what would the history of the novel look like if *Tristram Shandy* really *were* regarded as typical – if its place were securely in the middle of the mainstream, instead of being relegated to one of the side channels? That would be literary history as seen from the perspective of postmodernism.

The logic here is that of a celebrated essay by the twentieth-century Argentine writer Jorge Luis Borges. Borges, a seminal figure for postmodernism, claims in "Kafka and His Precursors" (1952) to have detected a series of precursors for the deeply paradoxical writings of Franz Kafka. But what a strange genealogy he traces: from Zeno's paradox to a text by a ninth-century Chinese writer to a pair of parables by Kierkegaard and a poem by Robert Browning to a story by the French novelist Léon Bloy and another by the British fantasy writer Lord Dunsany. These heterogeneous texts, spread across centuries, have little in common with each other, but each has something in common with Kafka: "Kafka's idiosyncrasy, in greater or lesser degree, is present in each of these writings, but if Kafka had not written we would not perceive it; that is to say, it would not exist" (Borges, 1964, 108). Reading *backward* from Kafka, we detect a Kafkan strain in these precursor texts that would not be visible *without* the perspective afforded by Kafka. That is the meaning behind the ordering of the nouns in Borges's title: Kafka first, then his precursors afterwards. "Each writer *creates* his precursors," Borges concludes. "His work modifies our conception of the past, as it will modify the future" (Borges, 1964, 108).

Tristram Shandy is a precursor of postmodernism – postmodern "before the fact," as we sometimes say. However, if postmodernism had never emerged, would we be able to detect the precocious postmodernism of Laurence Sterne? Or is Sterne's precociousness actually a *product* of the postmodernism that he supposedly prefigures and preempts?

Granted, this is a strange way to write literary history: in reverse, backward. Nevertheless, the principle of reverse-genealogy proves to be a powerful tool for reimagining precursor works in light of the postmodern present, as in projects such as the academic volume *Postmodernism Across the Ages* (Readings and Schaber, 1993) – the title alone signals historical paradox – or Steven Moore's alternative history of the novel (Moore, 2010, 2013). Moore, a scholar of twentieth-century literature, ranges backward in time as far as the novel's origins in the ancient world, and finds everywhere the traces of a tradition different from and parallel to the canonical story of the "rise of the (realist) novel" in eighteenth-century bourgeois culture. Apuleius, author of *The Golden Ass* (2nd century B.C.E.), is "a postmodernist *avant la lettre*" (Moore, 2010, 109); the eleventh-century Japanese novelist Lady Murasaki, author of *The Tale of Genji*, exhibits an "attitude toward fiction [that] sounds positively postmodern" (2010, 552); Henry Mackenzie's *The Man of Feeling* (1771) is "more like a postmodern novel than a premodern one" (Moore, 2013, 866). The German novelist Grimmelshausen's character Simplicius (1668) reminds Moore of Slothrop in Thomas Pynchon's postmodern novel *Gravity's Rainbow* (1973), while Charles Sorel's *L'anti-roman* (*The Anti-Novel*, 1633–34) reminds him of the postmodern fiction of Gilbert Sorrentino (Moore, 2013, 66, 191). Voltaire anticipates Kurt Vonnegut, Jr. (2013, 363), the seventeenth-century Chinese masterpiece *The Tower of Myriad Mirrors* anticipates "[Lewis] Carroll, Freud, Kafka, Jung, and Borges" ([CE] Moore, 2013, 450), and Swift's *Gulliver's Travels* (1726) anticipates William S. Burroughs's *Naked Lunch* (1959), Vonnegut's *Slaughterhouse-Five* (1969), and Hunter S. Thompson's *Fear and Loathing in Las Vegas* (1972) (2013, 694). *Don Quixote* introduces metafiction (Moore, 2010, 5) and Samuel Richardson, among others, practices it (2013, 713). Henry Fielding, Charlotte Lennox, and many others in Britain in the eighteenth century practice critifiction (2013, 758, 774), but so does at least one Japanese novelist around the year 1200 (2010, 580).

And so on, across the ages and around the world. This is, in one sense, sheer, irresponsible anachronism, but in another sense, Moore is reverse-engineering an alternative literary history, one in which *Tristram Shandy* would figure centrally rather than on the margins (Moore, 2013, 813–16) – one in which postmodernism creates its own precursors, modifying the past retrospectively.

To put it another way: Moore is revisiting the "tradition of learnéd wit" that he himself identified (Moore, 1986), running from Petronius's *Satyricon* through Rabelais, Swift, *Tristram Shandy, Moby-Dick*, and *Ulysses* down to postmodern novels such as *Gravity's Rainbow*, Sorrentino's *Mulligan Stew*, David Foster Wallace's *Infinite Jest*, Mark Z. Danielewski's *House of Leaves*, and beyond (Moore, 2013, 48, 634, 941–2). That tradition overlaps in part with the one mapped by the Soviet-era Russian literary historian Mikhail Bakhtin (1984 [1929, 1963], 112–32), who traced the roots of the novel back to popular carnival practices, which left their imprint on the ancient genre of Menippean satire. It is the Menippean genre, reconstituted at intervals over the course of literary history – in the middle ages, then again in the Renaissance (Rabelais, Cervantes, Grimmelshausen), then later in the fiction of Swift, Voltaire, Sterne, and others – that transmits carnival attitudes, practices, and motifs down to the modern novel. Bakhtin ends his history with Dostoevsky; in effect, he reads history backward to create a reverse-genealogy of Dostoevsky's fiction, just as Moore reads backward to create the alternative history that culminates in postmodernism.

Other alternative histories leap into view when we read backward from postmodernism. For instance, postmodern performance art seems to revive the dramaturgy of seventeenth-century Stuart court masques. Ranging from the Happenings and Fluxus events of the fifties through the "actions" of Viennese Actionism and the street and guerilla theater associated with anti–Vietnam War protests, down to Robert Wilson's theater of images, Laurie Anderson's multimedia performances, and Matthew Barney's *Cremaster* films, postmodern performance is too various for easy generalization, but much of it involves spectacle, mixed media, weak or incidental narrative, and often some degree of audience participation. The Stuart masques combined music, dance, allegorical verse drama, and the most advanced theatrical devices of their time, and brought actual courtiers onstage as actors and dancers. Masques were ephemeral in every respect – unrepeatable gestures of conspicuous consumption, meant to be staged only once or twice, but also short-lived as a genre, rendered abruptly obsolete by the English Civil War. However, their DNA survived in various offshoots and analogues – pageants, masquerades, holiday pantomimes, fantastic operas – and it is perhaps through these channels that masque practices came to inform postmodern performance. However it was transmitted, the masque genre seems to be everywhere in postmodernism, not only in performance art but even in narrative texts like Sorrentino's "Masque of Fungo" (incorporated in *Mulligan Stew* [1979]), James Merrill's narrative poem *Scripts for the Pageant* (1980), and John Ashbery's prose "Description of a Masque" (1984) (see "Prospero's Books").

Read in reverse, theater history is retrospectively reshaped, and court masque becomes an unlikely precursor of postmodernism. Similar reconfigurations emerge when we read the history of poetry in reverse. Viewed from the perspective of postmodern practices of concrete, shaped, visual, illegible, and erased poetry (Dworkin, 2003; McHale, 2005; Bray, 2012), an alternative tradition of pattern poetry comes to light (Higgins, 1987). Widely distributed in space and time, from Western Europe to India and China, and from the Hellenistic era to the Latin Middle Ages to the baroque period and the experimental fringes of modernism, pattern poems have rarely been admitted to the literary canon. (George Herbert's shaped poems – "Easter Wings," "The Altar" – are the exceptions that prove the rule.) They constitute not so much a continuous tradition as disconnected episodes of experiment and innovation. Or rather, they *do* constitute a tradition, but only retrospectively, from the moment that concrete poetry and other postmodern practices turn them into precursors.

Another postmodern poetic practice, that of *procedural writing*, has even more radical retrospective consequences. Involving the implementation of predetermined *rules* or *constraints*, proceduralism is practiced in a variety of ways by poets ranging from the New York School and the OuLiPo group beginning in the fifties (see Chapter 2) to the L=A=N=G=U=A=G=E poets in the seventies and eighties (see Chapter 3) to the Conceptual and Flarf writers around the turn of the millennium (see Chapter 5). Postmodernist procedural poetry sheds a new and estranging retrospective light on past poetries of formal constraint (McHale, 2000b). Haiku and tanka in the Japanese tradition, sonnets, sestinas, canzones, and villanelles in the Western tradition, and all the other complicated fixed forms that have emerged over the long history of poetry, appear in this estranging perspective as *procedures*, anticipating the proceduralism of the postmodernist schools. The OuLiPians, in their slyly self-mocking way, would call all these fixed forms *anticipatory plagiarism* (Mathews and Brotchie, 1998, 207–8): plagiarism of OuLiPian practices, but *in advance,* ahead of time. Not only fixed forms, but even rhyme and meter, all the traditional apparatus of poetry, now appear in retrospect as anticipation of postmodernism – which is what happens when literary history is read in reverse.

2. Changing Dominants

Demanding closer attention is the relationship between postmodernism and its immediate precursor – modernism. After all, that relationship is inscribed in the very term *postmodernism* itself: whatever the prefix *post-* means (merely *after*, or *consequently*?), postmodernism manifestly has *something* to do with modernism. Is it something *other* than modernism, or just a continuation of modernism into the second half of the century – more of the same? How one views the likelihood of postmodernism's *divergence* from modernism partly depends on one's sense of how different the late-twentieth-century world is from the early twentieth-century world in which modernism arose. If we are still essentially experiencing the same modern conditions, the same "modernity," that early twentieth-century thinkers, writers, and artists experienced and responded to – *A Singular Modernity*, as Fredric Jameson puts it (2002) – then perhaps it would make better sense to approach postmodernism as the persistence or renewal of modernism. However, if the experience of modernity has mutated into something else – call it "postmodernity" – then perhaps we should expect modernism, too, to mutate along with it.

The world obviously *did* change around mid-century, in multiple, complex ways, or at least the rate of change accelerated. Modernist-era world wars, fought with conventional weapons, gave way to regional conflicts, spasms of genocidal violence, international terrorism, and the perennial threat of nuclear annihilation. The old empires collapsed, giving way to neocolonial exploitation, and the former imperial subjects flooded into the European metropoles. Monopoly capitalism mutated into multinational capitalism and overheated consumerism. The powerful new modernist-era mass media (advertising, cinema, radio) ramified into an entire media ecology and a world saturated by simulations and virtual realities. New gender roles ("the New Woman") gave way to a postmodern proliferation of gender identities. The breakdown of the master narratives that had once structured nineteenth-century society, begun in the modernist era (Kern, 2011), continued and deepened, becoming a defining trait of the so-called postmodern condition. In short, since the conditions in which modernism arose in the first half of the twentieth century underwent so many changes in the second half of the century, it only stands to reason that art and culture would change, too, in order to keep pace with that changing world.

Changes in the world drove the pace of cultural change from *outside*, so to speak, but there were also mechanisms driving the pace from *inside*. Here, the case of literature, and the novel in particular, is revealing. When a literary genre has temporarily exhausted its possibilities, it renovates or replenishes itself by shuffling the hierarchy of its features, subordinating the features that had formerly been dominant, and promoting formerly subordinate features to positions of dominance (Jakobson, 2002 [1935]). This is what happened to the novel around mid-century: it underwent a *change of dominant*.

The modernist novel explored *interior experience*. A key constituent of much modernist fiction is embodied consciousness – the mind in its engagement with the world – which underlies and motivates many of modernism's experiments in narration, perspective, the representation of interiority, temporality, and language, as well as its problematizing of knowing and unknowing (Weinstein, 2005). Modernist fiction's dominant was *epistemological*, knowledge-oriented. Preoccupied with *what we know* and *how we know it*, with the accessibility and reliability of knowledge, it pursued epistemological questions.

Consider William Faulkner's canonically modernist novel *The Sound and the Fury* (1929). In successive chapters it dives into the interior monologues of three brothers, one of them an intellectually disabled adult, another an obsessed and suicidal adolescent, the third a crook and a liar, utterly unreliable. If interior monologue is one marker of this novel's modernism, another is its dislocation of time: the first chapter occurs on April 7, 1928, the third chapter on the day *before* that, the last chapter on the day *after*, but the second chapter flashes back eighteen years, to 1910. It should be clear, even from this cursory description, that *The Sound and the Fury* poses special challenges for the reader. It is notoriously difficult to read, taxing our ingenuity and interpretative resources to the utmost. We must read between the lines, fill in the gaps, link up widely dispersed details, solve puzzles, and distinguish solid clues from red herrings.

In short, it requires of us many of the same reading skills required by popular detective novels – not coincidentally, a genre that emerged contemporaneously with modernist fiction, in the first decades of the twentieth century. Crimes are committed in *The Sound and the Fury*, in fact, but solving them isn't really the point. The point, for the reader, is rather to try to fathom the novel's deeper mysteries: the mystery of the disabled brother's inconsolable sadness; the mystery of the suicidal brother's obsession; the mystery of the crooked brother's deceit, self-delusion and self-loathing; the mystery of the missing sister's hold on all of them. A modernist novel like *The Sound and the Fury* is a detective story, in a sense, but the detective is the reader. In the end, it is a novel about the difficulty of knowing anything for sure, or anything at all – an epistemological novel.

The modernist novel's radical exploration of epistemology, so conspicuously displayed in *The Sound and the Fury*, exhausted itself in the middle decades of the twentieth century, in such texts as Faulkner's *Absalom, Absalom!* (1936), Jean-Paul Sartre's *La Nausée* (1938), Samuel Beckett's *Murphy* (1938), Vladimir Nabokov's *The Real Life of Sebastian Knight* (1941), Malcolm Lowry's *Under the Volcano* (1947), and Alain Robbe-Grillet's *La Jalousie* (1957), among many others. What emerged from modernism's mid-century impasse was a different set of priorities for fiction. Already anticipated in the closing chapters of *Absalom, Absalom!* (McHale, 1987, 8–11), this new mode privileged questions of *world-making* and *modes of being* over questions of *perception* and *knowing*: It was *ontological* in its orientation, where modernism had been epistemological. Where modernism asked, "Who knows what, how do they know it, and how reliably?" the new mode – postmodernism – asked,"Which world is this? What is to be done in it? Which of my selves is to do it?" (Higgins, 1978, 101, quoted in McHale, 1987, 10).

The distinction was never absolute. Embodied consciousness persisted in postmodernist fiction, though it was relegated to the background. Modernist fiction also asked ontological questions alongside its epistemological questions, and postmodernist fiction continued to ask epistemological questions alongside its ontological ones. The difference was one of priority: in modernist fiction, epistemological questions take priority over ontological ones; in postmodernist fiction, it's the other way around. So the changeover from modernism to postmodernism isn't a matter of something absolutely new entering the picture, but of a reshuffling of the deck; what was present but "backgrounded" in modernism becomes "foregrounded" in postmodernism, and vice versa, what was "foregrounded" in modernism becomes "backgrounded" in postmodernism. To put it differently, what changed was the *dominant* – "the focusing component of the work of art," which "rules, determines, and transforms the remaining component" and "guarantees the integrity of the structure" (Jakobson, 2002 [1935], 82).

Embodied consciousness persisted in postmodernist fiction, though it was relegated to the background. However, postmodernist fiction did not take the world for granted as a backdrop against which the adventures of consciousness could be played out but rather foregrounded the world itself as an object of reflection and contestation through the use of a range of devices and strategies. Postmodernism multiplied and juxtaposed worlds; it troubled and volatilized them.

Compare *The Sound and the Fury* with Pynchon's *Gravity's Rainbow* (1973), a historical novel about the immediate aftermath of the Second

World War, the development of the V-2 rocket in the Third Reich, and the victorious Allies' scramble to obtain the German technologies and expertise that would form the basis of their space programs and of the prolonged nuclear standoff we call the Cold War. Like *The Sound and the Fury,* it involves multiple quests for knowledge. A number of characters are trying to find out what happened at the last launch of a V-2 by a rogue German rocket commander in the waning days of the war, while the novel's hero, an American lieutenant named Tyrone Slothrop, is trying to find out what was done to him in his infancy when he was handed over to a behaviorist psychologist for experimentation. However, something strange happens to these quests for knowledge in the course of the novel: they bog down in a proliferation of possibilities and alternatives; they dissolve in ambiguity and uncertainty; they lose their way.

Responsibility for this petering out of the novel's epistemological quests rests with the instability of its world. The world of *Gravity's Rainbow* is riddled with secondary worlds and subworlds, little enclaves of alternative reality, so many of them that in the end they fatally weaken and overwhelm the novel's "main" world. We slip in and out of movies and staged performances; indeed, the whole novel seems to collapse into a war movie on its last page. We fall into characters' hallucinations and fantasies, often without knowing that we've done so until much later; we mistake subjective realities for the outside world. Under such conditions, it's no wonder that quests for reliable knowledge run aground, and the novel's various detectives, Slothrop included, lose themselves in thickets of alternative reality and hallucination. Quests for knowledge succumb to the proliferation of worlds; questions of epistemology give way to questions of ontology: "Which world is this? What is to be done in it? Which of my selves is to do it?"

Pynchon achieves the full-blown postmodernism of *Gravity's Rainbow* not all at once, but in stages. He begins with a complicated but still recognizably modernist historical novel, *V* (1963), then makes the transition to postmodernism in *The Crying of Lot 49* (1966; see Chapter 2), before taking the final step in *Gravity's Rainbow* (see Chapter 3). Other writers follow a similar trajectory: Samuel Beckett, from the attenuated modernism of *Molloy* (1950), through the transitional stage of *Malone Dies* (1951) to the dizzying ontological puzzle of *The Unnamable* (1952); Vladimir Nabokov, from the modernism of *Lolita* (1955), through the finely balanced ambiguity of *Pale Fire* (1962) to the fabulous world-making of *Ada* (1969); Alain Robbe-Grillet, from *La Jalousie* (1957), a classic New Novel (*nouveau roman*), by way of *Dans le labyrinth* (1959) to *La Maison de rendez-vous* (1965), a *New* New Novel (*nouveau nouveau roman*), or in other words a postmodernist novel; Carlos Fuentes, from *La muerte de Artemio Cruz* (1962), an interior-monologue novel, by way of the ambiguous *Cambio de piel* (1967) to the alternate-history fantasia *Terra nostra* (1975); and so on (McHale, 1987, 12–25).

Other literary genres – let alone other art forms or media – are harder to fit into this tidy (perhaps overly tidy) picture of the change of dominant. Even poetry (or *especially* poetry?) proves less amenable to this kind of analysis than novels (McHale, 2004b). Nevertheless, if other forms of cultural expression undergo different processes of "postmodernization" than the novel, at different rates of change, with somewhat different starting points and endpoints, the changeover does seem to have been general, and to have climaxed (as I will argue in Chapter 3) sometime in the 1970s–80s. If the whole range of culture – architecture, dance, performance, the visual arts, the moving image, etc. – did not become postmodern all at once or all in the same way, it *did* eventually, somehow or other become postmodern.

3. The Last Avant-Garde

"A work can become modern only if it is first postmodern," J.-F. Lyotard once notoriously asserted; "postmodernism is not modernism at its end, but in a nascent state, and this state is recurrent" (Lyotard, 1993, 13). Some regard this, understandably, as a fatuous remark (e.g., Mepham, 1991, 145), or downright crazy (Jencks, 1986, 42), dismissing it as mere paradox-mongering. It *is* paradoxical and counterintuitive, but calculatedly so. Lyotard wants to provoke us to think about the way modernism, or even a *succession* of modernisms, is consolidated – the process by which certain works and tendencies are canonized, made integral to our picture of "the modern," while others are left out, too radical or deviant or just too intransigently odd to assimilate. It is these leftovers that remain available for use as models in the *next* phase of culture – the *next* modernism, including postmodernism. Postmodernism in this sense, thus, precedes the consolidation of modernism – it is modernism before it has been "edited," with the unassimilable parts left *in*.

For Lyotard "postmodernism" is the name for the avant-garde impulse *within* modernism. He identifies it with that part of modernist art that resists being domesticated and reduced to a familiar period style – the intransigent or intractable part of modernism. Not everyone agrees with Lyotard's conflation of the postmodern with the radical avant-garde, to say the least (see Chapter 3); nevertheless, he seems to have captured an important aspect of postmodernism's emergence. If the epistemologically oriented modernism described in the previous section represents something like *mainstream* modernism, then the avant-garde is that part of modern-era culture that could not be absorbed into the mainstream and was left out of that description. Missing from that description, for instance, was Gertrude Stein, the expatriate American writer, long-time resident of Paris, who tried to emulate the Cubist painting of her friend Pablo Picasso and his circle, but by using words, sentences, and paragraphs instead of paint and collage; Raymond Roussel, an eccentric poet, playwright and novelist, who devised elaborate procedures for producing texts that were utterly unpredictable and unprecedented; and the Dada artists of the Great War years, whose protest against the Europe-wide cultural suicide transpiring around them took the form of art that sought to destroy art itself. Artists and practices such as these, while contemporaneous with mainstream modernism, and overlapping with the mainstream in various ways – Stein's mentoring of the modernist writers and artists in Paris is a famous example – nevertheless got edited out of the modernist picture.

Which is what qualifies them to serve as models for postmodernism. Jameson calls Stein, Roussel, and Marcel Duchamp (a leading Dada figure) "genealogical precursors" of postmodernism and "outright postmodernists, avant la lettre" (Jameson, 1991, 4). Duchamp and Dada, modernist leftovers, become models in the post–Second World War years for various neo-avant-garde and neo-Dada tendencies (Miller, 2009), especially the Fluxus group, a loose international affiliation of musicians, writers, and performance and intermedia artists. Fluxus included, at one time or another, George Maciunas (Fluxus's founder), George Brecht, Joseph Beuys, John Cage, Robert Filliou, Al Hansen, Dick Higgins, Alison Knowles, Jackson Mac Low, Nam June Paik, Yoko Ono, Daniel Spoerri, and many others (see Chapter 2). As for Gertrude Stein, though a celebrity in her own time, she was not emulated as a writer until the emergence in the fifties of the New York School of poets (John Ashbery, Barbara Guest, Kenneth Koch, Frank O'Hara, James Schuyler), who like Stein before them were deeply influenced by the visual art of their contemporaries, especially the paintings of the Abstract Expressionists (Ward, 1993; Lehman, 1998). The New York School poets also participated in the rediscovery of Roussel, a precursor they shared with the avant-garde OuLiPo group in Paris (see Chapter 2).

Other neo-avant-garde tendencies of the fifties and sixties, while not so obviously modeled on particular modernist-era precursors, nevertheless emulated the avant-garde *attitude* of the earlier decades. They adopted a stance of *resistance* to contemporary culture and society, refusing to ingratiate themselves with their audience or even risking alienating it altogether through willful difficulty and obscurity or an aggressive tone and calculated offensiveness. This avant-garde of resistance took a somber, philosophical turn in Europe – understandably, given Europe's cata-strophic recent history. Thus, Samuel Beckett fed his own experience as a fugitive from the German occupiers of France into his avant-garde play *En attendant Godot/Waiting for Godot* (1953), launching the Absurdist tendency in world theater (Gavins, 2012). The German-language poet Paul Celan (born Paul Antschel), a Holocaust survivor, produced poetry that sought to express the inexpressibility of the Shoah, as did his Francophone counterpart Edmond Jabès, each by distinctive means – Celan by extreme difficulty and proliferating negatives, Jabès by erasure and blank space (McHale, 2005). A number of the postwar European avant-gardes, especially in French, were colored by the existentialist philosophy of Jean-Paul Sartre. Alternatively, as in the case of the *nouveaux romanciers* (Robbe-Grillet, Nathalie Sarraute, Michel Butor, Claude Simon, and others) and the *Tel Quel* circle (Phillipe Sollers, Julia Kristeva, Roland Barthes, and others; see Chapter 4), they reacted vigorously *against* existentialism (Marx-Scouras, 2012).

The postwar avant-gardes of resistance in the United States were generally more exuberant, energetic, even playful. Their campaign of resistance was fought on two fronts – against a timid and reactionary high culture, on the one hand, and the apparently irresistible rise of the mass culture of advertising, television and consumerism, on the other. The American avant-gardes of the fifties and sixties developed an aesthetics of *spontaneity* and *improvisation*, often modeled on contemporary jazz, just then entering its be-bop phase. This "culture of spontaneity" (Belgrad, 1998; Lee, 2012) is reflected in various ways in Abstract Expressionist painting, also called "Action" painting (Jackson Pollock, Willem DeKooning, Franz Kline, Mark Rothko, and others), in the writings of the irrepressible Beats (Jack Kerouac, Allen Ginsberg, William S. Burroughs, Lawrence Ferlinghetti, and others), and in the multifarious activities of the faculty and students at Black Mountain College. An experimental institution near Asheville, North Carolina, Black Mountain shaped or supported the work of composers and choreographers (John Cage, Merce Cunningham), poets (Charles Olson, Robert Creeley, Ed Dorn, Robert Duncan), and visual and conceptual artists of all kinds (John Chamberlain, Robert Rauschenberg, Cy Twombly, Ray Johnson).

Some of these avant-garde tendencies, victims of their own success, were ultimately absorbed into the culture they sought to resist – the Abstract

Expressionists into mainstream high culture of the museums and the universities, the Beats into the pop culture of television and celebrity. Others, such as the Black Mountain group, remained largely on the margins, forming a sort of permanent opposition to mainstream culture, high and low alike.

Sometime around 1958, according to Dick Higgins's dating, the postwar neo-avant-grade and neo-Dada movements achieved a kind of critical mass, and a corner was turned. That was the year, according to Higgins, when artists stopped asking "cognitive questions" – in effect, what I have been calling epistemological questions – and started asking "post-cognitive" ones instead (Higgins, 1978, 101) – ontological questions, in effect. Sally Banes places the threshold date a little later, around 1963, but she is looking at a somewhat different array of tendencies and practices than Higgins, namely the Greenwich Village avant-garde performance scene of the early sixties, which included Fluxus (Higgins's circle), but also groups like the Living Theatre, the Open Theatre and the Judson Dance Theater, and tendencies like Happenings, Pop Art and underground filmmaking (Banes, 1993). In neither case, Higgins's dating or Banes's, does the threshold date exactly coincide with the onset of postmodernism. Banes is especially clear on this point. The early sixties art scene "laid the groundwork," she writes, for "two distinct branches of vanguard art": on the one hand, the continuation of the avant-garde into the seventies; on the other, "the deeply ambivalent, ironic, reflexive art of the Eighties and Nineties" – what I will call "peak postmodernism" (Chapter 3).

Were these neo-avant-gardes, the ones that flourished in the fifties and sixties and then gave way to postmodernism, the "last avant-gardes," as some people have asserted (e.g., Lehman, 1998)? In other words, did Fluxus, the New York School, the Black Mountain group, the Greenwich Village experimentalists and the others represent the last occasion when artists *behaved* like the avant-gardists of the modernist era, forming communities, expressing solidarity, issuing manifestos, creating performance spaces and publishing venues, and so on? That doesn't quite appear to be the case. Later groups, notably the L=A=N=G=U=A=G=E writers, the Downtown artists of the eighties, and the apparently immortal and indestructible OuLiPo group, all behaved in exactly those ways, yet they all seem to me to belong to postmodernism (see Chapter 3).

So the postwar neo-avant-gardes don't appear to be the "last avant-gardes" after all. Nevertheless, there are important discontinuities between the postwar avant-garde episode and the postmodernism that arises in the sixties and peaks in the seventies and eighties. The postmodernism of the later decades does not seem to be a direct continuation of the avant-garde tendencies of the immediate postwar. Rather, those avant-gardes left to postmodernism a legacy in the form of a *toolkit* from which the postmoderns selected their own tools, taking them up, using and developing them in their own ways and for their own purposes. This inherited toolkit included, among other things, a deeply skeptical and ironic attitude toward both the prestige of high culture and the consumerist appeal of mass culture, balanced by an openness to using all kind of material, high and low; a willingness to override category distinctions among genres and media, and to mix and match them freely; a whole repertoire of procedures for producing texts and other artworks, including chance procedures, artificial rules and constraints, the use of "found" materials, procedures for cutting up and rearranging those materials, and so on; and, above all, extreme self-consciousness about art-making, a willingness to reflect on *everything* about the process and its products. These are among the tools with which postmodernism would be shaped.

Postmodernism is sometimes regarded (e.g., by Charles Jencks) as retreating or recoiling from avant-gardism, in favor of populism and accessibility. Conversely, it is, sometimes regarded (e.g., by J.-F. Lyotard) as the continuation of the avant-garde impulse by other means (McHale, 2012a). As well shall see, it is both.

Chapter 2

Big Bang, 1966

1. Crash

"Oh Mama, can this really be the end,/To be stuck inside of Mobile with the Memphis blues again?" Bob Dylan sings in one of his very greatest songs, released in 1966 on his ambitious double album *Blonde on Blonde*. The condition captured by the song, of being at an impasse, "stuck" in a place that is itself (punningly) "mobile," seems strangely at odds with Dylan's own hectic mobility over the previous year or so, during which he had literally electrified folk music at the Newport Folk Festival, toured the world relentlessly with his rock band (soon to be known simply as The Band), and recorded three landmark albums – *Bringing It All Back Home* and *Highway 61 Revisited* in 1965, then *Blonde on Blonde* – that not only propelled folk music into folk-rock but also made as strong a case as any to date for regarding rock music as art. Yet the immobilized blues singer of "Stuck Inside of Mobile" can't escape, can't even get a message through, can't hide, has no sense of time, and wants out (Marqusee, 2003, 194–5):

> And here I sit so patiently
> Waiting to find out what price
> You have to pay to get out of
> Going through all these things twice.
> Oh Mama, can this really be the end . . .   (Dylan, 1974, 38)

Dylan in 1996 seems so much an innovator, poised at the very *beginning* of something new, that one can't help but wonder what possible *end* he could be worrying about: the end of the tour? the end of the road? the end of the world? And what is it exactly that he wants to avoid repeating? Himself?

Ends and beginnings also preoccupy the other rock ensemble at the height of its powers in 1966 – The Beatles. Consider "Tomorrow Never Knows," the final track of The Beatles' own highly innovative album of that year, *Revolver*, the recording on which they invented not only the concept album but also psychedelic music (unless that actually happened on their single "Rain," recorded during the same sessions; LeBlanc, 2002, 202). Cribbing from *The Tibetan Book of the Dead*, his voice framed by a guitar solo played in reverse (Reising, 2002, 251), so that musical time literally runs backward, John Lennon sings here about "play[ing] the game existence to the end/Of the beginning" (Aldridge, 1991, 121).

The end of the beginning: in their songs of 1966 both Dylan and The Beatles seem uncannily to anticipate the break – breakthrough *and* breakdown – that they each underwent that year. Back home in Woodstock, New York, after his series of grueling and confrontational concerts backed by The Band, Dylan had some sort of motorcycle accident – how serious remains unclear (Hajdu, 2001, 292–5). Whether forced by his injuries to abandon touring for the time being or just using the accident as a pretext for doing so, he literally went underground, down into the basement studio of his band's house near Woodstock, to reacquaint himself with the raw materials of his own musical tradition (Marcus, 1997), emerging a year later having reinvented himself as a much sparer, more severe songwriter on *John Wesley Harding*: a new beginning. Like Dylan, The Beatles, too, stopped touring in 1966, after an unsatisfactory tour in North America and Asia; also like Dylan, they disappeared into the recording studio, reinventing themselves continually over the next several years, first of all as *Sergeant Pepper's Lonely Hearts Club Band*. Unlike Dylan, however, The Beatles never reemerged from the studio to perform together as a touring band: the end of a beginning.

Dylan's accident also interrupted publication of his book *Tarantula*, due to appear in 1966, but delayed until 1971 (Hajdu, 2001, 222). The story was different, and sadder, for Dylan's friend Richard Fariña, a fellow folksinger who performed and recorded with his wife Mimi, Joan Baez's sister. In 1966 Fariña finally published the novel he had been working on for several years, his first, called *Been Down So Long It Looks Like Up to Me*, and then shockingly was himself killed in a motorcycle accident after a book-signing party (Hajdu, 2001, 283–90). That same year, the poet Frank O'Hara, too, was killed in a motor-vehicle accident that changed forever the group identity and dynamics of the New York School of poets (John Ashbery, Barbara Guest, Kenneth Koch, James Schuyler, and a host of younger poets; see Lehman, 1998). Is it any wonder that the urban legend that "Paul is dead," which sprang up in 1969, fixed on 1966 as the date of Beatle Paul McCartney's allegedly fatal car accident?

"On or about December 1910," Virginia Woolf wrote of the onset of the modernist era, "human character changed." On or about the year 1966, something changed in culture; something ended and something else began. Major innovators at the cutting edge of popular music, Dylan and The Beatles, reoriented their careers, abandoning public performance – temporarily in one case, permanently in the other. The Canadian poet Leonard Cohen reoriented his career, too, but in the opposite direction, publishing his second and last novel, the difficult and controversial *Beautiful Losers*, in 1966, then renouncing literature for the life of a singer-songwriter. In the spring of the previous year, the leading pop artist Andy Warhol had announced his retirement from painting, the medium in which he had made his career (Warhol and Hackett, 1990, 113, 115). His retirement was only temporary as it turned out, but by 1966 Warhol had reoriented his art practice toward film, installation, and performance, "dematerializing" it in ways that would become increasingly typical of the fine arts in the later sixties and seventies (Lippard, 1997). Instead of making silkscreens, Warhol now ushered viewers into art environments, such as the roomful of shiny, bobbing, helium-filled pillows called *Silver Clouds*, perhaps anticipating what Fredric Jameson (1991, 101) would later call the "antigravity of the postmodern" and Milan Kundera, even more negatively, the "unbearable lightness of being" (see Chapter 4). Beginning in 1966, Warhol also staged mixed-media performances under the title of Exploding Plastic Inevitable, featuring collaborations with a short-lived rock band that would have an enormous impact in the long run, though its visibility was much lower in its own time than either Dylan's or The Beatles' – The Velvet Underground.

Fiction, too, underwent abrupt renunciations and changes of direction in or about the year 1966, and not just in the case of the songwriter-novelists Fariña and Cohen. With his novel of 1966, *The Crystal World*, the British New Wave science-fiction writer J. G. Ballard completed a tetralogy of science-fiction novels begun in 1962, in which he ended the world four times over, by air (*The Wind from Nowhere*), water (*The Drowned World*), fire (*The Burning World*, aka *The Drought*), and now finally earth. Having exhausted the four elements – and with them the venerable science-fiction *topos* of apocalypse – Ballard started over, reorienting his fiction. In 1966 he wrote the first of the stories that would form part of his innovative story cycle *The Atrocity Exhibition* (1969) (Ballard, 1990, 11, 83). In these stories Ballard developed a new style – dense, disjointed, and bristling with technical vocabularies – and introduced new themes of technological fetishism and perverse sexuality. His new approach would culminate in his notorious novel of eroticized auto accidents, *Crash* (1973), and would contribute to shaping the poetics of a younger generation of science-fiction writers, the cyberpunks (see Chapter 3).

Abrupt career changes, impasses and renunciations, interruptions and breakdowns, crashes literal and figurative, endings and beginnings: these are the hallmarks of the year 1966 at the cutting edge of culture. Nowhere is this pattern of interruption and breakdown more conspicuous than at the conclusion of what many regard as the signature novel of 1966, *The Crying of Lot 49*, by Richard Fariña's college friend and occasional sidekick, Thomas Pynchon (see Fariña, 1969). Pynchon's heroine, a suburban housewife named Oedipa Maas, has inadvertently uncovered what she suspects might be a centuries-long international conspiracy to subvert the postal service – unless it is a hoax, or pure paranoia on her part. Proof, one way or another, will be forthcoming at a stamp auction where agents of the conspirators – if they exist – will bid for a "lot" of counterfeit stamps. Oedipa joins the bidders in the auction room, the auction (or "crying") begins – and the novel simply stops, as if it had somehow stalled out right at the crucial moment. "Settl[ing] back to await the crying of lot 49," Pynchon's heroine is left suspended, stranded high and dry – as is the reader (Pynchon, 1967, 138). Nothing is resolved; the novel *crashes*. Oh Mama, can this really be the end?

2. Bang

When did postmodernism begin? What if we said, more or less arbitrarily, that it began in 1966 – the year when Dylan, The Beatles, Leonard Cohen, Andy Warhol, J. G. Ballard, and others stopped doing what they had been doing and started doing something else; the year when some people broke through and others broke down, and some did both.

This is manifestly an absurd way to write cultural history (isn't it?): assemble a year's worth of coincidences and accidents (some of them literal, even fatal) and then assert that they form a *pattern* of ends and beginnings. Surely *any* year would yield just as many such coincidences and could be made to serve a similar argument about the onset of something or other. When Woolf asserted that human character changed "on or about December 1910," she didn't expect to be taken seriously; she only wanted to capture, in an appropriately arbitrary and tongue-in-cheek way, some sense of the abruptness of change that her generation experienced in the years of cultural modernization that preceded the Great War of 1914–1918. For Woolf and her contemporaries, it felt *as if* everything changed in the space of a month or so. Other months, other years, might have served her argument equally well: for instance, those months in 1899 when Sigmund Freud published *The Interpretation of Dreams* and Joseph Conrad *Heart of Darkness* (Kolocotroni, 2006); or the months in 1912 when the American expatriate in London Ezra Pound invented Imagism, helped launch one seminal modernist little magazine, and radically transformed another one (Kinnahan, 2006); or even the days in July 1916 when, in the monumental blood-letting of the battle of the Somme, human character arguably really *did* change (Stevenson, 2006).

Of course, Woolf knew very well that cultural change, even change as abrupt as the onset of modernism, actually takes place not over the span of a month or even a year, but gradually, incrementally, over the course of decades. Nevertheless, she had good enough reasons for treating December 1910 as *representative* of the entire period of the transition to modernism. In 1910, among other things, the art critic Roger Fry introduced the English public to advanced French painting with an exhibition of Post-Impressionist artists; the brief Edwardian period ended with the death of Edward VII, and the governing Liberal Party in England threatened to abolish the House of Lords; and Woolf herself suffered a nervous breakdown, though in a lighter moment she also helped perpetrate a bizarre hoax on the Royal Navy (Stansky, 1996; for a different version of 1910, see Harrison, 1996). Ends and beginnings, breakthroughs and breakdowns.

If dating modernism's onset to 1910 is a somewhat arbitrary gesture, then so too is identifying the onset of postmodernism with some specific year. The transition to postmodernism, like the earlier transition to modernism, is a process, not a punctual event. Though earlier onset dates have sometimes been advanced, the consensus view seems to be that postmodernism emerged over the course of the "long sixties," the span of years from the mid-fifties to the early seventies (Jameson, 1988; DeKoven, 2004). This is a reasonable and defensible position, for even if elements of what would later be called post-modernism can be traced back to the late thirties or even earlier – maybe much earlier – these elements converge only in the sixties to form something like a period style.

An experience of abrupt and radical cultural change, indeed of *multiple* changes in rapid succession, characterizes the era of the long sixties in something like the way it did Woolf's era. So strong was the sense of being swept over by successive *waves* of change that almost *any* year between, say, 1954 and 1975 would be a plausible candidate for representative year, in the spirit of Woolf's "on or about December 1910." Thus, for example, the avant-garde Fluxus artist Dick Higgins once specified 1958 as the year when artists stopped asking what he called "cognitive questions" about knowledge and interpretation and starting asking "post-cognitive" ones about being and doing (Higgins, 1978, 101) – in effect (though he doesn't use the term), when they became postmodern. Sally Banes identifies a different year, 1963, associating it with the onset of a countercultural artistic practice that sprang up first of all in

New York's Greenwich Village, at the intersections among overlapping circles of pop artists, dancers and performance artists, "underground" filmmakers, and others (Banes, 1993). Persuasive cases could readily be made for the "revolutionary" years 1967 (e.g., Hellmann, 2006) and 1968 (e.g., Kurlansky, 2004), the years of Swinging London and the Summer of Love, of *Sergeant Pepper's* and *Rolling Stone* magazine, of the Tet Offensive in Vietnam, the May Events in Paris, and the Prague Spring. Charles Jencks, as we shall see later, dates the onset of postmodernism to 1972, in fact to a specific month, July of that year – even to a specific day and hour! – while Andreas Killen somewhat more soberly dates it to the year 1973 (Jencks, 1984, 9; Killen, 2006) (see Chapter 3).

Each of these years could be viewed as a microcosm of the long sixties, and each of them could plausibly be treated as a symbolic onset date for post-modernism, but in each case, the *version* of postmodernism that could be said to begin in each of these years would be somewhat different. Higgins's post-cognitivism, for instance, reflects the achievement of a sort of "critical mass" around 1958 by the neo-Dadaist avant-gardes that had emerged since the war, including Higgins's own Fluxus cohort (see Belgrad, 1998; Miller, 2009); his postmodernism would amount to a continuation of this avant-garde. A postmodernism pegged to 1967 might be more oriented toward the explosion of popular youth culture, while one pegged to 1968 would be more likely to emphasize the legacy of liberationist politics and mass movements. The postmodernism that Jencks traces back to that particular day in July 1972 begins in architectural theory and practice and expands outward from there, and so on.

What if we tried the thought experiment of dating postmodernism's onset to the symbolic year 1966? Granted, 1966 has certain disadvantages as a candidate for Year Zero of postmodernism, compared to some of the other years that have been proposed. Unlike, say, 1968, it is rarely cited as a pivotal year in world-historical terms, despite the fact that (among many other things) the feminist National Organization for Women (NOW) and the black-separatist Black Panther Party were both founded in 1966, and Mao Zedong launched the Cultural Revolution in China in that year. However, epochal turning points in world-historical events do not necessarily coincide with major changes in culture, and vice versa, nor do changes in different spheres of culture necessarily coincide with each other. Cultural transitions and world-historical epochs are not necessarily in sync, and asynchronicity, slippage, and semi-autonomy prevail across the several partial, overlapping histories that together constitute the history of culture (Frow, 1997, 28–30). Nineteen sixty-six perhaps illustrates this asynchronicity.

Moreover, in other respects, 1966 seems a strong candidate for Year Zero of postmodernism – at least as likely a candidate as 1910 ever was for the onset year of modernism. Nineteen sixty-six was above all a year in which avant-garde tendencies converged, mingled, and cross-pollinated with developments in popular culture, to explosive effect. The elements of a nascent postmodernism, already accumulating throughout the preceding decades, converged around 1966, forming a dense core, waiting only for the big bang of that year to propel them outward throughout culture and forward into the future.

For instance, this is the year when European art cinema achieved high visibility worldwide with films such as Bergman's *Persona*, Truffaut's *Fahrenheit 451*, Godard's *Masculine Feminine,* and especially, right at the end of the year, Antonioni's *Blow Up*, while American "underground" cinema reached its own creative apogee in Warhol's *Chelsea Girls.* Characteristic themes and styles of the counterculture (a term that would not actually enter the lexicon until 1969) emerged in the fiction of 1966, not only in the novels of Fariña and Cohen, but also in Charles Wright's Harlem novel *The Wig* and the Beat novelist William Burroughs's *The Soft Machine*, originally published in 1961 but reissued in a revised version in 1966. Alongside this countercultural fiction one could find aesthetically ambitious novels by Pynchon, John Barth, Christine Brooke-Rose, B. S. Johnson, Jean Rhys, and others, as well as first novels by novelists who would later go on to become leading postmodernists, including Robert Coover, William Gass, Joseph McElroy, and Gilbert Sorrentino. In 1966, as we have seen, the British science-fiction author J. G. Ballard changed directions, while on the other side of the Atlantic his American counterpart Philip K. Dick continued to overproduce, sometimes (though not always) to brilliant effect. Truman Capote and Hunter S. Thompson independently invented the nonfiction novel (or helped to reinvent it), while the poets John Ashbery and Allen Ginsberg both published long poems reflecting avant-garde methods of composition.

Conspicuous art- and music-world careers, as we have already seen, reached impasses, stalled out, and seemed to recoil back upon themselves in 1966, as illustrated by the cases of Warhol, Dylan, The Beatles, and Leonard Cohen. This same pattern of *turning back on oneself* recurs elsewhere in cutting-edge culture, not only in the worlds of fine art and popular music, but even in the academic humanities disciplines. Here, it is not career trajectories that turn back on themselves, but *language itself* in the newly emergent schools of structuralism and poststructuralism. In effect, 1966 witnessed the emergence of not only self-conscious popular music (Dylan, The Beatles) and self-conscious fiction (metafiction), but also self-conscious critical reflection in the mode that would eventually come to be known simply (or not so simply) as *theory*.

If identifying 1966 as a microcosm of the long sixties is an arbitrary gesture – as it no doubt is – it is arbitrary in the same way as Woolf's singling out of 1910, and with something of the same purpose: to experiment, to provoke, to make strange. One asks oneself, if 1966 marks the beginning of postmodernism, then what does that version of postmodernism – the one that begins in 1966 – look like? To begin to answer that question, we must look more closely at some of the cultural artifacts and tendencies of 1966.

3. Complexity and Contradiction

In the Italian director Michelangelo Antonioni's film about Swinging London, *Blow-Up,* released in 1966, the severe, stripped-down architecture of the *Economist* complex, designed by Alison and Peter Smithson, serves to signify urban regimentation and alienation, providing a suitably hostile backdrop for the anarchic antics of a mime troupe, with which the film opens (Steiner, 2006). The architecture critic Rayner Banham, in his book of the same year, gave this architectural style a name, calling it *The New Brutalism* – but not in a pejorative sense. In fact, the term New Brutalism referred approvingly to the use of exposed, undecorated materials, such as *béton brut,* raw concrete, which in Banham's view was one of the signs of this style's aesthetic honesty and integrity: what you see is what you get. It was a sign, in other words, of New Brutalism's adherence to the aesthetic standards of architectural *modernism*: integrity, functionality, expression of the materials, and renunciation of decoration. Antonioni's use of this style to connote alienation anticipates the sorts of critiques of high-modernist architecture that would eventually provoke the search for some alternative to modernism – the search for a *postmodernist* architecture.

If we take the word of Charles Jencks, architecture critic and propagandist for postmodernism, that critique climaxed in 1972 with the spectacular demolition of a failed modernist housing project (see Chapter 3) and the near-simultaneous appearance of a key text of architectural theory, *Learning from Las Vegas* by Robert Venturi, Denise Scott Brown, and Steven Izenour. The hole that the destruction of the Pruitt-Igoe project blew in architectural history, in Jencks's view, would be filled by the postmodernism of Venturi, Brown, and Izenour. Like everything else in cultural history, however, *Learning from Las Vegas* has a prehistory, including (among other things) an earlier book of architectural theory by Venturi himself, *Complexity and*

Contradiction in Architecture, published six years earlier, in 1966 – the same year as *Blow-Up*'s implicit critique of modernist architecture.

It is in *Complexity and Contradiction in Architecture* that Venturi first mounts his polemic against modernist purism and his defense of what he calls the "honky-tonk elements" of the urban and ex-urban landscape (1977, 104) – its pop-cultural and commercial elements, its signage, iconic forms, and visual busyness, its *bad taste*. He argues for an alternative set of values to those of modernism: not unity and simplicity but complexity and contradiction; not clarity and the expression of materials but ambiguity and the principle of "both-and"; not "Less is more," Mies van der Rohe's modernist slogan, but "Main Street is almost all right." It is Venturi's embrace of the complexities and contradictions of Main Street that would over time evolve into the postmodernist appreciation of the Las Vegas Strip in *Learning from Las Vegas*.

Apart from Venturi's *Complexity and Contradiction*, 1966 also saw the publication of the Italian architect Aldo Rossi's *Architecture of the City* [*L'architettura della cittá*], which proposed a vision of architectural historicism and urban form at odds with orthodox modernism (Lobsinger, 2006). Rossi resists the modernist tendency to view the city in exclusively *functionalist* terms, arguing that, apart from its economic, administrative, circulatory, and other functions, a city is also a repository of *history* and *memory*. Reluctant to apply too dogmatically the modernist dictum that "form follows function," he remains open to the possibility that in cities, especially in older cities, function can sometimes follow form, in the sense that inherited urban elements – monuments, ancient buildings, squares and plazas, entire quarters (his example is the Roman Forum) – can continue to shape the city even after their function changes or disappears altogether. Rossi's approach clearly has something in common with Kevin Lynch's earlier insights (in *The Image of the City* [1960]) into the role of urban landmarks in making cities navigable and livable – insights that would later inform Jameson's critique of postmodernism (see Chapter 3). Rossi also evidently shares something with the American urbanist Jane Jacobs, whose defense of urban complexity (in *The Death and Life of Great American Cities* [1961]) influenced Venturi's postmodernism (Laurence, 2006).

Clearly, then, if one were intent on making the case for 1966's threshold status as a kind of Year Zero of postmodernism, one place to begin would be the architectural theories of Venturi and Rossi, which seem to anticipate the postmodernism of later decades. Nevertheless, a little skepticism is in order. In Rossi's case, it is important to appreciate the way *The Architecture of the City* intervenes in a specifically Italian conversation about urban form

(Lobsinger, 2006, 28–9). The book's concerns are not automatically transferable to other contexts, other conversations, perhaps least of all to the North American context, where (arguably) architectural postmodernism first emerges. For instance, Rossi takes it for granted that no city would ever intentionally destroy its own greatest monuments. No doubt he is thinking of the Italian cities, or maybe the European cities more generally, where the greatest monuments *were* preserved and where the most dangerous threats to them came from outside – in particular, from wartime bombing, which as late as 1966 was still fresh in European city planners' minds. Yet in the United States, only a few years earlier, in 1964, New York City had permitted one of its greatest architectural landmarks, Pennsylvania Station, to be demolished in the name of efficiency, progress, and optimized profits. The difficulty of translating Rossi's concerns to a North American context is confirmed by the fact that the book was not actually, *literally*, translated into English until 1982, too late to have much impact on the emergence of an architectural discourse on postmodernism in the Anglophone world. So the question arises, how postmodernist is *The Architecture of the City* really?

Similarly, the more closely we scrutinize Venturi's *Complexity and Contradiction*, the harder it is to overlook its backward-looking, high-modernist tendencies. Could there be anything more modernist sounding than Venturi's phrase, "the obligation toward the difficult whole," his formula for an architecture of complexity and contradiction (1977, 88)? *Obligation, difficulty, wholeness*, these are all *modernist* values, much more than they are postmodernist ones. *Pleasure* instead of obligation, *accessibility* instead of difficulty, *plurality* instead of wholeness: these are the postmodernist alternatives, in the view of someone like Jencks.

Venturi's concepts of complexity, contradiction, ambiguity, and paradox are all explicitly derived from modernist poetics – from T. S. Eliot and the New Critics William Empson and Cleanth Brooks. It is they who are Venturi's true spiritual contemporaries, rather than anyone of his own generation, such as John Ashbery or Jacques Derrida. Instead of turning for aesthetic models to, say, Ashbery's *Rivers and Mountains*, which appeared in 1966, Venturi looks back to Eliot's canonically modernist *Waste Land* of 1922; instead of looking to the contemporary discourse of poststructuralists such as Derrida, whose American debut occurred in 1966 at a famous conference at Johns Hopkins University, Venturi relies on retrograde New Critical concepts.

Nevertheless, however regressively modernist or distinctively local Venturi and Rossi actually were, it was out of their ideas and insights that a "language of postmodernist architecture" was synthesized a decade later by propagandists like Jencks. In the genealogy of postmodernist architectural discourse, Venturi and Rossi circa 1966 are, perhaps inadvertently, founding fathers.

4. The Tipping Point

As the French-born American novelist Raymond Federman tells it (1993, 113–4), he sat down to begin composing his first novel, *Double or Nothing* (1971), on October 1, 1966, in Paris. Unflaggingly self-reflective and experimental, *Double or Nothing* is a model of the American brand of postmodernism that Federman himself preferred to call *surfiction*, a term he coined. Federman himself would go on to publish over a dozen other surfictions in both French and English, and would help direct the Fiction Collective, a consortium of authors dedicated to the publication of advanced fiction.

Tempting as it is to trace the onset of postmodernism in fiction to that October day in 1966, the evidence won't support such a dating – and in any case, Federman was a notorious self-fictionalizer, and his story is as untrustworthy as any of his novels, a personal myth rather than a sober matter of fact. In plain fact, most of the cutting-edge novels of 1966 stop short of surfiction in the Federman mode. Rather, they are in something like the same situation as Robert Venturi's architectural theory, poised on the very brink of postmodernism while exhibiting for the most part a kind of aggravated modernism. Rarely fully postmodernist, the cutting-edge novels of 1966 are epistemological fictions pushed to the breaking point but seldom toppling over into the fiction of ontology (see Chapter 1).

Nineteen sixty-six is a threshold year for fiction in the sense that a number of major novelists who would subsequently make the transition to postmodernism published their first novels in that year. A list might include Robert Coover's *The Origin of the Brunists*, William H. Gass's *Omensetter's Luck*, Joseph McElroy's *A Smuggler's Bible*, and Gilbert Sorrentino's *The Sky Changes*. All of these novels are characterized by a modernist focus on the interior lives of characters – many of them experiencing extreme psychological states – and on the way different characters perceive the same exterior reality differently. The narrative techniques here are those of high modernism – internal focalization through one or more characters, interior monologues cast in the first-person or the third-person (free indirect) modes, juxtaposed perspectives of multiple characters, and so on – and the models are the classic modernist novels of Joyce, Woolf, Faulkner, and others. The

British novelist B. S. Johnson's *Trawl* also belongs to this group because, even though this is not his first novel, Johnson here *retreats* to modernist-style interior monologue after the metafictional breakthrough of 1964's *Albert Angelo* – literally a breakthrough, involving (among other things) punching a physical hole through several pages of the text.

Each of these novelists would sooner or later leave behind the edgy, aggravated modernism of these early novels and pass over into one version or other of postmodernism. Coover would make the transition by way of *The Universal Baseball Association Inc., J. Henry Waugh, Prop.* (1968), his novel of an obsessive game player who slips across the ontological border into his own game, and he would seal his transformation in his stories of world-building and -unbuilding in *Pricksongs and Descants* (1969), followed by the carnivalesque historical fantasy of *The Public Burning* (1977). Gass would shift by way of the transitional stories of *In the Heart of the Heart of the Country* (1968) to the experimental book-making of *Willie Master's Lonesome Wife* (also 1968), a metafictional reflection on authorship printed on colored pages and in varying and distorted typefaces, sometimes juxtaposed with nude photographs of the wife of the title. Sorrentino would make his transition to postmodernism in *Imaginative Qualities of Actual Things* (1971); McElroy, despite some ambitious experiments in various modernist modes, perhaps not until *Women and Men* (1987). Even Johnson, after his retreat to modernism in *Trawl*, would return to the postmodernist mode, if not in *The Unfortunates* (1969), his notoriously randomized novel-in-a-box – which in fact proves to contain a rather tame interior monologue – then in his later full-blown metafictions, *Christie Malry's Own Double Entry* (1973) and *See the Old Lady Decently* (1975).

The *brinksmanship* of the novels of 1966 – their quality of remaining poised at the very brink of postmodernism, without quite toppling over into it – is readily illustrated through two examples, one relatively unknown, the other celebrated: Charles Wright's *The Wig* and Pynchon's *The Crying of Lot 49*. A dark and extravagant satire of American success stories of the Horatio Alger type, *The Wig* signifies on – that is, ironically reenacts and rewrites (see Gates, 1988) – that indispensable novel of African-American modernism *and* postmodernism, Ralph Ellison's *Invisible Man* (1952). Just as Ellison's nameless protagonist discovers the ambivalent pleasures of masquerade when, late in the novel, he inadvertently assumes the identity of Rinehart, a shape-changing Harlem trickster figure – preacher, pimp, brawler, lover – so Wright's narrator, Lester Jefferson, experiences a dubious liberation from his racial identity when he straightens and bleaches his African-American hair. In the background of Lester's narrative of his slapstick and cartoonish adventures in racial passing, we catch brief, ambiguous glimpses from time to time of an alternative reality that does not quite coincide with contemporary Harlem, circa 1966 – glimpses of "an America of tomorrow," as Wright calls it in an author's note. There is no way to confirm the reality of this alternative America, since everything we know about it reaches us through the filter of Lester's subjectivity and narrative voice, and this indeterminacy persists right to the end, when Lester abruptly falls into the hands of the sinister undertaker Mr. Fishback, who apparently castrates him. Or does he? Have we slipped with Lester into some parallel world of gothic horror? Is he dead and narrating posthumously? Or hallucinating? Has the novel itself switched into the allegorical mode? We are left suspended, hesitating among possibilities; nothing is resolved.

Similarly, Pynchon's Oedipa Maas in *The Crying of Lot 49* accumulates evidence pointing to the existence of an alternative reality parallel to the world of her everyday experience, a secret order of things invisible to her up till now. She suspects she has uncovered "another mode of meaning behind the obvious" (1967, 137) – unless, of course, it is all a fabrication, either a hoax of which she is the victim, or the projection of her own paranoia. *"Shall I project a world?"* Oedipa asks herself (1967, 59), but in the end she cannot decide whether she has only projected a world or actually discovered one. The alternative world in which a conspiratorial organization called the Tristero really exists seems to infiltrate her reality throughout the novel – and not just that particular alternative reality, but others as well. The novel abounds with episodes of what appears to be "another world's intrusion into this one" – miracles, apparitions, communications from beyond the grave or from the ghost in a machine, one world interfering with another like "a kiss of cosmic pool balls" (1967, 88, 92). However, communications break down, messages fail to get through, and none of her otherworldly encounters can be independently verified, leaving us with nothing but Oedipa's unreliable perceptions and overtaxed imagination. By the novel's close, as we have already seen, her epistemological difficulties have forced her into a corner from which she cannot exit. If other worlds really *do* exist here, we will not learn about them from Oedipa Maas.

This is the typical condition of the novels of 1966: pushed into the corner, poised on the brink. Nevertheless, a few novels of that year actually do topple over the edge into something like full-blown postmodernism. One that does so is Leonard Cohen's *Beautiful Losers*, in which the fantastic and the everyday appear to mingle; for instance, a sex-toy acquires sentience and a grotesque will of its own, threatening its human users. As in *The Wig* and *Lot 49*, however, the fantastic here is subjectivized by the presence of a mediating character – two of them, in fact, one of whom narrates the novel's first section, the other the second section, and both of whom are dreamers and fantasists, prone to exaggeration and hallucination, and thoroughly unreliable. Everything changes, though, in the epilogue. Cast in the third person, and thus presumably objective, it narrates how one of these characters (it's not entirely clear which one) literally, physically disintegrates – as Pynchon's protagonist Tyrone Slothrop later would in *Gravity's Rainbow* (1973) – and then reassembles himself as, of all things, a movie of the R 'n' B singer Ray Charles projected onto the sky! Where Pynchon's Oedipa stops short of projecting a world, Cohen lurches into the alternative-reality mode and, allowing the subjective frame to fall away, morphs his character into a literal, fantastic projection.

Similar breakthroughs from the epistemological into the ontological occur in Barth's *Giles Goat-boy* and Brooke-Rose's *Such*. Where *The Wig* allows only fleeting glimpses of a dubious alternative reality – which may prove after all to be merely subjective – *Giles* constructs a robustly substantial one. Part updated pastoral, part cybernetic science fiction, part campus novel, and part Cold War allegory, the world of *Giles* is framed by layers of mock documentation – disclaimers, cover letters, postscripts – claiming to authenticate the text but in fact throwing it into a limbo of deauthentication: a whole world under erasure, there but not there. In *Such*, Brooke-Rose, the most French-oriented of all the British experimentalists of her generation, follows in the footsteps of the French New Novelists (*nouveaux romanciers*), who had themselves made the transition from modernism to a kind of postmodernism in the years leading up to 1966. (As it happens, the English translation of Alain Robbe-Grillet's *La Maison de rendez-vous*, arguably his first fully postmodernist novel, appeared in 1966, though the French original actually dates from the year before.) The world of *Such* is double – two worlds, that of everyday reality and that of a fantastic world-to-come. The novel's protagonist, having undergone a near-death experience, finds himself slipping back and forth across the boundary between the world of his everyday life – which he now perceives in strangely altered ways, in science-fiction terms of cosmic radiation, waves and particles, magnetic fields – and a bizarre wonderland or *paraworld* lying presumably beyond death.

Indeed, paraworlds of various kinds – worlds within worlds, alternative universes, worlds next door – are one of the signatures of 1966. Brooke-Rose's *Such* is hardly the only example. For instance, parareality is an obsessive preoccupation in almost all of Philip K. Dick's science fiction of that year, if we take into account both the novels he actually published during 1966 – all of them written or at least begun much earlier, in 1963 or 1964 – as well as the ones he wrote in that year but would not publish until several years later. The paraworld motif appears in a classic form in *The Crack in Space*, one of Dick's minor novels of 1966, where the crack of the title gives access to a parallel earth. It also appears in both *Now Wait for Last Year* and *The Unteleported Man*, where drugs facilitate the passage to alternative realities, as well as in his masterpiece *Ubik* (written 1966, published 1969), where the characters gradually realize that what they have taken to be everyday reality is only a simulation – that they are all actually dead, and that what they are experiencing is a posthumous shared hallucination of life.

Dick's preoccupation with paraworlds no doubt reflects his own experiences with hallucinogenic drugs, which in the mid-sixties were in some quarters regarded as gateways to alternative realities. For instance, Robert Crumb, the underground cartoonist whose work anticipated and inspired the postmodern graphic novels of the eighties (see Chapter 3), attributed the invention of some of his most memorable characters (including Mr. Natural, Flaky Foont and his trademark "Keep on Truckin'" figures) to an LSD experience he underwent in 1966 (Crumb and Poplaski, 2005, 132, cited in Round, 2013, 340). If Dick's pararealities are similarly psychedelic in origin, then this perhaps helps explain their resemblance to the floating worlds implied or visited in some of the songs from The Beatles' *Revolver*. The Beatles, too, were notoriously experimenting with hallucinogens in the months leading up to the *Revolver* sessions. John Lennon "float[s] *up*stream" in "I'm Only Sleeping" and "float[s] *down*stream" in "Tomorrow Never Knows" (Aldridge, 1991, 92, 121); in both songs he glimpses the kinds of paraworlds he would later visit in "Strawberry Fields Forever" (released as a single the next year) and "Lucy in the Sky with Diamonds" (from the *Sergeant Pepper's* album, also 1967). "Tomorrow Never Knows" borrows its language from the evangelist of psychedelic experience, Timothy Leary, who had in turn borrowed it from *The Tibetan Book of the Dead*; so this particular paraworld – the world that begins when we "play the game existence to the end" – is also a world beyond death, a world-to-come like those in Brooke-Rose's *Such* and Dick's *Ubik*.

Parareality is also associated with the drug counterculture in William Burroughs' novel *The Soft Machine*, reissued in 1966, in which interplanetary vistas out of science fiction are juxtaposed with gritty junkie naturalism. However, the definitive drug paraworld of 1966 must surely be the one glimpsed in the song "White Rabbit," written by Grace Slick and performed and recorded by her that year with her first band, The Great Society, prior to her joining The Jefferson Airplane (which would release a different version of the song the next year). Reinterpreting Lewis Carroll's *Wonderland* and *Looking-Glass* worlds as anticipations of psychedelic experience, Slick's song had a transformative impact on almost all subsequent versions of *Alice*, down to the present; but that's a different story.

5. High and Low

Early symptoms of the erosion of hierarchical distinctions between "high" and "low" culture, typical of the full-blown postmodernism of later decades (see Chapter 3), began to appear around 1966. Of course, the mingling of the high and low spheres of culture – of legitimized, canonized, and institutionalized culture with popular or mass culture – is not by any means exclusive to postmodernism (despite what its apologists sometimes seem to imply). Indeed, as the Russian Formalist already observed nearly a century ago (Tynjanov, 2000 [1924]), high culture often draws on the resources of low culture to renew itself, upgrading popular genres and materials and turning them into vehicles for high art. This process of renewal through the infusion of new blood from "below" is embraced more openly in some periods than in others. Canonical high modernism, for example, fearful of competition from the new mass media, denied that it had any commerce with low culture, and tried to maintain a "great divide" between the high and the low (Huyssen, 1986). Meanwhile, the avant-garde wing of modernism, including Dadaism and Surrealism, gleefully embraced low-culture elements (Varnedoe and Gopnik, 1990). Postmodernism revives the modernist-era avant-garde's receptivity to elements of low culture. Traffic between high and low culture was already conspicuous in the late fifties and early sixties, especially in the United States, where visual artists such as Warhol turned to pop culture – comics, advertising, celebrity photographs – for their imagery. By 1966 that traffic had intensified.

By then, for instance, cutting-edge literature had become "contaminated" by the imagery, themes, and styles of the "lowest," least reputable and most abject genres of writing, including pornography and science fiction (Fiedler, 1972). Constraints on literature's freedom to use obscene language and to represent sexual behavior had been eased by a series of high-visibility trials of celebrated "dirty books," invariably decided, sooner or later, in favor of the alleged "pornographers." Among the books tried and ultimately acquitted during the late fifties and sixties were Allen Ginsberg's long poem *Howl*, D.H. Lawrence's *Lady Chatterley's Lover*, Henry Miller's

Tropic of Cancer, and most recently Burroughs's *Naked Lunch,* whose banning in Boston was successfully appealed before the Massachusetts Supreme Court in 1966. A number of novels of that year took full advantage of the new freedom to represent explicit sex acts, both hetero- and homosexual, including Barth's *Giles Goat-Boy,* Burroughs's *Soft Machine,* Cohen's *Beautiful Losers,* Fariña's *Been Down So Long,* Pynchon's *Lot 49,* and Wright's *The Wig.*

Science fiction, too, infiltrated advanced literature in 1966, as we have already noticed more than once. Brooke-Rose's *Such,* Barth's *Giles Goat-Boy,* Burroughs's *Soft Machine,* Wright's *The Wig:* all of these cutting-edge novels exhibit science-fiction premises, motifs, or language, sometimes even full-scale science-fiction worlds (Barth's cybernetic future, Burroughs's Venus). Strikingly, science fiction had not yet penetrated mass-market popular culture as it would later on, in the seventies and eighties. Still generally stigmatized as adolescent entertainment, associated with pulp magazines, Hollywood "B" movies and comic-books, it continued to occupy a relatively narrow niche in pop culture of the mid-sixties. That would all change after the debut of *Star Trek,* whose first season was broadcast on the NBC network in 1966, laying the foundations for science fiction's ubiquity throughout popular culture in later decades. Meanwhile, only a few notable science-fiction films appeared in 1966, the most ambitious of them being not a Hollywood movie at all, but a European art film: François Truffaut's *Fahrenheit 451,* based on the 1953 novel by Ray Bradbury.

Not only did advanced art exploit the resources of popular culture in 1966, but also vice versa, popular genres aspired to the condition of cutting-edge art. Science fiction, again, is a case in point. The genre had already made strides to shed the stigma of pulp fiction, achieving something like *literate* status in the fifties (the era of Arthur C. Clarke, Isaac Asimov, Robert Heinlein, and others). Now, in the mid-sixties, it sought to take the next step, from *literate* to *literary* status. Such literary aspirations were associated with the emergent "New Wave" of science fiction, including writers such as Brian Aldiss, Michael Moorcock and J. G. Ballard in the United Kingdom, and Samuel R. Delany, Thomas Disch, Harlan Ellison, Ursula LeGuin, Joanna Russ, and others in the United States. Apart from Ballard, whom we have already considered, Delany did important work in 1966, publishing a transitional novel, *Babel-17,* about an alien language that is literally "a virus from outer space" (in the words of Burroughs's slogan, later popularized by the performance artist Laurie Anderson; see Chapter 3).

On the fringes of the New Wave, Philip K. Dick continued to sustain the frenetic pace of production that characterized his work throughout the mid-sixties. At first glance, Dick seems to have had a relative poor year in 1966, bringing out three rather slapdash novels dating from 1963 to 1964 – *The Crack in Space, Now Wait for Last Year,* and *The Unteleported Man* – though he also wrote and published at least one superior short story, "We Can Remember It for You Wholesale." However, if we take into account what Dick actually *wrote* in 1966, rather than what he published, a different picture emerges. Apart from "We Can Remember It," his actual output for 1966 included the novels *Do Androids Dream of Electric Sheep?* (published 1968) and *Ubik* (1969). I have already touched on *Ubik,* a seminal text of postmodern science fiction. *Do Androids Dream,* of course, was adapted by Ridley Scott as the film *Blade Runner* (1982), while "We Can Remember It" became the basis for Paul Verhoeven's *Total Recall* (1990), a successful vehicle for Arnold Schwarzenegger. Arguably, then, Dick's output for 1966 has as strong a claim to launching postmodern science fiction as Ballard's, or as the premiere of *Star Trek.*

If cutting-edge art, including art cinema like Truffaut's *Fahrenheit 451,* proved receptive to science fiction in 1966, it tended to struggle harder in the face of the challenge posed by popular music. In at least two of the major art films of that year, Godard's *Masculine Feminine* and Antonioni's *Blow-Up,* European directors tried, with only partial success, to come to terms with global youth culture, especially as reflected in pop and rock music. Of the two, *Blow-Up* is the more prescient, featuring as it does an explosive scene of the British blues band The Yardbirds performing in a London club; the budding pop star or *yé-yé* girl of *Masculine Feminine* pales by comparison. (A few years later Godard would engage more robustly with rock music than he was able to do in 1966, incorporating documentary footage of The Rolling Stones recording "Sympathy for the Devil" in *One Plus One* [1968].) Some of the artists of 1966 were simply more receptive to rock music than others. At one extreme we might locate Pynchon, who in *Lot 49* seemed to find nothing in the mid-sixties garage-band scene but opportunities for satire, and at the other, Warhol, who gave up painting to collaborate with The Velvet Underground, or Leonard Cohen, who went as far as to abandon a literary career for one as a singer-songwriter.

What these artists were, in various ways and with various degrees of success, struggling to respond to were the new-found ambitions of popular musicians. Nineteen sixty-six was the year when major rock performers – including Bob Dylan, The Beatles, The Mothers of Invention, Brian Wilson of The Beach Boys, and not least of all The Velvet Underground itself – began to think of themselves as avant-garde artists and to make a case for being thought of in those terms by others. In other words, 1966 was the year when *rock 'n' roll* began to morph into *rock*.

Nineteen sixty-six was crowded with rock breakthroughs: the first double album in rock history, Dylan's ambitious *Blonde on Blonde*; the first album by Frank Zappa's Mothers of Invention, *Freak Out!*, poised between rock and parody; *Pet Sounds*, the most sophisticated album The Beach Boys had so far produced, and, above all, The Beatles' *Revolver*. This was the year when rock 'n' roll music, impatient of its status as a commercial product, began to aspire to the condition of art, as reflected in the way rock musicians began to enter into artistic dialogue with each other, over the heads or behind the backs, so to speak, of their commercial handlers. The Beach Boys sought to emulate The Beatles, and The Beatles in turn took inspiration from The Beach Boys. John Lennon tried to imitate Dylan in "Norwegian Wood" (from *Rubber Soul* [1965]), and Dylan, ungracious as ever, replied by parodying Lennon in "Fourth Time Around" (from *Blonde on Blonde*), which closes with the pointed lines, "I never asked for your crutch,/Now don't ask for mine" (Dylan, 1974, 351; see Marqusee, 2003, 176). If intra-art dialogue of this kind (however ungracious) is one measure of an artistic field's maturity, then rock in 1966 was maturing rapidly.

Moreover, the invention of the psychedelic style in music can be dated to 1966 – specifically, to the sessions during which The Beatles recorded "Tomorrow Never Knows," the last cut on *Revolver*, and "Rain," the B side of their 1966 single "Paperback Writer" (LeBlanc, 2002, 202). Above all, however, 1966 marks the emergence of the rock album as a unified artwork. Here, too, credit for the breakthrough belongs to *Revolver*, arguably the first rock album designed to be experienced as an integrated whole, with motifs, both musical and verbal, recurring across the album from cut to cut (Reising, 2002, 251–2). Nevertheless, even as *Revolver* aspires to a higher degree of integration than any rock album to date, it also seems more eclectic and heterogeneous than almost any rock album to date, each of its songs seeming to belong to a different sound-world from all the others (Reising, 2002, 236). On the one hand, then, *Revolver* anticipates highly integrated albums like The Beatles' own *Sgt. Pepper's Lonely Hearts Club Band* or later "concept" albums by The Who, Marvin Gaye, David Bowie, Pink Floyd, and others. On the other hand, *Revolver* also anticipates the radical stylistic and thematic eclecticism of The Beatles' *White Album* (1968). Balancing its centripetal and centrifugal tendencies, *Revolver* stands poised between integration and disintegration, unity and diversity, concentration and dispersion – between, some might say, modernism and postmodernism.

6. Made, Unmade, Ready-Made

Julio Cortázar, author of the story on which Antonioni's *Blow-Up* is distantly based ("Las babas del diablo" [1959]), was also represented in the cultural scene of 1966 by another text: *Hopscotch*, the English translation of his 1963 novel *Rayuela*. Cortázar, along with Jorge Luis Borges, was among the first of the Latin American "Boom" writers to be widely read in the Anglophone world (see Chapter 3). Among the novels of the Boom, *Hopscotch* has a special claim to fame: it offers the reader two different sequences of chapters to choose from, one proceeding straight through from the first chapter to the fifty-sixth, the other zig-zagging (or "hopscotching") through the book in an alternative order that includes extra chapters not present in the "normal" sequence. Less radical than Marc Saporta's novel-in-a-box *Composition No. 1* (1961), somewhat more radical than B. S. Johnson's *The Unfortunates*, Cortázar's novel exemplifies what would later be called *interactive* fiction, anticipating the hypertext fictions and computer games of the nineties (see Chapter 4). It exposes to view the process by which readers, even in the case of more conventional novels, actively participate in the *making* of storyworlds – the *constructive* dimension of fiction.

If *Hopscotch* lays bare the process of construction on the reader's side of the transaction, then its opposite number in the cultural scene of 1966 is Daniel Spoerri's *An Anecdoted Topography of Chance*, which lays bare the process on the *writer's* side. Here Spoerri describes, item by item, in exhaustive detail and with an abundance of backstory, all the clutter that had accumulated on his picturesquely messy coffee table as of a particular date and time, October 17, 1961, at 3:47 p.m. Spoerri, in other words, produces his text by following a specific *procedure*, which, if in one sense it is *accidental* – the accidents of a messy life determine the precise content of the description – in another sense is entirely *systematic*. We can follow Spoerri's process of composition as it unfolds: nothing is subjective or mysterious about it, nothing secret or hidden. Published in French in 1962, *An Anecdoted Topography* appeared in Emmett Williams's English translation in 1966 from Something Else Press, founded and run by the Fluxus artist Dick Higgins. (John Barth would mock Spoerri's book, sight unseen, along with Something Else Press itself and the avant-garde generally, in his influential manifesto, "The Literature of Exhaustion," published the next year.)

Reading in *Hopscotch*, writing in *An Anecdoted Topography*: in both cases, *processes* are laid bare, upstaging and eclipsing the actual *product*. The focus on process, a general tendency throughout twentieth-century art, especially in the postmodern era, is here applied to literature. Process-driven, or procedural, writing is an emergent feature of 1966, taking a number of forms, among them writing according to *rule*, writing under *constraint*, writing subject to *chance*, and *found* writing. In every case, the "suspension of disbelief" that is supposed to be a condition for fiction is deliberately jeopardized, and the storyworld, revealed to be a construction of the reader or the writer (or both), is placed under erasure – there but not there.

A relatively transparent example of procedural writing comes from John Ashbery's 1966 collection *Rivers and Mountains*: every line of his poem "Into the Dusk-Charged Air" contains the name of one of the rivers of the world, beginning with the Rappahannock and ending about 150 lines later with the Ardèche. More elaborate and opaque are the procedures evidently applied by Ashbery's friend Harry Mathews, another writer associated with the New York School, in his 1966 novel *Tlooth*. *Tlooth* observes one conspicuous constraint – it systematically withholds the gender of any of its characters, including its narrator, until near the end – but it also appears to have been generated, in whole or in part, in accordance with a number of arbitrary rules – rules invisible to the reader, and largely impossible to reconstruct. Mathews' procedures seem to have been modeled on those practiced by the eccentric early twentieth-century French writer, Raymond Roussel, who composed some of his texts, including his novels *Impressions d'Afrique* (1910) and *Locus Solus* (1912), by punning on idioms, clichés or lines of verse and then devising scenes and events that *literalized* those puns. Evidently Mathews followed something like the same procedures in *Tlooth*, or at least in parts of it.

A figure of an earlier generation, a favorite author of the Surrealists in the twenties and thirties, Roussel was largely forgotten after his death in 1933 but enjoyed a surprising revival in the fifties and early sixties. Mathews had discovered him thanks to Ashbery, who participated in the revival of Roussel's reputation in the fifties, at about the same time that he was also rediscovered by the *nouveaux romanciers* and other French intellectuals, including Michel Foucault (whose first book, published in 1963, was devoted to him). Thus, by the mid-sixties Roussel was widely regarded as a model for cutting-edge procedural writing. He was certainly viewed in this light by the writers of the Ouvroir de Littérature Potentielle [Workshop of Potential Literature], or OuLiPo for short (Motte, 1986; Mathews and Brotchie, 1998). Founded in 1960 by Raymond Queneau and others and dedicated to the practice and promotion of proceduralism and other literary experiments, the OuLiPo group in 1966 was still a secretive coterie. It would not emerge into public view until 1973 – the same year that Harry Mathews became a member (see Chapter 3).

Rousselian word-games constitute one wing of proceduralism, circa 1966; Burrough's cut-ups constitute another. Around 1959 the Beat writer William S. Burroughs had begun literally to slice up texts – sometimes his own, sometimes those of others – with a razor or scissors, and to piece them back together differently to produce a kind of verbal collage. Alternatively, he would fold one text in half and lay it on top of another, reading across the fold to discover new splices of the two texts. *The Soft Machine,* the first of his full-length novels to employ cut-ups and fold-ins, appeared in 1961; he rewrote it in 1966 to make it somewhat more accessible, and again in 1968 for a U.K. edition. Collage was also a feature of Allen Ginberg's procedural poem of 1966, his monumental *Witchita Vortex Sutra*, composed orally during a trip through the Midwest, incorporating the language of signage and headlines seen from a bus or car window, and the songs and news reports heard on the radio. If Spoerri's or Mathews's procedures are in some metaphorical sense "mechanical," Ginsberg's are *literally* machine-made, mediated by a machine – recorded on a portable tape-recorder (cutting-edge consumer technology in 1966) bought with money given to Ginsberg expressly for that purpose by none other than Bob Dylan (Marqusee, 2003, 190–2).

Burroughs in *The Soft Machine*, and even more so Ginsberg in *Witchita Vortex Sutra,* illustrate the use of *found* materials in writing. The artistic procedure of incorporating materials found in one's surroundings, rather than invented from scratch, is one of the great aesthetic discoveries of the twentieth century (Antin, 1972). The cubists practiced it when they glued scraps of newspaper or chair caning onto their canvases; so did the surrealists when they treated objects found in flea-markets (*objets trouvés,* found objects) as sculptures; so did the Dadaist Marcel Duchamp when he exhibited a urinal or a snow-shovel in a gallery and declared it a *ready-made* artwork; and in recent decades, so do hiphop artist when they build sonic textures out of samples of others' music. The radicalism of found-art practices lies in the challenge they pose to the pervasive ideology of art-making as *self-expression* – an ideology to which Ginsberg, for one, certainly subscribed. Nevertheless, in texts like *Witchita Vortex Sutra* he allowed artistic expression to be dictated in part by the verbal "objects" that he happened to encounter in his wanderings through the world. His friend Frank O'Hara (who died prematurely in 1966) similarly collected verbal found objects during his lunch-hour strolls through Manhattan, and incorporated them in his *Lunch Poems* (1964) and other texts. Other examples of found writing in 1966 include Ashbery's sampling of material from a corny, old-fashioned boys' book called *Three Hundred Things a Bright Boy Can Do* in his long poem "The Skaters," and Leonard Cohen's use of material culled from Jesuit accounts of the seventeenth-century Iroquois saint, Catherine Tekakwitha, in *Beautiful Losers.*

Ginsberg's technique in *Witchita Vortex Sutra,* and even more so his tool, the portable tape-recorder, are in a sense *journalistic*: he reports what he found on a trip through the American Midwest during a year of increasing escalation of U.S. involvement in the war in Vietnam. Of course, a long poem is not the usual genre for reportage, so in reading *Witchita Vortex Sutra* we inevitably experience a certain tension between *factuality* and *lyricism.* A comparable tension is found in another of the literary inventions (or re-inventions) of 1966, the so-called *non-fiction novel* – journalistic reportage in which fact-finding is wedded with the formal methods of novelistic fiction. Such conflation of journalism and fiction is hardly unprecedented – it had already appeared as early as the eighteenth century, for instance in Daniel Defoe's *Journal of the Plague Year* (1722) – but it re-emerged in 1966 in Truman Capote's crime narrative, *In Cold Blood,* and Hunter S. Thompson's *Hell's Angels,* and would come to be identified over the course of the next decade with the so-called New Journalism of Tom Wolfe, Norman Mailer, Michael Herr, Joan Didion, and others (Wolfe and Johnson, 1973).

When Burroughs cuts up texts by other writers – classic modernists such as Joyce, Eliot, and Kafka are among his favorite targets – he samples from them, but in a sense he also *rewrites* them. Rewriting, too, can be viewed as literary procedure, one with a long history, but which assumes a special centrality in postmodernism (Calinescu, 1997; Moraru, 2001). One need only think of all the many adaptations, recyclings, remakes, and re-envisionings of canonical texts that appear during the postmodern decades – all the versions of Shakespeare, Jane Austen and *Alice,* for instance – some of them cynically commercial, others parodic but in the strangely neutral or "blank" way that Jameson calls "pastiche" (1991, 16–7), still others critical, polemical, or subversive. Examples of the latter type include the rewritings of *Robinson Crusoe* by Michel Tournier (*Vendredi* [1967]) and J.M. Coetzee (*Foe* [1986]), as well as Kathy Acker's *Great Expectations* (1983) and *Don Quixote* (1986). Once again, the onset of this renewed postmodern practice of rewriting can be dated rather precisely to 1966, specifically to Tom Stoppard's rewriting of *Hamlet* as an absurdist drama in *Rosencrantz and Guildenstern Are Dead* and Jean Rhys's re-envisioning of Charlotte Brontë's *Jane Eyre* through a feminist and postcolonial lens in her novel *Wide Sargasso Sea.*

Burroughs rewrites other writers, but he also rewrites himself, not only when he cuts up or folds in his own texts, but when he re-edits *The Soft Machine* for its 1966 re-issue. This practice of *self*-rewriting overtakes other texts of 1966 as well. Gilbert Sorrentino, for instance, would rewrite *all* of his early novels later on, in the eighties – *Steelwork* (1970) as *Crystal Vision* (1981), *Imaginative Qualities of Actual Things* (1971) as the trilogy *A Pack of Lies* (1985, 1987, 1989), and his road-novel of 1966, *The Sky Changes*, as *Blue Pastoral* (1983) (Mackey, 1997, 84–5). In a similar spirit of self-revision, John Barth would revisit and rewrite all six of his early novels, including *Giles Goat-boy*, in *LETTERS* (1979). This practice of *doubling back on oneself* – in this case, returning to one's own texts and re-imagining them – is another of the signatures of 1966.

7. Strange Loops

Barth doubled back on his own career when he rewrote *Giles* as part of *LETTERS* thirteen years later – but this was nothing new, for he had already doubled back when he wrote *Giles* itself. *Giles* rewrites his preceding novel, *The Sot-Weed Factor* (1960), a parodic historical fiction in which Barth had inadvertently (or so he says) recreated the archetypal pattern of the hero monomyth popularized by the mythographer Joseph Campbell in *The Hero with a Thousand Faces* (1949) (Barth, 1984, 41–54). Having recreated the monomyth without meaning to, he decided in his next novel to revisit it self-consciously, reflecting knowingly and ironically on the heroic pattern; the result was *Giles Goat-Boy*. Such doubling-back also occurs inside *Giles*, locally, on a miniature scale. In one episode, trying to escape from the Library with enemies in hot pursuit, Giles interrupts a librarian who is reading a "large novel" to ask her for directions. She answers "as if that question … were exactly what she expected," and Giles reflects that her "simple answer" prevented his tale from being cut short, "an endless fragment" – words which the librarian herself murmurs under her breath (*"-less fragment"*) (Barth, 1966, 724–5). In short, the book that the librarian is reading must be *Giles Goat-Boy* itself, and having come to the scene in which she herself appears, she quotes her own lines from it, and Giles's, verbatim. The novel doubles back upon itself.

We call such doubling-back, at whatever level it occurs, *recursion* or *self-reference* (Hofstadter, 1979). Though it is a feature of postmodernism generally, and of the "big bang" moment of 1966 in particular, it would be an exaggeration to say that 1966 *discovered* recursion. If any historical moment deserves the credit for that, it would be the moment of modernism's onset, in the years preceding the Great War (Everdell, 1997, 347–8). Nevertheless, 1966 certainly *re*discovered recursion. Recursion's fingerprints are all over the terminology of the time, wherever the Greek prefix *meta* appears: *metalanguage* (Jakobson, 1960), language that refers to *language itself*, whether in the specialized vocabularies of grammarians and linguists or in everyday conversation, when we need to clarify each other's meanings ("What did you mean by that?"); *metafiction* (Gass, 1970), fiction that acknowledges and reflects upon its own status *as fiction*, as in the encounter with the librarian in *Giles* (as well as in a great many other postmodernist novels of 1966 and thereafter); *metatheatre,* theatre that exposes its own theatricality to view, as in Stoppard's *Rosencrantz and Guildenstern* (but also in *Hamlet* itself, the play that Stoppard rewrites); and so on.

The cultural artifacts of 1966 seem, time and again, to *fold back* on themselves or to *tuck themselves back into* themselves, bending themselves into all kinds of strange loops (Hofstadter, 1979, 10, 691). To visualize such forms, one might think in terms of familiar topological paradoxes like the Klein bottle, whose inside is also its outside, or the Möbius strip, a loop with a twist whose outer surface is continuous with its inner surface. Pynchon provides an image of this sort of paradox when, near the beginning of *The Crying of Lot 49*, he has his heroine Oedipa contemplate a painting, *Bordando el manto terrestre* (*Embroidering the Earth's Mantle*) – which actually exists, it turns out, having been painted by the émigré Spanish surrealist Remedios Varo in 1961 (see Figure 1). *Bordando el manto terrestre* represents a strange

Figure 1. Remedios Varo, *Bordando el manto terrestre* (1961). Oil on masonite. 39 3/8 in. × 48 3/8 in. (100 cm × 123 cm).

loop: a group of girls, sequestered in a tower, embroider a tapestry that tumbles out the windows of their tower and becomes the world – evidently the very world in which their tower is itself located. Oedipa recognizes this paradoxical figure as an image of her own situation, trapped in the tower of her own solipsism, which creates the world around her. It also mirrors, on a miniature scale, the novel *The Crying of Lot 49* itself. (Technically, this is called a *mise en abyme*; see Chapter 3.)

Recursion and the figure of the strange loop spill over from one cultural level to another in 1966, and from genre to genre. Recursion penetrates even to the science-fiction genre, which might at first glance seem inhospitable to self-reflection. However, consider Delany's *Babel-17*, a novel about language – perhaps one of the world's first metalinguistic science fictions. Even more brazenly, in Dick's science-fiction novel of 1966, *The Unteleported Man*, emigrants to a distant world are given a book, *Dr. Bloode's True and Complete Economic and Political History*, in which, like the librarian from *Giles Goat-Boy*, they read their own experiences, repeated verbatim from elsewhere in *The Unteleported Man* itself. Even The Beatles' pop songs loop back on themselves in 1966:

> Dear Sir or Madam will you read my book,
> It took me years to write, will you take a look?
> Based on a novel by a man named Lear,
> And I need a job,
> So I want to be a paperback writer. . . .
> It's a dirty story of a dirty man,
> And his clinging wife doesn't understand.
> His son is working for the Daily Mail,
> It's a steady job,
> But he wants to be a paperback writer. . . .   (Aldridge, 1991, 114)

The speaker, who wants to be a paperback writer, has written a novel about a man whose son wants to be a paperback writer – strange loop.

Nineteen sixty-six is the year of *meta* on the pop charts and at the cutting edge of fiction, but also in universities and research centers housing the academic humanities disciplines. New metalanguages appear, as though in response to the heightened self-conscious of culture itself. For example, the academic study of narrative emerged as a subdiscipline, and began to acquire its own metalanguage, not once but twice in 1966, in two different contexts, independently of each other: in North America, with the appearance of a landmark work of synthesis, Robert Scholes and Robert Kellogg's *The Nature of Narrative*; and in France, with the publication of a special issue of the journal *Communications* that announced the arrival of what its subtitle called "the structural analysis of narrative" (*Recherches sémiologiques: l'analyse structural du récit*). Empirical and historicist, Scholes and Kellogg keep their theorizing low key; not so the French, who make bold claims for the scientific status and universal scope of their theories, and who already display the flair for neologism that would be one of the hallmarks of *narratologie*, the scientific study of narrative. The special issue's roster is a who's who of Francophone narrative theory: Roland Barthes, Claude Bremond, Umberto Eco, the film theorist Christian Metz, Tzvetan Todorov, and Gérard Genette, among others. Structuralism had arrived.

In fact, structuralism had been gradually percolating into humanities disciplines for some time, but in North America it had penetrated no farther than linguistics and anthropology. That all changed in 1966. This was the year when Jacques Ehrmann edited a special issue of *Yale French Studies* that surveyed structuralism not only in linguistics and anthropology, but also in art, psychoanalysis, and literature. Even more crucially, it was the year of a celebrated conference at the Johns Hopkins University which introduced *post*structuralism for the first time to the United States (Macksey and Donato, 1972), notably in the person of Jacques Derrida, who delivered a seminal lecture there, "Structure, Sign, and Play in the Discourse of the Human Sciences." In both these venues, the *YFS* special issue, and the Johns Hopkins symposium, structuralists and those who would soon come to be called poststructuralists mingled – the structuralists Claude Lévi-Strauss and Michael Riffaterre alongside the poststructuralists Jacques Lacan and Geoffrey Hartman in the *YFS* special issue, Barthes and Todorov alongside Lacan and Derrida at Johns Hopkins (though Barthes at this point was already more than halfway along his intellectual trajectory from structuralism to poststructuralism). Thus, structuralism and poststructuralism were introduced *simultaneously* in 1966, which perhaps helps explain why the American academy leap-frogged over structuralism (which never really attained much of a foothold in North American intellectual life) and jumped directly to poststructuralism, a commanding influence in the seventies and eighties. If this curious situation does not exactly reflect the rediscovery of *meta*, it certainly reflects its *Americanization*.

Another way to put it would be to say that, with the arrival of poststructuralism in North America, "theory" was born, in the freestanding sense of the term that became so familiar in subsequent decades: not theory *of* this or that – not, for instance, theory *of* narrative, as structuralist narratology aspired to be – but theory *in general*, what in other eras might have been called *speculation*, or even indeed *philosophy*. Freestanding theory, which would come to be associated with the most conspicuous names of 1966, Derrida and Lacan – with the crucial addition of Michel Foucault, who happened to be absent from both the *YFS* special issue and the Johns Hopkins symposium of that year – would go on to enjoy a protracted career in the postmodern academy. Theory, however, is not the *cause* of postmodernism; that is, post-structuralism does *not* constitute the blueprint for the production of post-modernist artworks or other forms of cultural expression, as some people have rashly concluded. Poststructuralism is not the theory of which postmo-dernism is the practice. Rather, theory in the freestanding sense is itself one of the *symptoms* of postmodernism (Jameson, 1988, 194), on a par with post-modernist novels, poems, films, buildings, cities, and so forth.

It would be fruitless to try to summarize here the poststructuralist theory that would emerge in the years after 1966, given its diversity and complexity. Perhaps it would be enough to emphasize here its fundamental skepticism about language – in particular, about the capacity of language to reflect or represent reality. Instead, from the poststructuralist point of view language should be seen as *constructing* reality, or rather constructing *a* reality, since the reality it constructs is neither inevitable nor natural – just the way things are – but arbitrary, and shot through with disparities of privilege and power attributable to the structure of language itself. For these reasons, the apparent "naturalness" of language needs to be contested, and its structures *deconstructed*.

Viewed in this way, poststructuralism shares something in common with another landmark of theoretical reflection, also dating from 1966, that never quite entered the canon of "theory": the sociologists Peter Berger's and Thomas Luckmann's *The Social Construction of Reality*. According to Berger and Luckmann, reality is a kind of collective fiction – a novel that we are all writing together – constructed and sustained by processes of socializa-tion, institutionalization, and everyday social interaction, and especially through the medium of language. Socially constructed reality is complex, a jostling assemblage of "subuniverses of meaning," reflecting the word-views of different social classes, religious sects, occupations, and so on. Individuals experience a multiplicity of private and peripheral realities – dreams, play, fiction – but these alternative realities are all subordinated to the shared social reality of everyday life, which is experienced as "paramount" (Berger and Luckmann, 1966, 24).

The relevance of Berger's and Luckman's approach to the cultural artifacts of 1966 should be obvious. Recall, for instance, *The Crying of Lot 49*. Pynchon's heroine Oedipa undergoes a series of encounters with diverse "subuniverses of meaning," each associated with a different subculture, breakaway sect, or subversive cell, all previously invisible to her, crowding the peripheries of what she had always taken for "paramount reality." She experiences, one after another, a variety of "minor" or "satellite" realities – a painting, a movie, a play, games, dreams, moments of intoxication, and hallucination. The result of all this ontological experimentation is not to confirm her confidence in paramount reality but the reverse, to shake it to its very foundations – in effect, to deconstruct the fiction of the comfortable suburban everyday life with which she began. Hence the pain and confusion – but also the potential liberation – in the question she asks herself: "*Shall I project a world?*"

*

Breakdowns and breakthroughs, self-reflection and strange loops, paraworlds and subuniverses of meaning, proceduralism and rewriting, avant-pop, and "theory": these are some of the building blocks of the postmodernist poetics that would emerge in the decades after 1966, Year Zero of postmodernism. It was the end of the beginning.

ALICE

1. Curious *Alice*

"Things then did not delay in turning curious": so begins Chapter 3 of Thomas Pynchon's 1966 novel, *The Crying of Lot 49*. Pynchon's heroine, Oedipa Maas, having undertaken to execute the will of her deceased lover, Pierce Inverarity, finds herself dislodged from her comfortable suburban life and exposed to the first of what will prove to be a long series of Californian subcultures, micro-worlds and alternative realities. It would be commonplace to say that she has tumbled down a rabbit hole, or passed through the looking glass. Such commonplace phrases, of course, have entered our everyday language from the two books that the cleric and Oxford don C. L. Dodgson, using the pen name Lewis Carroll, wrote for children in the mid-nineteenth century: *Alice's Adventures in Wonderland* (1865) and *Through the Looking-Glass and What Alice Found There* (1871). These everyday phrases are more than usually appropriate in the case of *Lot 49*, as Pynchon signals by his conspicuous use of the keyword "curious." "Curious" is a something like a synecdoche of *Alice in Wonderland* – a part that stands for the whole (see Schor, 2013, 69–84). It occurs no fewer than twelve times in *Wonderland* (one occurrence per chapter, on average), most memorably at the beginning of Chapter 2: "'Curiouser and curiouser,'" cried Alice (she was so much surprised, that for the moment she quite forgot to speak good English)" (Carroll, 1971, 14). Alice herself had been punningly characterized a couple of pages earlier as "this curious child" (Carroll, 1971, 12). Pynchon's Oedipa is another such curious child, grown up to be a curious young woman: eager to know, as her name, Oedipa, suggests, but also curious in the sense of "strange" – a stranger in a strange land.

The presence of the keyword "curious," in such a conspicuous position, identifies *Lot 49* as a rewrite of *Alice in Wonderland* – one of many in the postmodern era. Fast-forward to the early years of the new millennium. William Gibson, founder of cyberpunk science fiction, is also alluding to *Alice* when, in his novel *Pattern Recognition* (2003), he has his own heroine, Cayce Pollard, reflect on the slightly uncanny unfamiliarity of London from an American visitor's perspective, calling it the "mirror world":

> The switch on [the] Italian floor lamp feels alien: a different click, designed to hold back a different voltage, foreign British electricity. . . . . Mirror world. The plugs on appliances are huge, triple-pronged, for a species of current that only powers electric chairs, in America. Cars are reversed, left to right, inside; handsets have a different weight, a different balance; the covers of paperback books look like Australian money. (Gibson, 2003, 2–3)

Cayce has passed *Through the Looking-Glass*, and what she finds in this mirror-world of London seems to be modeled, in a more or less oblique way, on Alice's experiences in the looking-glass world. *Pattern Recognition*, too, is a rewrite of *Alice* – though at the same time it is also a rewrite of *The Crying of Lot 49*, and of Gibson's own first novel, *Neuromancer* (1984), the book that launched cyberpunk (see Chapter 3).

2. Postmodern *Alice*

The rewriting or recycling of canonical texts is a typical postmodern practice. Sometimes parodic, sometimes not, it occurs throughout the postmodern decades, but its breakthrough moment might be 1966, the year of Tom Stoppard's *Rosencrantz and Guildenstern Are Dead* and Jean Rhys's *Wide Sargasso Sea*, rewritings of *Hamlet* and *Jane Eyre*, respectively. Rewriting the classics is always an act fraught with a kind of patricidal violence, but never more so than when the text being manhandled in this way belongs to the prehistory of postmodernism itself – a precursor of postmodernism. This is the case, for instance, with Shakespeare's *The Tempest* (see "Prospero's Books"), as it is with *Don Quixote*, which is rewritten over and over again by postmodernists – by Borges in his story "Pierre Menard," then by Robert Coover, Carlos Fuentes, John Barth, Paul Auster, Kathy Acker, and many others. Lewis Carroll's *Alice* is another such precursor text, postmodern before the fact – always already postmodern – and thus a source of multiple rewritings, partial and complete, overt and covert, throughout the postmodern decades.

Of course, many versions of *Alice* predate 1966, beginning almost as soon as Dodgson's original books appeared. Nearly 200 literary imitations, revisions, or parodies appeared between 1869 and 1930 (Sigler, 1997), and if the number of popular adaptations fell off after the twenties, this was more than compensated for by the intense interest that the Anglophone high modernists (Woolf, Eliot,

Joyce, and others; see Dusinberre, 1987) and the Continental surrealists (Breton, Aragon, Ernst, Dalí; see Jones and Gladstone, 1998, 244–5) took in Lewis Carroll. Nor are *Alice* versions restricted to print. There had been stage adaptations of *Alice* from the very beginning, with Dodgson himself collaborating as early as the 1880s on stage productions, which would be revived annually at Christmas until 1939. Beginning in the thirties, *Alice* crossed over into film, and then in the post–Second World War period into television. Kamilla Elliot in 2003 counted nearly fifty film and television versions – surely not an exhaustive total, given the entertainment industry's erratic record keeping.

So Lewis Carroll's books have been a source of rewrites, remakes, and adaptations since the very beginning. Nevertheless, *Alice* underwent a revival in the postmodern decades of the seventies, eighties and nineties, with a proliferation of versions (some of them admittedly rather remote from the originals). One scholar (Israel, 2000) documents at least ten "literary" novels on *Alice* themes from the eighties and nineties – not all of them postmodern in form or spirit – by writers such as Emma Tennant, David Slavitt, Pat Barker, A. M. Homes, and even Whoopi Goldberg. She identifies almost the same number of "genre" fictions (fantasy and science fiction) from the same decades by John Crowley, Jeff Noon, Philip Pullman, Jonathan Lethem, and others, as well as a number of films, television shows, and plays, including Wim Wenders' *Alice in the Cities* (1974); Jim Henson's *Labyrinth* (1986); Gavin Millar's *Dreamchild* (1985), scripted by Dennis Potter; plays by Susan Sontag and Christopher Hampton; and even an episode of *The X-Files* ("Paper Hearts," broadcast in December 1996). Other *Alice* versions from these decades include Philip José Farmer's *Riverworld* series of science-fiction novels (1971–83), in which the historical Alice Liddell Hargreaves, the real-life model for Dodgson's character, makes an appearance; Angela Carter's stories "Flesh and the Mirror" (1973), "Wolf-Alice" (1979), and "Alice in Prague" (1993), the last of these inspired by Jan Švankmajer's stop-action animated *Alice* (1988); and at least three *Alice* versions by the Japanese novelist Haruki Murakami, one per decade from the eighties through the new millennium: *Hard-Boiled Wonderland and the End of the World* (1985), *The Wind-Up Bird Chronicles* (1994–95), and *After Dark* (2004), a version of *Looking-Glass*. Among the many theatrical adaptations – one source reports as many as 150 new productions between 1979 and 1988 (Jones and Gladstone, 1998, 242–3) – the one directed by Robert Wilson, with songs by Tom Waits (Hamburg, 1992) is particularly notable. Film versions include Terry Gilliam's *Jabberwocky* (1977), Richard Rush's 1979 film of Paul Brodeur's novel *The Stunt Man* (1970), James Cameron's science-fiction horror movie *Aliens* (1986) and, incredible though it sounds, even a pornographic musical version (1976). *Alice* characters and motifs also figure in graphic novels such as Grant Morrison and Dave McKean's *Arkham Asylum* (1989) and Neil Gaiman's *Sandman* series (1989–96).

A cluster of *Alice* versions appears right around the turn of the millennium (see Brooker, 2004), including a British television film of *Looking-Glass* in 1998, an NBC television adaptation in 1999, and in the same year, the Wachowski siblings' film, *The Matrix*, with its several explicit allusions to *Alice*. Also dating from the turn of the millennium are American McGee's horror videogame adaptation of *Alice* (2000; a sequel appeared in 2011), Jeanette Winterson's novel *The PowerBook* (2000) (see Torpey, 2009), J. G. Ballard's *Super-Cannes* (2000), Katie Roiphe's *Still She Haunts Me* (2001; Brooker, 2004, 182–4), and a Royal Shakespeare Company production (2001–02), adapted by Adrian Mitchell (Brooker, 2004, 68–9), the same radical poet who, back in 1966, had adapted Peter Weiss's play *Marat/Sade* for the director Peter Brook. Another cluster appears around the end of the new millennium's first decade, including the Walt Disney Company's spectacular 3-D film version of *Alice in Wonderland* (2010), directed by Tim Burton; a cable-television mini-series on the Syfy channel (December 2009); a long philosophical poem, "Alice in the Wasteland" (2009), by the American avant-garde poet Ann Lauterbach; and even an iPad application for children (spring 2010), a sort of interactive digital reinterpretation of a child's pop-up book, based on Carroll's text and John Tenniel's illustrations. It is the range of cultural levels and media platforms that seems most striking: from mass-market entertainment to the avant-garde, from print to film and television to digital media, Alice seemed to be everywhere for several months in 2009 and 2010. Other *Alice* versions from the new millennium include Gibson's *Pattern Recognition*, mentioned earlier; Terry Gilliam's film *Tideland* (2005); Robert Coover's short story "Alice in the Time of the Jabberwock" (2005); at least two graphic novels, *Lost Girls* (2006), written by Alan Moore and drawn by Melinda Gebbie, and Bryan Talbot's *Alice in Sunderland* (2007), a local history in the form of graphic narrative; and even (if obliquely) Christopher Nolan's celebrated film *Inception* (2010).

So ubiquitous are allusions to *Alice* in postmodern novels in particular that the presence of *Alice* might almost be considered a *marker* of literary postmodernism: if *Alice* appears, the novel is likely to be postmodernist; if not, maybe not. Examples include Guillermo Cabrera Infante's *Tres tigres tristes* [*Three Trapped Tigers*] (1965), Angela Carter's *Several Perceptions* (1968), John Fowles's *The French Lieutenant's Woman* (1969), Pynchon's *Gravity's Rainbow* (1973), Don DeLillo's *Ratner's Star* (1976), Alasdair Gray's *Lanark* (1981), Paul Auster's *City of Glass* (1985), Salman Rushdie's *The Satanic Verses* (1988), Alison Habens's *Dreamhouse* (1994), Zadie Smith's *White Teeth* (2000), and Junot Díaz's *The Brief, Wondrous Life of Oscar Wao* (2007), as well as several novels I have already mentioned, including *Lot 49* and *Pattern Recognition*. Indeed, so ubiquitous are *Alice* allusions that one might legitimately wonder whether there are *any* novels that we generally regard as "postmodern" that do *not* allude somehow or other to *Alice*.

When did this proliferation of postmodern *Alice* versions begin? I believe its onset can be dated rather precisely.

3. *Go Ask Alice*, 1966

Even in the light of the long history of *Alice* versions, 1966 has a special status as a landmark date – the year in which *Alice* versions attained a sort of "critical mass" and also underwent a significant reorientation.

Alice versions abound in and around that year, roughly from the centennial of *Wonderland* in 1965 to that of *Looking-Glass* in 1971. In 1966, no fewer than three televised *Alice* versions aired, one animated, two live action, including Jonathan Miller's notable adaptation for the BBC. This was the same year, of course, as Pynchon's *Lot 49*, as well as Christine Brooke-Rose's *Such*, another *Alice* version, if a more remote one. In 1967, Ralph Steadman, who would later go on to collaborate with the New Journalist Hunter S. Thompson on several memorable books, illustrated *Alice in Wonderland*. Nineteen sixty-seven also marks the posthumous publication of Flann O'Brien's (Brian O'Nolan's) *The Third Policeman*, a darkly comic version of *Alice*. Between 1967 and 1970, Joanna Russ published four sword-and-sorcery stories, later collected as *The Adventures of Alyx* (1983), about a resourceful adventuress seeking her fortune in strange lands; the last of these stories, "The Second Inquisition" (1970), is especially rich in *Looking-Glass* motifs. Nineteen sixty-eight saw the appearance of Angela Carter's *Several Perceptions*, a contemporary picaresque in which Alice's Wonderland dream is collapsed into a climactic all-night house-party. In that same year the first of the American composer David Del Tredici's multiple musical settings of songs and episodes from the *Alice* books was premiered. In 1969, the French philosopher Gilles Deleuze published *Logique du sens*, which commented extensively on Lewis Carroll's nonsense, and the Surrealist artist Salvador Dalí produced a set of woodcut illustrations of *Wonderland*. In 1970, the British artist Peter Blake, best known for creating the cover of the Beatles' *Sergeant Pepper's Lonely Hearts Club Band* album, began a series of *Alice* silkscreens. The following year, 1971, the uncategorizable German artist Sigmar Polke painted his own *Alice in Wonderland*, appropriating one of Tenniel's illustrations (Alice's interview with the caterpillar) and brushing it onto patterned fabric to obtain a disorienting "layered" effect. Finally, in the wake of the successful 1969 re-release of *Fantasia*, the Disney studio's 1951 animated version of *Wonderland* was itself re-released and screened for newly receptive audiences on college campuses across the United States (Brooker, 2004, 208).

No doubt the impulse to commemorate the centennials of *Wonderland* and *Looking-Glass* had something to do with the upsurge *Alice* versions in the later sixties. However, the real trigger for the proliferation of *Alice* rewrites and adaptations at this moment, and their qualitative transformation, seems to have been a single event, datable to the year 1966. That event was the appearance of Grace Slick's song "White Rabbit" as performed first in 1966 by The Great Society, and then a year later by the San Francisco acid-rock band Jefferson Airplane:

> One pill makes you larger
> And one pill makes you small
> And the ones that mother gives you
> Don't do anything at all
> Go ask Alice
> When she's ten feet tall

And if you go chasing rabbits
And you know you're going to fall
Tell 'em a hookah smoking caterpillar
Has given you the call
Call Alice
When she was just small. . . .

"White Rabbit" enormously enhanced *Alice'*s pop-culture visibility, but for a new audience – not children, but adolescents and young adults. It also launched the psychedelic reinterpretation of *Alice*. These two factors together seem to have created the impetus for the proliferation of postmodern *Alices*.

Controversial for its endorsement of psychedelic experience, but an inescapable hit on late-sixties radio, "White Rabbit" is a catalyst. From 1966 on, not only do the sheer numbers of *Alice* versions surge, but a certain threshold is crossed, a certain critical mass is achieved. We might say that, post-1966, in the aftermath of "White Rabbit," *Alice goes viral*. One measure of the change is the fact that, whereas before 1966 versions of *Alice* engaged mainly with the "original" texts, after 1966 versions typically engage with Dodgson's originals *but also with at least one other previous version*. For example, A. M. Homes's novel *The End of Alice* (1996) rewrites both *Alice* and Vladimir Nabokov's *Lolita* (1955/58), which is itself a version of *Alice* (Israel, 2000); Nabokov, it turns out, had actually translated *Alice's Adventures in Wonderland* into Russian in 1923. Alison Habens's *Dreamhouse* rewrites both *Alice* and Angela Carter's *Several Perceptions*. Jonathan Lethem's *As She Climbed Across the Table* (1997) rewrites both *Alice* and DeLillo's *Ratner's Star*, which slyly acknowledges its indebtedness to *Alice* through the titles of its two parts (part one: "Adventures"; part two: "Reflections"). The Wachowskis' *The Matrix* rewrites *Alice* but also "White Rabbit," notably in the scene when Morpheus offers Neo a choice of capsules, blue or red: choose the blue pill and "the story ends," but choose the red one and "you stay in Wonderland, and I show you how deep the rabbit-hole goes." ("One pill makes you larger/And one pill makes you small/And the ones that mother gives you/Don't do anything at all.") Jeff Noon's *Automated Alice* (1996) rewrites both *Alice* and Gray's *Lanark*. Gibson's *Pattern Recognition* rewrites both *Alice* and *The Crying of Lot 49*; Gibson's heroine Cayce Pollard, who visits the "mirror-world," is a version of Alice, but at the same time also a version of Pynchon's Oedipa Maas. The Syfy channel's *Alice* rewrites both Dodgson's *Alice* and *The Matrix*, and, arguably, so does Nolan's film *Inception*, while Tim Burton's *Alice in Wonderland* rewrites both *Alice* and *The Wizard of Oz*, one of the most influential of all *Alice* versions, and so on, throughout the postmodern decades.

4. Trips vs. Missions

"White Rabbit" introduces a new and transformative understanding of Carroll's *Alice* books as reflecting or anticipating psychedelic experience. It emphasizes, for the first time as far as I can see, the literally hallucinatory quality of the *Alice* world – its abrupt, unmotivated juxtapositions and transformations, its disjointedness and sense of *non sequitur*, its illogic and mutability. The reframing of *Alice* in terms of psychedelic experience very quickly became a commonplace of popular culture, not only among advocates of the drug subculture – Thomas Fensch, for instance, published an annotated edition of *Wonderland*, under the title *Alice in Acidland* (1970), that identified all of Carroll's supposed allusions to drug experience – but also in antidrug polemics such as the bestseller *Go Ask Alice* (1971), allegedly the diary of an anonymous young drug user. (The latter was in fact a hoax, though that did not prevent it from being adapted as an ABC television *Movie of the Week* in 1973.) I would venture to say that *all* the *Alice* versions subsequent to 1966–67 are colored to some greater or lesser degree by this psychedelic reinterpretation; they are all more or less influenced by the model of *Alice* as *trip*.

This reorientation of *Alice* is readily traceable in popular music, beginning with the Beatles. Lennon and McCartney's song "Lucy in the Sky with Diamonds," from *Sergeant Pepper's Lonely Hearts Club Band* (1967), was widely interpreted as a song about psychedelic experience, partly on the basis of its suggestive initials – *LSD* – but mainly because of its hallucinatory imagery: "Picture yourself in a boat on a river, with tangerine trees and marmalade skies." John Lennon would later protest (not entirely convincingly) that the song never had anything to do with drug experience at all, but drew its inspiration wholly, and innocently, from *Alice*:

> The images were from *Alice in Wonderland*. It was Alice in the boat. She is buying an egg and it turns into Humpty Dumpty. The woman serving in the shop turns into a sheep, and next minute they're rowing in a rowing boat somewhere – and I was visualizing that . . . . It's not an acid song. (*The Beatles*, 200, 242)

Not just the "boat on the river," incidentally, but also the last verse's "train in a station, with plasticine porters with looking glass ties," seems derived from *Alice* – not *Wonderland* in this case, but the episode from *Looking-Glass*, memorably illustrated by Tenniel, in which Alice travels by railway through the Third Square. In any case, Lennon's defense of the song's innocence seems somewhat disingenuous: given the pervasive psychedelic interpretation of *Alice* as trip, nothing prevents "Lucy in the Sky with Diamonds" from being *both* a version of *Alice* (as Lennon claims) *and also* a song about drug experience.

Reinterpreting *Alice* as an acid trip, as Grace Slick does in "White Rabbit," is of course grossly ahistorical; LSD wasn't even synthesized until 1938, and Dodgson, as far as we know, never dabbled in any of the hallucinogens actually available at his time. However, the psychedelic interpretation reframes *Alice* in ways that make it available for reappropriation in updated circumstances. It makes Carroll's novels contemporary with The Beatles' explorations (beginning in *Revolver*) of worlds up- or downstream from our own, and with Philip K. Dick's paraworlds of science fiction; it (post)modernizes *Alice*. Viewed in this light, the ontological *playfulness* and *experimentalism* of Wonderland and the looking-glass world become salient: their status as alternative realities, accessible through special portals (rabbit hole, looking glass); their multiplicity of pocket universes or microworlds, differing in scale, in the sorts of beings that inhabit them, in their physics and even their logic, revealed to us as Alice travels across them, from one subuniverse to the next; their ontological paradoxes, such as the classic strange loop of *Looking-Glass*, Chapter 4, when Alice is shown the sleeping Red King who, alarmingly, is said to be dreaming Alice, as Alice is dreaming *him*; and so on. To read *Alice* as a trip is to read it as an experiment in world-making and – unmaking, and thus as a precursor of postmodernism – always already postmodern.

The trip model also emphasizes the *weak narrativity* of Lewis Carroll's original books (see McHale, 2001). Eventful though they are, literally event-*filled*, they are also episodic, disjointed, weakly plotted, picaresque in structure rather than strongly end-oriented. "Picaresque" seems exactly the right term for the structure of *Alice's Adventures*, whose very title seems designed to evoke the tradition of *Don Quixote, Joseph Andrews, Roderick Random*, and so on. One might have expected *Through the Looking-Glass* to be the more firmly plotted of the two books, given its overarching narrative of a chess endgame, but in fact this is not really the case. Notice that *Through the Looking-Glass* is subtitled, not "what Alice *did* there," but what she "*found* there," emphasizing accidental encounters and passive receptivity over purposeful action. Here, the plotting suffers from Alice's lack of agency. While she does have a definite purpose in *Looking-Glass* – to become a queen when she reaches the Eighth Square – Alice seems powerless to affect her progress toward that goal very materially. Though she is permitted a bird's-eye view of the chessboard and players from the hill at the beginning, once she descends to the level of the board she literally loses sight of the narrative in which she participates; she is, after all, only a pawn in someone else's game.

Only weakly narrativized, the *Alice* books are literally *pointless* in the sense of *refusing to make a point*. In contradistinction to nearly every other children's book of that era, and by Dodgson's conscious design, they teach no moral, deliver no warning, offer no model of behavior for a child to emulate. They are also pointless in the sense of literally *going nowhere*. It is perhaps misleading to refer to them as novels at all, picaresque or otherwise. They are, rather, Menippean satires (see Chapter 1), and in common with other texts of this genre (or anti-genre), they use narrative structure not to drive a sequence of events toward a conclusion or *telos*, but mainly as an excuse for juxtaposing a series of "numbers" or "turns" (in the variety-show sense): encounters with colorful characters, usually inconclusive; conversations, often baffling or agonistic, but in any case inconsequential; recitals of poems; and performances of songs. Narrative in the *Alice* books does not so much advance as *pause* and *linger*, then pause again, and then pause some more.

It is this aspect of the *Alice* books that the trip versions capitalize on, in the aftermath of "White Rabbit." Indeed, trip versions of *Alice* are arguably more faithful to the spirit of Carroll's originals than any others. Be that as it may, *pure* trip versions of *Alice* are rare, perhaps for obvious reasons. The purest expressions of the trip model occur in non-narrative or weakly narrative genres, for instance in musical adaptations or in lyrical or discursive poetry. Ann Lauterbach's "Alice in the Wasteland," itself a verse Menippean satire, is one example. Another is David Del Tredici's obsessive series of musical settings of *Alice* material, beginning with

Pop-Pourri in 1968 and continuing down to *Dum Dee Tweedle* in 1992, a total of at least nine works in all. If the various pieces were assembled into a cycle and performed on successive nights, Del Tredici's *Alice* would rival Wagner's *Ring* in scale – except that, unlike the *Ring*, they would not yield a continuous narrative, but only disjointed episodes, lacking narrative's connective tissue. The effect would be, like *Alice* itself, diffuse, meandering – *trippy*.

This psychedelic model of *Alice* as trip is one of two major types of *Alice* versions that I detect in the postmodern (or post-1966) era. If the trip model capitalizes on the weakness of narrativity in Carroll's *Alice* books, the alternative model responds to the originals' weak narrativity by seeking to ameliorate it – to repair the deficiency by *narrativizing Alice*. Narrativized versions link up the disjointed episodes of the originals, stringing them together on a single narrative thread; they supply the missing connective tissue and bring narrative order to the disorder of the trip. They give Alice *something to do*, devising a *mission* for her to undertake, whether in the action-hero sense of *Mission: Impossible* or in the missionary sense of saving the heathens, or both. Narrativizing is the typical solution to *Alice*'s trippiness on the part of commercial movie and television adapters of the books. Walt Disney's animators, for instance, reflecting on the 1951 animated version of *Alice in Wonderland*, frankly admit that they never overcame the antinarrative tendencies of Carroll's *Alice* – though they certainly tried. Disney himself, they write,

> liked the idea of a young girl living in her own dream yet not realizing why everything was so strange. . . . Unfortunately, either he lacked the energy to make a strong feature out of the episodic story material or he failed to communicate his uncertain feelings to his staff . . . . [T]he result was a very interesting, disjointed film with moments of high entertainment and other sections that seemed mild or puzzling. (Johnston and Thomas, 1993, 105)

"Peculiar actions and visual gimmicks can hold an audience only for a limited time," the animators go on to say, "and there is always a problem with the continuity once that crucial point has been passed" (Johnston and Thomas, 107). For "continuity," read "narrativity." In this case, by the animators' own admission, the project of narrativizing *Alice* failed. It is surely no accident that, almost two decades later, their film would acquire a new audience of college students who valued it precisely for its *trippy* qualities, in other words, for its *failed* narrativity.

The CBS television adaptation of 1985, directed by Harry Harris, compensated for the story's weak narrativity by attributing a motivation to Alice – precisely, the drive to *get out of* Wonderland, once she has fallen into it. Nick Willing, director of the 1999 NBC adaptation, gives Alice the *opposite* motivation: she flees *into* Wonderland in order to avoid having to perform a song at her parents' garden party. "The main thing I insisted on," Willing is reported as saying,

> is that Alice is asked to sing a song and is scared. The reason I did that is I felt the book is a collection of anecdotes, sketches written at different times and then cobbled together in a book. It is not written as a story with a

> beginning, middle and end. And our modern movie sensibility has to have an emotional pull for us to stay with a character. (quoted in Brooker, 2004, 217–8)

Finally, Tim Burton, director of the 2010 Disney version, seems as self-conscious as any of his predecessors about the decision to narrativize *Alice*. As quoted in the *New York Times*, he seems quite clear in his own mind about which model he chose, and why. Other versions, he is reported to have said, "always end[...] up seeming like a clueless little girl wandering around with a bunch of weirdos" (Rohter, 2010, 12) – which is to say, they ended up as trips. Burton evidently regards the narrative weakness of other versions as sufficient justification for imposing a robust narrative of his own. He motivates Alice's trip by giving her a mission that of liberating Wonderland from the capricious tyranny of the Red Queen – the same mission, coincidentally, that the Syfy channel's contemporaneous version sends *its* Alice on.

Missions, trips: surely it is no coincidence that these are the same terms that came to be associated with the American experience in the Vietnam War during the very years when *Alice* emerged as a touchstone of postmodernism. The same tension between *missions* and *trips* that characterizes postmodern versions of *Alice* also characterizes representations of Vietnam, for example in Michael Herr's *Dispatches* (1977), Tim O'Brien's *Going After Cacciato* (1979), Francis Ford Coppola's *Apocalypse Now* (1979), and Stanley Kubrick's *Full Metal Jacket* (1987). Recall, for instance, the nightmarish episode in Coppola's film in which Captain Willard encounters a leaderless unit defending a hallucinatory, illuminated bridge, firing at unseen North Vietnamese while listening to Jimi Hendrix on a tape deck: trip conflated with mission. Some of these Vietnam representations explicitly acknowledge *Alice* as their model. Several episodes of O'Brien's *Cacciato*, for instance, allude more or less obliquely to *Alice*, while Herr, describing senior officials' collective lapse into irrationality in the aftermath of the 1968 Tet Offensive in Vietnam, writes, "The Mission Council joined hands and passed together through the Looking Glass" (Herr, 1978, 74).

The tension between trip and mission makes itself felt particularly acutely in two related *Alice* versions, both already mentioned above, that roughly bookend the postmodern decades: Pynchon's *The Crying of Lot 49* (1966) and Gibson's *Pattern Recognition* (2003). *Lot 49* begins unmistakably as a quest narrative, but "things [do] not delay in turning curious," and before long the quest bogs down in proliferating information and tangential encounters. Oedipa Maas's mission mainly provides a narrative excuse for a trippy, *Alice*-like tour of various Californian subcultural enclaves and underworlds. Ultimately, the quest itself falters and finally is suspended, *stalling out* just before its resolution and leaving us, like the heroine herself, awaiting the crying of lot 49. The trip compromises the mission.

Gibson's *Pattern Recognition*, simultaneously a version of *Lot 49* and of *Alice*, actually involves two missions. Gibson's heroine, Cayce Pollard, is commissioned to track down the creator of a series of mysterious and hypnotically attractive online video clips, while at the same time she seeks to confirm the fate of her father, who disappeared on September 11, 2001, in the vicinity of the World

Trade Center towers. Each of these quests interrupts the other, and neither achieves entirely satisfactory closure. The fate of the lost father is almost but not quite ascertained, while the quest for the source of the online footage, though it does yield the identity of the creator, leaves many other mysteries unresolved. The footage itself, an unfinished fragment of narrative in which *almost nothing happens*, exhibits just the sort of weak narrativity that characterizes the very novel in which it appears; it constitutes, in other words, a scale model or *mise en abyme* of *Pattern Recognition*. Like Pynchon's *Lot 49*, *Pattern Recognition* ends up taking us on a literally pointless grand tour of the heroine's world, involving episodic encounters with grotesque and colorful characters in exotic "mirror-world" locales. Here, too, the trip compromises the mission.

If the trip sometimes interferes with the mission in recent *Alice* versions, the reverse is also possible: even the trippiest versions sometimes display traces of narrative momentum. Surprisingly, this is the case even with the text that I have been treating as foundational for the model of *Alice* as trip, Grace Slick's song "White Rabbit." What is most striking about this song's lyrics, which supposedly advocate for blissful, hedonistic psychedelic experience, is their surprising *aggressiveness*, their *pushiness*. These lyrics are imperative, importunate, issuing orders: "Go ask Alice"; "Call Alice." Their tone is that of a proselytizer for psychedelic experience, in the spirit of Timothy Leary or Ken Kesey in his Merry Prankster phase (as well as many other psychedelic rock songs of that era). Far from blissfully trippy, "White Rabbit" seems charged with implicit narrativity. It seems, in fact, to be *assigning a mission*.

The same tension between trip and mission that is detectable in the lyrics is also reflected in the differences between two different arrangements of the song – the 1966 arrangement by Grace Slick's first band, The Great Society, and the definitive arrangement from 1967 by the Jefferson Airplane. The Great Society version begins with a long instrumental prelude, lasting nearly four and a half minutes of a six-minute, 15-second cut, in a wandering, vaguely Middle-Eastern modal arrangement that is distinctly trippy. The music circles, weaves, and doubles back on itself, apparently in no hurry to get anywhere. Only weakly narrative, the arrangement seems pointless, in something like the same way that the *Alice* books themselves are pointless. By contrast, the Jefferson Airplane's arrangement, brashly appropriated from Ravel's *Bolero*, is a marching, charging crescendo from beginning to end. Lasting all of two and a half minutes, sounding more *driven* than *drifting*, the Airplane's version climaxes with Grace Slick singing – or rather, bellowing – "Feed your head"; so urgent and purposeful is her delivery that it feels more like "*Off* with your head!" Clearly responding to the driving, end-directed dynamics of Jefferson Airplane's "White Rabbit," Hunter S. Thompson, in *Fear and Loathing in Las Vegas* (1972), has Dr. Gonzo, the drug-addled "Samoan attorney," demand to be electrocuted in his bath just as the song reaches its climax. (Raoul Duke, Thompson's surrogate in the story, does not comply.) The song's conflation of narrative closure and erotic climax, of sex drive and death drive, could hardly be dramatized more transparently. The mission overwhelms the trip.

The same contending impulses that I detect in many of the post-1966 *Alice* versions – the resistance to narrativity, on the one hand, and the impulse toward narrativization, on the other, or what I have been calling the trip *vs.* the mission models – also characterize postmodernism as a whole. On the one hand, post-modernism inherits from the modernist-era avant-gardes a suspicion of conventional models of coherence, legibility, and closure, all associated with dominant ideologies – in other words, a suspicion of narrative. This suspicion is reflected in postmodernism's various antinarrative strategies of metafictional self-critique and self-erasure, not least of all its recourse to weakly narrative genres such as Menippean satire. On the other hand, postmodernism also frankly embraces the populist pleasures of narrativity, reviving and recovering narrative – "replenishing" it, to use John Barth's term. The two impulses complicate and interfere with each other right across postmodern culture and right down the decades, from the sixties to the present – as they do, on a miniature scale, in so many of the *Alice* versions of the same period. In this sense, postmodern *Alice* is postmodernism in a nutshell.

Chapter 3

The Major Phase:
Peak Postmodernism, 1973–1990

1. Rebranding

Another big bang: on July 15, 1972, at 3:32 p.m. (according to Charles Jencks), several high-rise blocks of the Pruitt-Igoe public housing project in St. Louis, Missouri, were demolished, signaling (not for the first or last time) the failure of International Style modernist architecture to deliver what it promised – safe, healthful, inexpensive, and above all *rational* housing for the masses. Waiting in the wings to supplant modernism was a new mode of architecture, one hospitable to such *un*modernist qualities as popular appeal, historical allusion, legible symbolism, and pleasure: postmodernism. The outlines of this new mode could be glimpsed in a book of that same year, the manifesto *Learning from Las Vegas* by the architects Robert Venturi, Denise Scott Brown, and Steven Izenour.

That, at least, is Charles Jencks's story about the (literal) implosion of modernist architecture and the timely rise of postmodernism. It is a compelling one, especially in light of the fact that Pruitt-Igoe's prize-winning architect, Minoru Yamasaki, also designed New York's World Trade Center, the North Tower of which opened in December 1972; the dedication of the entire complex would follow the next year. Buildings whose destruction almost thirty years apart frames the postmodern era, both designed by the same architect – the coincidence is uncanny (Paperny, 2010; Williams, 2011, 94).

As compelling as it is, Jencks's story is perhaps too good to be entirely true. For one thing, as Jencks admitted all along, the failure of Pruitt-Igoe is only one of a multitude of symptoms of modernist architecture's exhaustion in the late sixties and seventies, if a strikingly iconic one. Moreover, the specific time of Pruitt-Igoe's destruction – 3:32 p.m. – which contributes so much to the story's air of circumstantial precision, turns out to have been fabricated (Jencks, 2011, 27). In any case, the demolition of the complex, though begun on that day in 1972, actually continued into the next year, 1973 (Killen, 2006, 211).

Indeed, by many people's account, Jencks was off by about a year, and it is 1973 that marks the real watershed between before and after – between a sixties that was still basically modernist, and the postmodernism of the seventies and eighties (Jameson, 1991, xx–xxi). It is certainly a watershed year in world-historical terms, in ways that 1966 was not. The Arab nations' oil embargo of that year, in the wake of the Yom Kippur war, heightened awareness of the world's dependency on fossil fuels and the vulnerability of its energy resources, and arguably planted seeds of a new sense of global inter-connection (Rodgers, 2011, 9). Nineteen seventy-three was also the year when details of White House involvement in the Watergate break-in emerged and the Nixon administration began to unravel, with long-term consequences for the American presidency. It was the year of the Paris Peace Accords, the beginning of the end of the Vietnam War, and consequently the beginning of the still ongoing contest over the meaning of the sixties, and it was the year of the U.S. Supreme Court's *Roe v. Wade* decision that legalized abortion nation-wide, marking the first round of the still-unresolved "culture wars" over gender and sexuality (Rodgers, 2011, 145). According to the intellectual historian Andreas Killen (2006), upon whom I have been mainly drawing, Americans around 1973 experienced a rupture in their history, a collective "nervous breakdown," and began to suffer from that inability to think histori-cally that Fredric Jameson would later identify as a key characteristic of the postmodernist sensibility.

Because of his focus on the United States, Killen overlooks one other world-historical landmark of 1973: the founding of the first fully neoliberal regime anywhere, in Chile, following Augusto Pinochet's bloody, CIA-backed coup (Harvey, 2005, 7–8). Neoliberal economics, which seeks to "liberat[e] indivi-dual entrepreneurial freedoms and skills within an institutional framework characterized by strong private property rights, free markets, and free trade" (Harvey, 2005, 2), is more typically associated with changes inaugurated a little later and with much less bloodshed during the years 1978–80, when Deng Xioping began the liberalization of the Chinese economy, and Margaret Thatcher and Ronald Reagan were elected as (respectively) prime minister of Great Britain and president of the United States. Nevertheless, Chilean neo-liberalization came first. "Not for the first time," writes David Harvey "a brutal experiment carried on in the periphery became a model for the formulation of policies in the centre" (2005, 9).

Harvey explicitly associates neoliberalism in economics with postmodernism in culture. Neoliberalization, requiring "the construction of a . . . market-based populist culture of differentiated consumerism and individual libertarianism," has "proved more than a little compatible with that cultural impulse called 'post-modernism' which had long been lurking in the wings but could now emerge full-blown as both a cultural and an intellectual dominant" (Harvey, 2005, 42). Harvey's formulation is circumspect here, and it allows for some slippage between economic neoliberalism and cultural postmodernism, which after all had been "lurking in the wings" since before neoliberalism's full emergence (whether one dates that to 1973 or to1978-80). Postmodern culture seems not *exactly* to coincide with the era of economic neoliberalism (which shows no signs of ending any time soon), just as it seems not *exactly* to coincide with the Cold War era, though chronologically it overlaps with both, reflecting them in various ways.

Killen, like Harvey, tries to synchronize cultural developments of 1973 with world-historical developments, arguing implicitly for a sort of across-the-board change in all domains of society and culture. Apart from the emergence of postmodernist architecture around 1973, Killen also cites the appearance on U.S. television screens of something that would later come to be called "reality TV," in the form of the PBS series *An American Family*, nearly twenty years in advance of MTV's breakthrough series *The Real World*. Other evidence for 1973 as a cultural threshold includes the flowering of a new, iconoclastic American cinema of directors operating outside the moribund studio system (Woody Allen, Robert Altman, Terrence Malick, Sam Peckinpah, Martin Scorsese); the ubiquity of Andy Warhol in American culture, both high and low; the short, raucous career of the New York Dolls, gender-bending rockers poised between glam and punk; and the publication, all in that same year, of such postmodernist literary landmarks as Thomas Pynchon's *Gravity's Rainbow*, J. G. Ballard's *Crash*, and Don DeLillo's *Great Jones Street*.

Such cultural indicators could be multiplied, of course, not all of them pointing in the same direction. (For instance, 1973 was also the year when B. S. Johnson, the most fully postmodern of the British novelists of the sixties, took his own life, ending prematurely a career of brilliant innovation; see Coe, 2004.) Moreover, as I have argued elsewhere (McHale, 2008), nearly all of Killen's cultural landmarks of 1973 are overshadowed by their precursors in the sixties, most of them dating to the *annus mirabilis* 1966 (see Chapter 2). The "directors' cinema" of 1973 has its roots in the underground film scene and European art-house cinema of ca. 1966. The Warhol of 1973 is overshadowed by the Warhol of the Exploding Plastic Inevitable and other innovative experiments of 1966, as the New York Dolls are by the innovations of the art-oriented rockers of 1966. Ballard's *Crash* is anticipated by the first stories in the *Atrocity Exhibition* cycle, dating from 1966, from which *Crash* would subsequently evolve. *Gravity's Rainbow* is anticipated by *The*

Crying of Lot 49, and *Learning from Las Vegas* by *Complexity and Contradiction in Architecture*. Nineteen sixty-six is the breakout year for all of these postmodernisms, while 1973 is the follow-through.

And yet, if postmodernism's actual onset falls somewhat earlier than 1973, nevertheless something *does* happen in that year in the cultural sphere. Another threshold is crossed – not a launch but a *re*launch, or better a *rebranding* (as we might say now). The situation in innovative fiction of the era is exemplary. Since the mid-sixties, a number of alternative *names* for the new fiction had been floated, without any of them achieving general acceptance: in the United States, for instance, *black humor, fabulation, surfiction* (Raymond Federman's coinage), and other candidates; in France, the manifestly inadequate *nouveau nouveau roman*. But throughout the early seventies, literary scholars had begun to use the term *postmodernism* – Leslie Fiedler from about 1970, Ihab Hassan from 1971, William Spanos from 1972 – so that, by the time of John Barth's important manifesto of 1979, "The Literature of Replenishment," it had become entirely normalized as *the* term for the period's fiction.

In short, around 1973, postmodernism acquired its *name*, signaling a new phase in its existence as a cultural category; or rather, it fully *became* a category for the first time, and so invited definition, refinement, reflection, theorization, and critique. From 1975, Charles Jencks began using the term in an architectural context, mapping the concept and extending its range in successive editions of his influential book, *The Language of Post-Modern Architecture*, from 1977 on. The term "postmodern" never appeared in Venturi, Scott Brown and Izenour's *Learning from Las Vegas*, but by the end of the seventies the sort of architectural practice they advocated, incorporating the legibility and populism of the Las Vegas Strip, had become identified all but universally with postmodernism. From its beachhead in architecture, the concept of postmodernism, and the aesthetic associated with it, radiated outward into the culture at large, from popular film and genre fiction to the art-world, from fashion and advertising to the academy.

What do we think of when we think of postmodernism? Mainly, the cultural forms and practices of postmodernism's "peak" period, from the emergence of the term itself in the mid-seventies through the end of the eighties, when a new threshold is crossed. Without pretending to exhaustiveness, it is possible to identify a number of characteristic forms and practices associated with the peak period: first, the discourse of "theory," which came to pervade the arts and humanities both inside and outside the academy in these years; second, the scaling up of metafictions from the smaller-scale works typical of the sixties to the "megafictions" that followed in the wake of

Gravity's Rainbow; third, the erosion of traditional hierarchical distinctions between the high and low strata of culture, across a range of cultural spheres; fourth, the special case of cyberpunk, which in the eighties began to "cross over" from the still somewhat marginalized enclave of science fiction to the culture at large, even serving as model and stimulus in the development of the Internet; fifth, the breakthrough of procedural writing to wider audiences, both through the success of OuLiPo writers such as Italo Calvino and Georges Perec and through the more overtly politicized practices of the L=A=N=G=U=A=G=E poets and Kathy Acker; and sixth, the return of representation in the visual arts of the eighties, a surprising reversion after the radical "dematerialization" of art by the conceptual movement in the early seventies. The site of many of these developments was a particular type of urban space, the contact zone between high and low culture, where high theory and street practice mingled and diverse career paths crossed. Duplicated in cities around the world, in the seventies and eighties that space was especially identified with Downtown New York – the capital of peak postmodernism.

2. "Theory"

If postmodernism came into its own in the period 1973–90, then part of its coming-of-age consisted of taking stock of itself. On or about the year 1966, postmodernism had been a practice – a set of practices – without a name; by 1973, a name had been proposed, but it was still casting around for an appropriate referent; by the Orwellian year of 1984, postmodernism had acquired its own theory, indeed a whole clutch of theories, some of them mutually incompatible (see Calinescu, 1987; Bertens, 1995). In less than a decade, postmodernism had escalated from a rumor to a clamor.

Early adopters of the term, mainly literary critics, associated it with one or another emergent phenomenon: with the irruption of popular culture and kitsch, in the case of Leslie Fiedler (1969); with the legacy of existentialism, in the case of William Spanos (1972); and in the case of Ihab Hassan (1971), whose approach was wider ranging and more eclectic, with the cultural consequences of technological transformation, among other things (Bertens, 1995, 29–52). These early attempts at definition look in retrospect like first drafts or trial runs for the theories that began to emerge from the mid-seventies on.

Crucial to the dissemination of the idea of postmodernism to fields beyond literature was Charles Jencks, as we have already seen. Beginning in 1975, in a series of manifestos and books published over the course of a decade or so, Jencks adapted insights from architects such as Robert Venturi, the Italian Aldo Rossi, and others (see Chapter 2) to develop a model of architectural postmodernism that offered an alternative to the functionalist purism of the modernist International Style. Key to Jencks's postmodernism was the notion of *double-coding*. Postmodern buildings, Jencks argued, such as the ones he championed by Venturi, Charles Moore, Michael Graves, Robert A. M. Stern, Frank Gehry, and others, appeal simultaneously to two different audiences: on one level, through their sophisticated reflection on design, structural techniques, and materials, to a minority constituency of architects and connoisseurs; on another level, through their decorativeness, their legibility, and their playful and pleasurable allusions to familiar historical styles of architecture, to a broader public of consumers. Jencks would eventually (1986) extend the range of double-coding to include the new figurative and narrative painting of Sandro Chia, Eric Fischl, Robert Longo, David Salle, and others (see section 7), and the "literature of replenishment" described by John Barth (1980) and conspicuously practiced by Umberto Eco (*The Name of the Rose*, 1980). Linda Hutcheon, in turn, would apply Jencks's model of double-coding more generally to postmodernist fiction of the type that she dubbed *historiographic metafiction* (1988) (see section 3). Hutcheon's was not the only theory of postmodernist fiction, of course. For instance, my own theory (summarized earlier in Chapter 1), hinging on the changeover from modernist fiction's exploration of epistemology (perception and knowledge) to postmodernism's showcasing of ontology (world-making, modes of being), appeared nearly simultaneously with Hutcheon's.

Jencks's notion of double-coding is only one version, albeit an influential one, of a larger, more encompassing thesis about postmodernism, articulated particularly powerfully by Andreas Huyssen (1984). This thesis holds that, in the postmodern era, the distinction between high culture and mass or popular culture that the modernists had striven so hard to maintain and police finally, definitively broke down; henceforth, high and low culture would mingle indiscriminately, for better or worse. This account of postmodernism, foregrounding its eclecticism, populism, and accessibility, had its critics, none more forceful than J.-F. Lyotard. Lyotard in 1982 associated postmodernism not with the encroachment of popular culture, but with the persistence of avant-garde experiment, identifying the postmodern with that part of modernist art that perpetually resists being domesticated and reduced to any familiar period style (Green, 2005, 40; McHale, 2012a). For Lyotard, "postmodernism" is the name for the avant-garde impulse *within* modernism; hence his notorious and paradoxical assertions that "A work can become modern only if it is first postmodern," and that "postmodernism is not modernism at its end, but in a nascent state, and this state is recurrent" (Lyotard, 1993, 13) (see Chapter 1).

Identifying postmodernism with the perpetual, "recurrent" avant-garde, against the grain of so many other approaches, was not, however, Lyotard's most influential contribution to the theory of postmodernism. More important was his thesis, developed in *La Condition postmoderne* (1979), that postmodernity is characterized by a general incredulity toward the master narratives that up until now have underwritten and sustained modern culture and society in the West (Lyotard, 1984). We no longer place our faith, Lyotard claimed, in the narratives of progress, enlightenment, and human liberation that once served to legitimate modernity. Skeptical of such "grand narratives," we postmoderns instead value the self-legitimating language games, or little narratives (*petits récits*), of affinity groups, local institutions, and subcultural enclaves. Where modern culture had aspired to universalism and "totality," postmodern culture prefers pluralism, particularism, and local knowledge (see Bertens, 1995, 123–131).

Lyotard's theory of postmodernism would seem, perhaps ironically, to preclude general theories of postmodernism – presumably including Lyotard's own. Charges of perpetrating a grand narrative and aspiring to totality, however, did not intimidate Fredric Jameson, who over the course of the eighties (1983, 1984, 1991) developed a comprehensive theory of post-modernism as the "cultural logic of late capitalism." Frankly acknowledging that his approach to postmodernism is a "totalizing" one, and unembarrassed by that fact (Jameson, 1991, 400), Jameson proceeds to identify a set of features characterizing postmodern culture across the board (Jameson, 1991, 1–54). These include a peculiar "depthlessness" attributable to post-modern culture's saturation with images; a weakening of our sense of histori-city; a "schizophrenic" fragmentation of postmodern cultural products that shatters temporal organization into disjointed moments of intensity; a new technological sublime, arising from technologies of electronic reproduction rather than the machine-age technologies of speed and power; and a distinc-tive new mutation of space, including the architectural spaces of our built environment, calling for new skills of orientation and navigation that Jameson terms "cognitive mapping." All of these cultural features, Jameson contends, heterogeneous though they maybe, derive from the underlying logic of the late-capitalist system (which perhaps ought to be identified with what Harvey and others call "neoliberalism"; see section 1).

Jameson proposes to group these theories *about* postmodernism – his own, Lyotard's, Huyssen's, Jencks's, and the rest – under the heading of "postmodernism theory," to distinguish them from what might ambiguously be called "postmodern theory." The latter presumably refers to *all* the varieties of theoretical discourse that arise during the postmodern period, but in fact the term "postmodern theory" is strictly speaking redundant, for "theory" itself, in the special sense that the term began to acquire from the mid-sixties on (see Chapter 2), is a postmodern phenomenon, and the success and proliferation of "theory" is itself a *symptom* of postmodernism. "Theory" in this special sense, writes Jonathan Culler, is not a theory *of* this or that particular object or practice – literature, for instance – but rather "an unbounded corpus of writing about everything under the sun" (Culler, 1992, 203). Heterogeneous though it is, "theory" in all its varieties shares the common project of "critiqu[ing] ... whatever is taken as natural" (Culler, 1992, 208). Its aim is to expose the cultural constructedness and contingency – and therefore the potential malleability and transience – of whatever falls within its purview: language, institutions, gender, identity, the self, the very category of the "human."

The history of "theory" in the period of peak postmodernism is in a sense the story of the piecemeal and belated reception in the Anglophone world of the writings of Continental thinkers, especially French thinkers: in a first wave, the philosopher Jacques Derrida, the psychoanalyst Jacques Lacan, the cultural historian Michel Foucault, and (more in the United Kingdom than the United States) the Marxist theoretician Louis Althusser; in later waves, Jean Baudrillard, Gilles Deleuze, and Félix Guattari, and the feminist theorists Hélène Cixous, Luce Irigaray, and Julia Kristeva, among others (see Baldick, 1996). Insofar as it implies passivity, "reception" is perhaps a misnomer, for in each case the assimilation of these thinkers was a vigorously active process, involving reframing and appropriation, even (from certain points of view) *mis*appropriation and *mis*comprehension (or "misprision," to use a term of art favored by Harold Bloom, himself one of the most vigorous of the misappropriators). Derrida's skeptical philosophy of language, for instance, assimilated to the academic New Critical project of literary close reading, yielded an "Americanized" practice of *deconstruction*, associated especially with the Yale School of Bloom, Paul DeMan, Geoffrey Hartman, Barbara Johnson, and J. Hillis Miller (Culler, 2007, 10–1). Foucault's reflection on the shifting relationships among power, knowledge and institutions, assimilated in the United States to a practice of historical criticism that was relatively weak on Marx but strong on archival research, yields a "New Historicism" spearheaded by Stephen Greenblatt, Louis Montrose, Catherine Gallagher, and others (see Jameson, 1991, 181–217). Differently appropriated in Britain by a more robustly Marxist indigenous tradition (associated with Raymond

Williams and others), it yields a practice of "Cultural Materialism," while, appropriated differently yet again in the context of the critique of colonialism developed by Frantz Fanon and others, it yields a discourse of postcolonialism (Edward Said, Homi Bhabha, Giyatri Spivak, and others).

The importation of Continental "theory" to Anglophone contexts inevitably provoked resistance, though this resistance to theory was itself theoretical, "anti-theory theory" (Culler, 2007, 73–96). A special case of resistance to theory was Anglophone feminists' suspicion of so-called "French feminisms," the theories of female creativity, identity, and difference associated with Cixous, Irigaray, and Kristeva, who were themselves in turn strongly influenced by Derrida and Lacan (Gallup, 1992). American feminists and gay/lesbian intellectuals in the seventies were preoccupied with more "hands-on" critique and reform – with political activism, the critique of patriarchal institutions and attitudes, the reclamation of neglected forerunners, and the "opening" and reform of the cultural canon – and so were initially somewhat unreceptive to imported feminist theory, which seemed to have ridden in on the coattails of deconstruction (Gallop, 1992, 6). Nevertheless, French feminism came gradually to color Anglophone feminist and gender discourses in the course of the period 1973–90, from Laura Mulvey in 1975 down to Judith Butler in 1990, with the watershed moment of theorization dating perhaps to 1980–81 (Gallop, 1992, 23).

French feminist theory posed special challenges because it seemed simultaneously to undermine or deconstruct gender categories, at a time when Anglophone feminists were struggling to reclaim and construct an identity for women, and conversely to identify women with their bodily experience, in effect naturalizing or "essentializing" the category "female," contrary to the general tendency of theory to critique "natural" categories (Baldick, 1996, 185). Possibilities for reconciling these apparently incompatible positions emerged in Butler's highly influential performative theory of gender as "a kind of persistent impersonation that passes as the real" (Butler, 1990, x; see Culler, 2007, 156–61), and in Donna Haraway's "Cyborg Manifesto" of 1985. For Haraway, the oppositional and liberatory possibilities of deconstructed subjectivity are captured in the "ironic myth" of the cyborg self – a hybrid subject, neither all-natural nor all-artificial, neither all-self nor all-other and, crucially, neither all-female nor all-male, but a composite, pieced together, and therefore capable of offering resistance to forms of domination that require individuals to be self-identical, one thing or another. "The cyborg," Haraway writes, "is a kind of disassembled and reassembled postmodern collective and personal self" (Haraway, 1991, 163). Haraway gestures toward a position that would later come to be called "posthumanism," already anticipated by Foucault in his critique of the supposed naturalness of the category "human."

Postmodernism embraces, then, both "theory" and the various forms of resistance to it. However, it is important not to *reduce* postmodernism to "theory," or (even more perniciously) to make postmodernism the practice of which "theory" is the theory (Nealon, 2013, xi–xii). For one thing, the historical record does not support such an understanding of the relationship between postmodernist practice and "theory." Though it may be the case that in a later generation of postmodernists – the generation that came of age in the nineties, let's say – schooling in "theory" predates practice and to some degree inspires or shapes it, this is demonstrably not yet the case with the generation of the peak period, most of whom were already practitioners of postmodern aesthetics before they became aware of the "theory" that their practice allegedly illustrates. There are exceptions – for instance, the OuLiPo writer Italo Calvino, who associated with the Paris structuralists; the post-modern science-fiction writer Samuel Delany, an adept of both semiotics and poststructuralism; the theoretically self-conscious experimental novelists Kathy Acker (see Siegle, 1989, 47–123) and Christine Brooke-Rose; and the American painter Mark Tansey, who incorporated both theoretical ideas and ironic portraits of theoreticians into his canvases. More typical, however, are the American surfictionists Raymond Federman and Ronald Sukenick, who began by emulating literary models – Beckett in Federman's case, Wallace Stevens in Sukenick's – and only belatedly discovered "theories" that might underwrite their practice (McHale, 2011). Typical, too, are the visual artists and writers who formed the Downtown scene in Manhattan towards the end of the seventies, including the image-appropriators of the so-called Pictures Generation (see section 7), to whom, by his own account, the theorist and publisher Sylvère Lotringer (Lotringer, 2003) introduced French theory (Baudrillard, Deleuze and Guattari, Paul Virillio) through his *Semiotext(e)* book series, beginning in 1983. These artists were *already* practicing an aesthetics of simulation and hyperreality that Baudrillard (for instance) the-orized, well before Lotringer ever brought him to their attention. Denial that their practice was theory driven or illustrated theory was a common refrain among Pictures artist such as Richard Prince, Sherrie Levine, and Barbara Kruger (Sandler, 1996, 326, 387, 391).

Did "theory" end with the end of peak postmodernism, around 1990? Have we witnessed the "death of theory" so eagerly anticipated and desired all along by those who resisted it? It is tempting, though probably irresponsible, to associate the death of theory with the premature deaths of so many of its Continental masters: Roland Barthes in a street accident, 1980; Foucault of

AIDS, 1984; Althusser in 1990, having killed his wife during an episode of mental illness in 1980; Deleuze by his own hand in 1995. Especially disturbing and disillusioning was the posthumous discovery, after his death in 1983, of DeMan's wartime journalism, published in a collaborationist journal in Belgium and tainted with apparent anti-Semitism, which for some people cast doubt on the integrity of DeMan's entire theoretical project. The DeMan controversy, raising issues about the ethical dimension of theory, perhaps set the stage for a reorientation toward ethics in literary theory in the nineties (e.g., Nussbaum, 1990; Phelan, 1996), reflected, for instance, in the belated rediscovery of the philosophical ethics of the French-Jewish thinker Emmanuel Levinas (e.g., Newton, 1995; Gibson, 1999).

Though many of those whose careers are identified with the rise of "theory" have died, sometimes in distressing circumstances, "theory" itself has survived down to the new millennium. If it is less conspicuous now than it was in the peak years of postmodernism in the seventies and eighties, this is only because it has become so pervasive as to pass largely unnoticed. Since the late eighties "theory" has especially animated the discourses of feminism, gender studies, and sexuality studies, and it underwrites what has come to be called "cultural studies." If postmodernism is not after all the practice for which "theory" is the theory, then perhaps the practice for which "theory" really *is* the theory is cultural studies (Culler, 2007, 246–7).

3. Megafictions

Nineteen seventy-three, apart from anything else, is the year of *Gravity's Rainbow*. Of all the evidence that Andreas Killen's amasses, it is Pynchon's novel that does the most to clinch his case for 1973 as a watershed in the history of postmodern culture. By almost anyone's account, *Gravity's Rainbow* figures as the most typical postmodernist novel – the model for all the postmodernist fictions that followed in the seventies and eighties, the one against which everything else would be measured.

Whatever criteria one proposes for postmodernism, *Gravity's Rainbow* appears to satisfy them. If postmodernism is characterized by incredulity toward the master narratives of Western culture, as Lyotard affirmed, then *Gravity's Rainbow* is a test case of postmodern incredulity, relentlessly questioning, exposing, and undermining cultural narratives about scientific knowledge and technological progress, about the nation and the people, about liberalism and democracy. A postmodern sceptic, Pynchon, like Lyotard, appears to place his faith in the "little narratives" that sustain small-scale separatist cultural enclaves, such as the ones that proliferate in "the Zone," a space of freedom, multiplicity and social improvisation that, according to *Gravity's Rainbow*'s version of history, flourished in Germany between the Third Reich's collapse and the consolidation of the Allied Occupation.

If postmodernism, as Jameson contends, expresses the underlying logic of late capitalism through such features as depthlessness and the waning of historicity, schizophrenic fragmentation, a new technological sublime, and more or less doomed and frustrated attempts at cognitive mapping, then no novel reflects the late-capitalist condition more faithfully than *Gravity's Rainbow*. Here the history of the Second World War is flattened out, reduced to Hollywood-movie simulations. The novel's hero, Tyrone Slothrop, undergoes a literal *disassembly*, so that by the end "it's doubtful if he can ever be 'found' again, in the conventional sense of 'positively identified and detained'" (Pynchon, 1973, 712). The new technologies of organic chemistry, ballistics, and cybernetics, all implicated in the development of the V-2 rocket, acquire an aura of sublimity, obsessing the novel's characters and dominating its world. Moreover, that world is rife with secret histories and paranoid conspiracy theories, making it a typical product of 1973 (Killen, 2006, 254–60), but also identifying it as yet another "degraded attempt" at cognitive mapping of the postmodern world, in Jameson's terms (1991, 38).

If, as I have argued myself, postmodernism in fiction is characterized by the subordination of modernism's epistemological issues to ontological ones, then *Gravity's Rainbow*, with its unstable world populated by beings of heterogeneous reality status, is paradigmatic. Pynchon's novel amounts almost to a *summa* of techniques and devices for foregrounding issues of ontology: techniques for pluralizing worlds, for proliferating levels of reality, for suspending reality between literal and figurative status, for unmasking the very process of bringing worlds into being. All narratives produce multiple possible worlds – potential states of affairs, subjective realities, plans, expectations, speculations, dreams, fantasies – but *Gravity's Rainbow* multiplies alternative realities to the point where they threaten to swamp the novel's "real world." Otherworldly visitations abound, as do subcultural enclaves, pocket utopias, and dissident realities, while historical figures make cameo appearances, and history bleeds into fiction (and vice versa). Paradoxes, confusion of narrative levels, and *trompe l'oeil* effects impede our efforts to reconstruct a stable storyworld. Entire episodes are placed under erasure: for instance, Franz Pökler, the troubled German rocket engineer, has a sexual encounter with a girl who may be his daughter and then defects with her to Denmark – but he also does *not* do any such thing: "Of course it happened. Of course it didn't happen" (Pynchon, 1973, 667). Characters' epistemological quests succumb to ontological uncertainty in a world – a plurality of worlds – where nothing is stable or reliably knowable.

If, finally, postmodernism is double-coded, in Jencks' sense of the term, then *Gravity's Rainbow* certainly seems to qualify. Difficult and demanding though it is, it also seems to cater shamelessly to our taste for "low" entertainment, offering all kinds of "mindless pleasures" (Pynchon's preferred title for the book): silly names and obnoxious puns, flagrant anachronism, cartoonish characters, abundant slapstick comedy, chase scenes, pornography, pop-song lyrics and musical-comedy song-and-dance numbers. Pynchon's complex style and high-culture allusions coexist with models and materials derived from popular genre fiction, cinema, and television, including the whole gamut of forties movie genres – war movies, musical comedies, romance, horror movies, and animated cartoons – not to mention superhero comics and radio shows. All the barriers between high and mass or popular culture seem to have broken down.

Or have they? Does *Gravity's Rainbow* really appeal, in the same way that (according to Jencks) postmodern buildings do, to two different audiences, one of connoisseurs and the other of pop-culture consumers entertained by its "mindless pleasures"? Or does its peculiarly postmodern forms of difficulty – difficulty of determining which world is which, what level we are on, what is real and what is not – combined with its daunting length (760 pages in the 1973 edition) preclude genuine popularity and relegate it instead to the ambiguous status of *cult novel*, appealing to a niche readership? That *Gravity's Rainbow* remains in print, and evidently sells steadily, does not absolve it of charges of cultishness or elitisim. Symptomatic of its ambiguously popular/elite status is the scandalous refusal of the Pulitzer committee to award *Gravity's Rainbow* the prize for fiction in 1974, contrary to the advice of its own board of experts (Krafft, 2012, 11).

In the ambiguity of its status, as in so much else, *Gravity's Rainbow* is a model for the novels that followed it during the peak decades of postmodernism. Like *Gravity's Rainbow*, these novels pose difficulties of a peculiarly postmodern kind, which, amplified by their inordinate length, seem to preclude the kind of universal, top-to-bottom appeal that Jencks's theory of double-coding predicts. We might call these novels *megafictions*. They include, for instance, Samuel Delany's *Dhalgren* (1974), Carlos Fuentes's *Terra Nostra* (1975), Don DeLillo's *Ratner's Star* (1976), Robert Coover's *The Public Burning* (1977), Gilbert Sorrentino's *Mulligan Stew* (1979), John Barth's *LETTERS* (1979), Alasdair Gray's *Lanark* (1981), Salman Rushdie's *Midnight's Children* (1981) and *The Satanic Verses*

(1988), William T. Vollmann's *You Bright and Risen Angels* (1987), and a number of others by these authors and their contemporaries. A related phenomenon is the revival of the long narrative poem during the peak decades, from Ed Dorn's *Gunslinger* (completed in 1975) and Kenneth Koch's *Seasons on Earth* (completed in 1977) to Derek Walcott's *Omeros* (1990). *Gravity's Rainbow*'s verse counterpart is James Merrill's epic-scale trilogy of otherworldly narratives, *The Changing Light at Sandover* (1976–82) (McHale, 2000c).

All of these novels and long narrative poems share with *Gravity's Rainbow* the features of *difficulty* combined with *length*. Not all difficulty is of a postmodern kind, of course, and not all long texts are difficult. Some of the difficult high-modernist classics, such as *Ulysses, In Search of Lost Time*, and *The Man Without Qualities*, were also inordinately long, and some of the long difficult novels of the peak postmodernist decades, such as William Gaddis's *JR* (1975) or Joseph McElroy's 1200-page novel *Women and Men* (1987), have more in common with them than with the novels of their postmodernist contemporaries. Bestsellers and genre fictions, which place a premium on accessibility, often run to several hundred pages; Margaret Mitchell's *Gone with the Wind*, for instance, is 423,000 words long, or over 500 pages. In the late sixties, with a few notable exceptions such as Barth's large-scale novel *Giles Goat-Boy* (see Chapter 2), ontological difficulty was the province of shorter texts: short stories like those by Donald Barthelme (such as "The Indian Uprising") or Robert Coover (such as "The Magic Poker"; see "Prospero's Books"); short novels such as Pynchon's own *The Crying of Lot 49,* not even 200 pages long (see Chapter 2). However, beginning with *Gravity's Rainbow* in 1973, ontological difficulty underwent a transformation of scale that produced postmodern narratives many hundreds of pages long.

Postmodern megafictions are various, and it is hard to identify common denominators among them, beyond their shared preoccupation with ontology. One structural feature that does recur, however, is directly related to their inordinate size and complexity. Many of them incorporate an internal scale-model *of themselves*: a *mise-en-abyme* (see McHale, 2007). In this as in nearly everything else, *Gravity's Rainbow* is exemplary. Folded into its complex storyworld is an episode in which the Floundering Four, bumbling comic-book superheroes, enact their adventures onstage in an outdoor amphitheater while at the same time infiltrating their own audience and uncannily *watching themselves* from the stands. Their adventures mirror those of the protagonist Slothrop in the novel's "real world," but so does their paradoxical straddling of two levels of reality. The episode duplicates *en abyme* the ontological complexity of *Gravity's Rainbow* itself. Because the global structure of a text of the scale and complexity of *Gravity's Rainbow* is so elusive, internal mirroring or *mise en abyme* can help make that structure more perceptible and graspable – but at the same time, as this example illustrates, it also complicates and destabilizes the world of the novel in which it appears.

Many of the other megafictions of the seventies and eighties also feature structures *en abyme* that function similarly to the one in *Gravity's Rainbow*: for instance, the "theater of memory" in the middle of Fuentes's *Terra Nostra*, and the card game at the end, in which other novelists' characters literally take a hand; London reconfigured on a movie-studio soundstage in Rushdie's *Satanic Verses*; the panoramic maps and allegorical frontispieces, all drawn by the author himself, in Gray's *Lanark*. A number of these scale models *en abyme* take the form of theatrical spectacles akin to the long-defunct masques of the Renaissance courts (see "Prospero's Books"), including those in Coover's *Public Burning*, Sorrentino's *Mulligan Stew*, and Merrill's *Changing Light at Sandover* (McHale, 2004b, 33–49; see Chapter 1). The recurrence of *mise-en-abyme* structures in some (but not all) of the long novels of the nineties – for instance, in David Foster Wallace's *Infinite Jest* (1996), Don DeLillo's *Underworld* (1997), Pynchon's *Mason & Dixon* (1997), and Mark Danielewski's *House of Leaves* (2000) – is one indicator of the persistence of postmodernism into that decade.

The category of megafiction overlaps with other genre categories often regarded as distinctively postmodern, including *historiographic metafiction* and *magical realism*. Jameson attributes to postmodern culture a weakening of historicity, yet one of the most typical forms of fiction to emerge during the peak phase is a postmodern mutation of the historical novel. Linda Hutcheon (1988) calls this distinctive fusion of historical fiction and postmodern self-reflexivity "historiographic metafiction," a genre capable of "complicitous critique" of its own postmodernity, and capacious enough to include Peter Ackroyd, Angela Carter, E. L. Doctorow, Umberto Eco, John Fowles, Ishmael Reed, Graham Swift, and D. M. Thomas, as well as Coover, Fuentes, Pynchon, Rushdie, and a great many others.

Historiographic metafictions challenge the master narratives of official, received history, and propose counter-histories – paranoid conspiracy theories, fantastic alternative histories, impossible, self-contradictory histories, and so on (McHale, 1987, 90–6; Berry, 2012, 137–8). Typically, story-rich and entertaining, historiographic metafictions reconcile metafiction with narrativity, bridging one of the fault lines that runs through postmodernist fiction (see "Alice"), and combining the metafictional difficulty of postmodernism with the accessibility of popular fiction; in short, they are double-coded. A number of the megafictions previously mentioned, including *Gravity's Rainbow, Terra Nostra, The Public Burning, LETTERS, Midnight's Children, Lanark,* and *The Satanic Verses,* qualify as historiographic metafictions, though not all of them do, and not all the novels that Hutcheon regards as paradigmatic of the genre – including Fowles's *The French Lieutenant's Woman* (1969), Doctorow's *Ragtime* (1975), and Swift's *Waterland* (1983) – quite qualify as megafictions, whether in terms of length or of degree of difficulty, or both. In other words, the two categories overlap without fully coinciding.

Revising official, received history in the mode of historiographic metafiction has sometimes proved to be a risky business. Powerful real-world forces are invested in the official narratives, and do not always tolerate self-reflexive retellings or counter-histories. Coover's *Public Burning,* for instance, a counter-historical retelling of the trial of the "atomic spies" Julius and Ethel Rosenberg in the fifties, appeared only after prolonged delays and several changes of publisher because lawyers feared legal action by Richard Nixon, whose libelous interior monologues dominate the novel (Coover, 2010). Much more menacing was the violence aroused by Rushdie's alleged blasphemy in *The Satanic Verses,* including book burnings in Bradford in the United Kingdom, riots resulting in fatalities in Pakistan and Kashmir, and finally a death sentence handed down on the author himself by the Ayatollah Ruhollah Khomeini, supreme religious leader of Iran, in his *fatwa* (religious ruling) of February 1989 (Appignanesi and Maitland, 1989; Pipes, 1990; Cohn-Sherbok, 1990). The so-called Rushdie affair dramatizes the real-world limits of a critique mounted through the medium of historiographic metafiction – but at the same it also perversely confirms the efficacy of that critique. The novelist certainly provoked the Ayatollah!

Rushdie's megafictions belong not only to the genre of historiographic metafiction but simultaneously to another genre often regarded as typically postmodern: magical realism. Again, some megafictions – such as Rushdie's and Fuentes's – are magical realist, but not all of them, while only some magical realist texts qualify as megafictions. Magical realism involves violations of natural or scientific law that cannot be explained away as subjective delusions or the effects of advanced technologies (as they might be in science fiction), but that also fail to provoke wonder or amazement in the novel's characters or narrator; rather, miracles here are generally accepted as routine and banal (McHale, 1987, 73–83). People ascend into heaven or survive falls from exploded jetliners, the dead return, communities are afflicted with plagues of insomnia or amnesia or butterflies, but no one finds any of this astonishing; what should be fantastic is blandly taken for granted.

The term "magical realism" (*lo real maravilloso*) originated with the Cuban novelist Alejo Carpentier in 1949, and it has been identified ever since with the Latin American literary renaissance, or *Boom*, that began in the forties and persisted through the decades of peak postmodernism. The genre is associated with writers such as Carpentier himself, as well as Jorge Luis Borges, Julio Cortázar, Gabriel García Márquez, Fuentes, Augusto Roa Bastos, Isabel Allende, and others. A common denominator of the *Boom* novelists' careers was their straddling of cultural divides between what were then still called "developed" and "developing" regions, or "First" and "Third" worlds. Many of them had one foot firmly planted, as it were, on their home soil, the other in Europe or North America: in Fuentes's case, one foot in Mexico City, the other in Washington, D.C.; in Cortázar's, one in Buenos Aires, the other in Paris; in García Márquez's, Colombia and Europe; in Allende's, Chile and California; and so on. This biculturalism – the writers' straddling of metropolitan center and postcolonial periphery, or First and Third worlds – seemed to inform their lived experience with a kind of ontological doubleness and vacillation that spilled over into their fiction. Magical realism, the product of this doubled experience, captures the situation where two world views coexist: that of Western science, skeptical toward miracles and intolerant of magic, and that of non-Western cultures, where magical explanations are not only tolerated but sometimes preferred (Faris, 1995 and 2004). Thus, magical realism expresses a form of resistance to cultural colonization by the scientific epistemology of the West and in that sense reflects a postcolonial perspective.

If magical realism constitutes "a point of convergence between postmodernism and postcolonialism" (Faris, 2004, 2), the convergence is hardly tension-free, and might more properly be called a point of contention. The assimilation of magical realism to international postmodernism – in effect, a First World appropriation of a Third World tendency – was already well under way by 1967, when John Barth included Borges alongside Beckett and Nabokov in his account of the "literature of exhaustion," and was completed by 1979, when he made García Márquez's *One Hundred Years of Solitude* an exemplar of the "the literature of replenishment," or postmodernist fiction. By the time my own book appeared in 1987, it was commonplace to assume that magical realism was little more than the name for a regional variant of international postmodernism (see also D'haen, 1995). To appropriate magical realism in this way meant de-contextualizing it, alienating it from its origins in the Latin American *Boom* movement – a process given further impetus, during the same period, by the dissemination of magical realism itself into literary territories far distant from its Latin American homeland. By the end of the eighties, it had extended its range as far as Central and Eastern Europe

(Milan Kundera, Milorad Pavić), the Asian subcontinent (Rushdie), Africa (Ben Okri), Palestine (Anton Shammas), even the literatures of "internally colonized" peoples in North America and elsewhere (Toni Morrison, Gloria Naylor; see "Prospero's Books"), perhaps even including feminists and other sexual dissidents (Angela Carter), all of whom sought to capitalize on the resistant, counter-narrative potential of magical realism (D'haen, 1997; Ortega, 1997; Aldama, 2003).

Finally, apart from overlapping with these other characteristic genres of the peak era of postmodernism, megafiction might also be credited with generating, through a kind of reaction formation, fictional writing of a kind diametrically opposed to itself – not *maximalist* fiction of the kind typified by *Gravity's Rainbow*, but its opposite, *minimalism*, or rather *multiple* minimalisms. One of these types of minimalism – the one with which the term itself is typically associated, though it has also been called "dirty realism" – favors short forms (short stories, short novels), a plain-spoken, stripped-down style, contemporary realism, and restrained or oblique expression of emotion. Writers working in this vein included Raymond Carver (who did not himself outlive the period, dying in 1988), Frederick Barthelme (brother of Donald, the metafictionist), Bobbie Ann Mason, Jayne Anne Phillips, Mary Robison and others. Another reaction against postmodernist megafiction, though in a different direction, was so-called Downtown writing, associated with the New York scene of the seventies and eighties (see section 8). Expressionist, self-consciously marginal and ephemeral, perversely and deliberately "minor," this variety of minimalism can be traced in the writing of Kathy Acker, Constance DeJong, Lynn Tillman, and others (Siegle, 1989). Though they do not share the postmodernist poetics of novels like *Gravity's Rainbow*, and in fact actively resist that mode, both of these minimalisms nevertheless belong to postmodernism in the sense of reflecting, in their drastically different ways, the condition of postmodernity.

4. Avant-Pop

By the mid-eighties, the postmodern brand had spread virally from its original host, architecture, to adjoining cultural fields, such as visual art and literature. Charles Jencks, who by then had been promoting the brand for a decade, detected its presence in Neoexpressionist and Transavantgarde painting (see section 7), and in novelists such as John Barth, David Lodge, and John Fowles. His main literary exhibit was a passage from the Italian novelist Umberto Eco, characterizing the "postmodern attitude." "I think of the postmodern attitude," writes Eco,

> as that of a man who loves a very cultivated woman and knows he cannot say to her, "I love you madly," because he knows that she knows (and that she knows that he knows) that these words have already been written by [the romance novelist] Barbara Cartland. Still, there is a solution. He can say, "As Barbara Cartland would put it, I love you madly." At this point, having avoided false innocence, having said clearly that it is no longer possible to speak innocently, he will nevertheless have said what he wanted to say to the woman: that he loves her, but her loves her in an age of lost innocence. If the woman goes along with this, she will have received a declaration of love all the same. Neither of the two speakers will feel innocent, both will have accepted the challenge of the past, of the already said, which cannot be eliminated; both will consciously and with pleasure play the game of irony. . . . But both will have succeeded, once again, in speaking of love. (Eco, 1984, 67–8; Jencks, 1986, 18; ellipses are Eco's.)

How does one make a declaration of love in postmodern-ese? By double-coding it – what else?

The Eco passage is brilliantly chosen. Not only does it illustrate the very structure of double-coding that Jencks had identified in postmodern architecture – sophisticated expression piggybacking on the "already said" of historical convention (in this case, the conventions of the romance genre) – but it also comes from a particularly appropriate source, the little pamphlet that Eco wrote in response to the astonishing international success of his first novel, *The Name of the Rose* (1980). *The Name of the Rose* is itself a model of postmodern double-coding in Jencks's sense. Reading it, "the reader seems to be reading two novels at once" (Richter, 1997, 258), both a popular genre fiction – in fact, a detective story and historical novel with gothic horror overtones, so several popular genres rolled into one – and at the same time a sophisticated *anti*-detective metafiction that reflects on its own fictionality. Erudite and full of intellectual in-jokes – which was only to be expected from an author who was a medievalist and professor of semiotics – it nevertheless crossed over to the mass market, becoming an international bestseller, its crossover success crowned by its adaptation in 1986 as a big-budget film starring none other than Sean Connery – James Bond himself!

In other words, the case of *The Name of the Rose* confirms the close relationship between double-coding as an intrinsic feature of postmodern artworks (novels, paintings, buildings) and the larger cultural phenomenon of *crossing over* from a niche or elite market to the mass market (or vice versa).

Both these phenomena, double-coding and crossing over, are symptoms of the same general development, identified by Andreas Huyssen – again, in the mid-eighties – as the breakdown of hierarchical distinctions between high culture and mass or popular culture. The mingling of high and low materials and genres – for example, of metafiction and genre fiction, or of modernist materials and Las Vegas signage – mirrors at the level of a work's construction the erosion of hierarchy at the level of the culture at large.

As early as the mid-sixties (see Chapter 2), the traffic between cultural strata had become freer, with high artists "stooping" to embrace popular, kitsch forms (advertising imagery, pop music, genre fiction), while pop artists (especially musicians like Bob Dylan, The Beatles, and The Velvet Underground) aspired to high art. By the mid-eighties, the cycle of exchange between high and low had sped up to the point where the stratification was itself compromised, and seemed on the verge of collapse. Examples abound of crossover in both directions, from low to high and vice versa, from high to low.

The career of the musician David Bowie, for instance, traces a rising trajectory from pop star to cutting-edge artist across the decade of the seventies, beginning with his highly theatrical performances in the persona of Ziggy Stardust, around 1972–73, through his role as an alien visitor in Nicholas Roeg's *The Man Who Fell to Earth* (1976), a science-fiction film poised between art-house fare and commercial product, to his collaborations with the avant-gardist Brian Eno on the ambitious "Berlin trilogy" of recordings from the end of the decade (*Low* and *Heroes*, 1977; *Lodger*, 1978). Following a similar rising trajectory from low to high is the genre of the *graphic novel*, rooted in the disreputable, low-art traditions of funny papers and superhero comic-books, but sharing some of the iconoclastic energies of the avant-garde underground comix of the sixties. The graphic novel's breakthrough to high art can be dated to 1986–87, with the appearance within a few months of each other of Frank Miller's *The Dark Knight Returns* (1986) and Alan Moore's and Dave Gibbons's *Watchmen* (1987), revisionist treatments of superhero conventions, as well as Art Spiegelman's nonfiction graphic narrative *Maus* (1986), based on his father's experience as a Holocaust survivor (Sabin, 1993, 87–95). Even steeper, perhaps, than the graphic novel's rise is the ascent of *graffiti art* in the late seventies and early eighties from the status of criminal nuisance, worthy only of eradication, to art-world legitimacy in the work of Keith Haring, Kenny Scharf and especially Jean-Michel Basquiat (see section 7).

Crossover in the opposite direction, from avant-garde to popular, can be observed, for instance, in the case of *minimalist music*. Associated with composers such as Terry Riley, Philip Glass, Steve Reich, and John Adams, musical minimalism begins as an avant-garde practice, heard in such venues as performance lofts in SoHo, New York's "urban artist colony" (Kostelanetz, 2003, 7; see section 8). Successive expansions of the audience for minimalist music occurred throughout the seventies and eighties, beginning with Glass's collaboration with the theater director Robert Wilson on the opera *Einstein on the Beach* (1975) – still pretty intransigently avant-garde – followed by Adams's topical opera, *Nixon in China* (1978), followed in turn by Glass's soundtrack for Godfrey Reggio's documentary cult-film *Koyanisqaatsi* (1982), and so on. By the end of the eighties, music by the British minimalist Michael Nyman could be heard regularly on the soundtracks of Peter Greenaway's art films (including *Prospero's Books*) as well as more popular ones (such as Jane Campion's *The Piano*, 1993), and by the new millennium Glass's soundtrack music was a staple of commercial movies (e.g., *The Hours*, 2002). Glass's trajectory from avant-garde to popular actually cuts across David Bowie's trajectory in the opposite direction, popular to avant-garde, when in the nineties Glass composes two symphonies (#1, 1992; #4, 1997) based on themes from Bowie's albums *Low* and *Heroes*.

A similar career path is traced by Laurie Anderson, an avant-garde performance artist whose art practice was incubated in the same Downtown New York scene as Glass's and Reich's. The unexpected success of her single *O Superman* on the UK pop charts in 1981 dramatically expanded her audience, and by the end of that decade she had contributed music to the soundtrack of Wim Wenders' art film *Wings of Desire* (1987; see "Angels in America") and had even hosted a short-lived program showcasing cutting-edge video art, *Live from Off Center* (1987), on the popular-music cable channel MTV. As in the case of Glass and Bowie, her trajectory from avant-garde niche to wider popularity intersects with that of another artist, the rock musician Lou Reed, a veteran of The Velvet Underground, Andy Warhol's collaborators back in 1966. Romantically involved since the late nineties, Anderson and Reed married in 2008 – a made-to-order emblem of the crossings between high and low in the peak era of postmodernism.

The crossover phenomenon at the level of careers and genres is distinguishable, at least in theory, from the intimate mingling of high and low *within* a particular artwork. Avant-garde jazz musicians mingle high and low in this way whenever they "cover" kitsch pop songs, as John Coltrane did, for instance, with a catchy but pallid number from *The Sound of Music*, "My Favorite Things" (a crossover hit for him in 1961, incidentally). The trumpeter Lester Bowie, a veteran of the intransigently avant-garde Art Ensemble of Chicago, did the same thing in his 1986 album of such covers, the title of which gives this practice a name: *Avant-Pop*. Extending the category to literature and beyond, the critic and editor Larry McCaffery showcased Avant-Pop writing in a pair of anthologies, the first of them a small-press book (1993), the second, crossing over, a commercial paperback (1995). Avant-Pop, according to McCaffery, exploits the resources of popular film, television, comics, rock music, advertising, and franchising in much the same way that high-modernist writing drew on classical mythology, Christian iconology, and the literary canon. Avant-Pop writing appropriates, recycles and repurposes the materials of popular mass-media culture, "combin[ing] Pop Art's focus on consumer goods and mass media with the avant-garde's spirit of subversion and emphasis on radical formal innovation" (1995, xvi–xvii). In other words, as Jencks would say, it is double-coded.

McCaffery's Avant-Pop literary canon includes fiction by Kathy Acker, Paul Auster, Robert Coover, Don DeLillo, Bret Easton Ellis, Steve Erickson, Steve Katz, Mark Leyner, Ronald Sukenick, Gerald Vizenor, William T. Vollmann, David Foster Wallace, Stephen Wright, and others both famous and obscure. Among this heterogeneous collection of writers, and the many others who might plausibly be grouped with them (see Olsen, 2012), two general types of Avant-Pop practice can be distinguished. The first involves absorbing pop-culture materials – brand names and advertising slogans, the language of genre fiction, entertainment-industry clichés, and so on – into "hostile" textual environments, where such materials, displaced from their normal contexts, are exhibited as specimens or subjected to irony. This is the case, for instance, with Acker's cut-and-paste fiction, which literally, physically appropriates and displays verbal material from sources high and low, or with the found-poetry practices of some of the L=A=N=G=U=A=G=E poets (see section 6). But the practice of pop-culture appropriation also figures in more conventional-looking texts, such as DeLillo's *White Noise* (1985) or Ellis's controversial and over-the-top *American Psycho* (1991), or even Manuel Puig's *Kiss of the Spider Woman* (*El beso de la mujer araña*, 1976), in which the cliché-ridden plots of Hollywood B-movies are retold in the context of a complex, metafictional narrative structure. (Puig's novel, perhaps ironically, was itself recycled as a pop-culture product, first as a commercial film in 1985, then as a Broadway musical in 1992–93.)

The other Avant-Pop type involves, not the piecemeal appropriation of pop-culture material, but the wholesale repurposing of a pop-cultural genre, as though the avant-garde text were *piggybacking* on the genre's conventions and style, the expectations it arouses, and so on. This is the case, arguably, with Miller's, Moore's, and Gibbons's repurposing of superhero conventions in *The Dark Knight Returns* and *Watchmen*. It is certainly the case with Sukenick's *Blown Away* (another text of 1986), which piggybacks on the conventions of low-budget exploitation films (see "Prospero's Books"), and Coover's story cycle *A Night at the Movies* (1987), which repurposes, one after the other, a whole series of Hollywood genres: the Western, slapstick comedy, musicals, romance, even cartoons, serials, travelogues, short subjects, and previews of coming attractions.

Especially conspicuous is the postmodern adaptation and repurposing of the detective story, which some have argued constitutes a separate genre of *metaphysical detective fiction* (Merivale and Sweeney, 1999). In such adaptations, the epistemological quest that motivates the classic detective story, and makes it a quintessentially *modernist* narrative structure (see Chapter 1), is frustrated and betrayed, and the detective's inquiry topples over from quest for knowledge into ontological doubt. Examples include Puig's *The Buenos Aires Affair* (1974) and Auster's *New York Trilogy* (1985–86) (see Bertens, 1997). However, the paradigm for this sort of deliberately sabotaged detective story is Eco's *The Name of the Rose* (McHale, 1992, 145–64), a "whodunit" modeled on the fiction of Conan Doyle, with a detective hero modeled on Sherlock Holmes, but displaced to fourteenth-century Italy. Eco's detective, William of Baskerville, ultimately solves the case and identifies the murderer, but only through consistent misinterpretation of the evidence and by relying on irrational associational leaps, calling into question the entire epistemological project itself – the very enterprise of achieving reliable knowledge through direct perception and ratiocination. "There was no plot," he is forced at the end to confess, "and I discovered it by mistake .... I arrived at [the murderer] by pursuing the plan of a perverse and rational mind, and there was no plan" (Eco, 1983, 492).

Needless to say, these two types of Avant-Pop practice – piecemeal appropriation of pop-culture materials, wholesale repurposing of pop-culture genres – are hardly mutually exclusive and often combine in one and the same text. DeLillo's *White Noise*, for instance, a text bristling with brand names, television messages, and other artifacts of consumer culture, also models itself on several popular genres, including the campus novel and the blockbuster disaster film. In this sense, the consummate Avant-Pop novel is *Gravity's Rainbow*, an enormous compendium of pop-culture materials – song-lyrics, advertisements, radio shows, comic books, chase scenes, slapstick – that masquerades as a Second World War action-adventure movie "for us, old fans who've always been at the movies (haven't we?)" (Pynchon, 1973, 760).

5. Cyberpunk

As we have just seen, when detective fiction is repurposed for postmodern uses, the outcome is profoundly inimical to the epistemology of detection, amounting to something like a highjacking of the genre, as in *The Name of the Rose*. Something quite different happens in the case of another popular genre, science fiction. Intrinsically ontological, a *world-building* genre, science fiction is much more compatible with postmodernism than detective fiction is, and so the postmodern repurposing of science fiction appears more a matter of *convergence* than highjacking. Already beginning to "postmodernize" itself as early as its New Wave phase in the sixties and seventies (see Chapter 2), science fiction undergoes a further mutation in the eighties into *cyberpunk*, which, by the end of the decade, is already well on its way to crossing over to mainstream culture.

The term *cyberpunk* itself, evidently coined by science fiction editor and critic Gardner Dozois, is the same sort of oxymoronic, portmanteau construction as *Avant-Pop*: one component (*cyber*) connoting the *advanced* (cutting-edge technology, in this case), the other (*punk*) connoting the abjectly popular. Moreover, it was the same critic, Larry McCaffery, the publicist of Avant-Pop, who also helped shepherd cyberpunk through its crossover from its science fiction niche to the postmodern mainstream, editing an influential casebook on cyberpunk and postmodern science fiction, *Storming the Reality Studio* (1991), and otherwise insinuating cyberpunk writing anywhere he could. McCaffery was schooled in the essentials of cyberpunk by the science-fiction writer and polemicist Bruce Sterling, whose 1986 anthology *Mirrorshades* established the canon of cyberpunk authors, including, among others, Pat Cadigan, Marc Laidlaw, Rudy Rucker, Lewis Shiner, and John Shirley, as well as himself and, of course, his friend and sometime collaborator William Gibson, author of *Neuromancer* (1984), the novel credited with launching the genre.

McCaffery, however, was hardly alone in identifying cyberpunk with postmodernism. Jameson, for one, concurred, but where McCaffery gleefully embraced the role of cheerleader for cyberpunk, Jameson tended to be skeptical, even mordant. Cyberpunk, he wrote, was "the supreme literary expression ... of late capitalism itself" (1991, 419) and "an outright representation of the present" (286). Complicit in the late-capitalist or neoliberal world order, cyberpunk, in his view, confirmed the failure of the utopian impulse in science fiction of the postmodern era. Cyberpunk's affinity for conspiracy theories and high-tech paranoia amounted to no more than a "degraded attempt" at the cognitive mapping of postmodernity (38).

There is a good deal of truth in Jameson's conflation of cyberpunk and "the imagination of the multinationals" (321), but not the whole truth, for no genre fiction, least of all science fiction, can directly or *im*-mediately (without mediation) reflect contemporary conditions, as his formulations suggest that cyberpunk does. Reflection of the immediate present will always be routed through and filtered or mediated by the conventions of the genre itself, which generally function as a *conservative* factor in literary history, a counter-vailing force to the pressure of contemporaneity, inhibiting literature's responsiveness to its historical moment. In the case of cyberpunk, a number of writers and critics, most vocally the science fiction novelist Samuel R. Delany (1988, 28–35), called attention to the new genre's *conventionality*, its reliance on familiar motifs and formulas. Delany complained that the novelty attributed to cyberpunk was overstated by mainstream readers and critics, new converts to the genre who, as outsiders to the science fiction world, were unfamiliar with its conventions. Gibson, in particular, was improperly credited with inventing motifs that actually have a long history in the science-fiction genre, including the female ninja or action hero (in the person of Gibson's hit-woman heroine, Molly Millions) and the most highly publicized of his supposed innovations, *cyberspace* itself.

It is not as though the cyberpunks never acknowledged their precursors. On the contrary, they were eager to claim the legacy of novels such as *Gravity's Rainbow* and J. G. Ballard's *Crash* (both dating from 1973, you will remember) or the fiction of Philip K. Dick (see Chapter 2), and they freely acknowledged cinematic precursors such as Ridley Scott's *Blade Runner* (1982, based on Dick's *Do Androids Dream of Electric Sheep?*, written in 1966), John Carpenters' *Escape from New York* (1981), and David Cronenberg's *Videodrome* (1983). Nevertheless, Delany had a point: what underinformed readers hailed as innovations on the part of Gibson and the others were often recycled generic motifs that had been in circulation for years, if not decades. Cyberspace, which Gibson claimed was inspired by his observation of the behavior of gamers in video-game arcades, certainly recycles the motif of *paraspace* in the science fiction of John Varley, Roger Zelazny, and others in preceding decades, going back at least as far as Dick's *paraworlds* of the mid-sixties (see Chapter 2). As for Gibson's other supposed innovation, the female action hero Molly, with her intriguing prosthetic enhancements such as retractable knife blades under the fingernails, she needs to be seen in the context of the previous decade's feminist science fiction by Ursula LeGuin, Alice Sheldon ("James Tiptree, Jr."), and especially Joanna Russ, whose female assassin, Jael, from *The Female Man* (1975), Gibson appropriates without acknowledgment. It is certainly the case that female precursors go largely unacknowledged by the cyberpunks. Moreover, from the point of view of demographic diversity, the first-generation cyberpunk group itself – straight, white and, with the exception of Pat Cadigan, all male – represents a step backward compared to the science fiction of the preceding decade, which had diversified itself both demographically and in terms of content, making room for identities and experiences that were *other than* male, white, and heteronormative.

None of which invalidates McCaffrey's or Jameson's view of the matter: cyberpunk does indeed converge with postmodern poetics. If we take *Gravity's Rainbow* to be the *summa* of postmodernist motifs and techniques in fiction (see the earlier material in this chapter), then it is easy to trace these same motifs and techniques in cyberpunk, with this difference: what in *Gravity's Rainbow* is likely to occur as a *formal* feature, or to hover between literal and figurative status, in a cyberpunk novel is much more likely to be *literalized* as an object or state of affairs in the storyworld itself – as a *reality*, typically a technological one. Indeed, this is a trait that cyberpunk shares with science fiction in general, which often proceeds by seizing on formal features or expressions that in most other contexts would be regarded as figurative and building or implying worlds in which those features or expressions make *literal* sense (see Chu, 2010).

Thus, for example, the worlds-within-worlds, or worlds *en abyme,* of *Gravity's Rainbow* and other postmodernist megafictions, are literalized technologically through the motifs of cyberspace and virtual reality in cyberpunk novels such as Gibson's first trilogy (*Neuromancer, Count Zero,* and *Mona Lisa Overdrive,* 1984–88), Cadigan's *Mindplayers* (1987) and *Synners* (1991), and Michael Swanwick's *Stations of the Tide* (1991; see "Prospero's Books"). The subcultural enclaves and dissident realities of *Gravity's Rainbow* (and of Berger and Luckmann's sociological theory of reality construction; see Chapter 2) are realized as *literal* micro-worlds – deep-space habitats, cities in orbit, space-colonies under domes – in Shiner's *Frontera* (1984), Sterling's *Schismatrix* (1986), Swanwick's *Vacuum Flowers* (1987), and elsewhere. The Zone of *Gravity's Rainbow,* a heterotopian space where fragments of multiple worlds mingle and jostle, is literalized in the Sprawl of Gibson's early stories and first trilogy, the Freezone of John Shirley's *Eclipse* (1987), and the future Los Angeles of Richard Kadrey's *Metrophage* (1988) (see section 8). Haraway's figure of the decentered, cyborg self (see section 2), ambiguously literalized in the disassembly of Slothrop over the course of *Gravity's Rainbow,* recurs in multiple variants across the cyberpunk corpus: as prostheses and all kinds of human/machine interfaces and hybrids in Sterling's *Schismatrix* and elsewhere; as nonhuman, artificial intelligences and robots in Rucker's trilogy of

Software (1982), *Wetware* (1988), and *Freeware* (1997); as host bodies possessed by implanted biological or biomechanical alternative selves in Rucker's trilogy, Sterling's *Schismatrix*, Lucius Shepard's *Green Eyes* (1984) and *Life During Wartime* (1987), Greg Bear's *Blood Music* (1985), and so on (see McHale, 1992, 243–67).

Even the sentence-level style of *Gravity's Rainbow* has left its mark on cyberpunk writing – reinforced, no doubt, by the comparably dense style of Ballard's *Atrocity Exhibition* (1969) and *Crash*. Here, it is not a question of literalizing anything, but of folding science fiction's world-building processes into the very texture of sentences, making implication (and its counterpart, active inference on the reader's part) do the work that exposition would do in more traditional types of science fiction. What results is cyberpunk's trademark "imploded" or "crammed" style, as in this passage from *Neuromancer,* where Gibson describes his heroine Molly receiving high-tech medical treatment for a broken leg:

> A transparent cast ran from her knee to a few millimeters below her crotch, the skin beneath the rigid micropore mottled with bruises, the black shading into ugly yellow. Eight derms, each a different size and color, ran in a neat line down her left wrist. An Akai transdermal unit lay beside her, its fine red leads connected to input trodes under the cast. (Gibson, 1984, 78)

We recognize the kinds of extrapolated medical technology implied by this diction – *micropore, derm, transdermal unit, trode* – or we can guess at them, but the sheer *density* of the passage, and the absence of glosses for any of the neologisms, creates a reading experience that is qualitatively different from reading most science fiction, though similar to reading Pynchon or Ballard.

Cyberpunk's crossover from its science-fiction niche to academic respectability was accomplished by about 1988, thanks largely to McCaffery's lobbying efforts. Its crossover to mainstream popularity was slower, however. The short-lived cyberpunk-flavored television series *Max Headroom* made an abortive bid for the popular market in 1987–88. *Total Recall* (1990), based on Dick's 1966 story "We Can Remember It for You Wholesale," succeeded as an Arnold Schwarzenegger vehicle but did little to enhance the genre's popularity. *Johnny Mnemonic* (1995), a Keanu Reeves vehicle based on the Gibson short story of the same name (1981), directed by the Downtown artist Robert Longo (see section 8), failed outright. Not until the very end of the nineties did cyberpunk achieve crossover popularity at the movies with the Wachowskis' film *The Matrix* (1999).

Nevertheless, cyberpunk left an indelible mark not only on science fiction but also on popular culture generally, and even, beginning in the early nineties, on the design of the Internet, whose engineers where manifestly influenced by Gibson's imagination of cyberspace – a word that he coined (but neglected to copyright). Arguably, other science-fiction extrapolations of a worldwide information network, such as the one in Delany's *Stars in My Pocket Like Grains of Sand* (1984, the same year as *Neuromancer*), came closer to anticipating the Internet that eventually materialized, but it was Gibson's coinage, and his imagery, that inspired the Internet's innovators (see Benedickt, 1991). Cyberspace, if not cyberpunk itself, went viral in the nineties.

6. Users' Manuals

Bruce Sterling, the impresario of cyberpunk, was also a master of the crammed or imploded style that is a trademark of the genre. He begins a 1984 short story, "Twenty Evocations," set in the same universe as his novel *Schismatrix*, with sentences like these:

> When Nicolai Leng was a child, his teacher was a cybernetic system with a holographic interface. The holo took the form of a young Shaper woman.

– and continues, a few paragraphs later, with sentences like these:

> Nikolai was on leave in the Ring Council with two men from his unit . . . . The first man was . . . a charming, ambitious young Shaper of the old school. The other man had a Mechanist eye implant. His loyalty was suspect. (Sterling, 1996, 313, 314)

Such sentences are difficult in the manner of cyberpunk, dense with implication, but hardly impenetrable, especially if one is already familiar with Sterling's future taxonomy of posthuman types, including the gene-splicing Shapers and the prosthetically enhanced Mechanists. But then, after the story's fifth paragraph, something seems to go wrong with the text, which begins to repeat itself, but in scrambled way:

> The holographic interface's loyalty was suspect. The cybernetic system helped him strip the valuables off his plastic eyes. . . . (Sterling's ellipsis)

The story rights itself in the next paragraph, but after paragraph ten the same thing happens again, as it does again after paragraph fifteen. Manifestly,

Sterling has practiced some kind of artificial *procedure* on his own text, cutting up its sentences and splicing them together differently, and doing so at regular intervals. His procedure is highly appropriate to this storyworld, literalizing at the sentence level its technological motifs of genetic engineering, prosthesis and artificial intelligence, but it is also risky, jeopardizing the status of the science-fiction world that Sterling has taken such pains to construct (McHale, 2004a). In taking that risk, Sterling establishes his avant-garde credentials, and by extension those of the cyberpunk genre itself.

Proceduralism, the application of preestablished *rules, constraints,* or *practices* in the production of texts, is one of the places where the postmodern avant-garde and popular culture converge and cross. Thus, just as the cyberpunk science fiction writer Sterling approaches proceduralism from one side of the high/low divide, so does the avant-gardist Kathy Acker from the *other* side. In *Empire of the Senseless* (1988), for example, she appropriates textual material from William Gibson's seminal cyberpunk novel, *Neuromancer,* reworking it by applying her own procedures. Rewriting Gibson, she deletes some (but not all) of his original techno-speak, while interpolating oddly irrelevant details of her own. Compare Gibson's sentences about Molly's physiotherapy, quoted in the preceding section, with Acker's version:

> A transparent cast ran from her knee to a few millimetres below her crotch, the skin mottled *by blue purple and green patches which looked like bruises but weren't. Black spots on her nails, finger and toe, shaded into gold.* Eight derms, each a different colour size *and form,* ran in a neat line down her right wrist *and down the vein of the right upper thigh.* A transdermal unit, *separated from her body,* connected to the input trodes under the cast by means of thin red leads. *A construct.* (Acker, 1988, 33–4; my emphases).

What should we call this: sampling, in the music-production sense? Plagiarism? Parody? The Paris Situationists of the sixties might have called it *détournement* (Miller, 2012); Jameson calls it *pastiche,* which he defines as postmodern "blank parody," lacking the pointedness, the "ulterior motives," of satire (Jameson, 1991, 16–17).

As it happens, Acker began her career of plagiarism, pastiche, and proceduralism in 1973–74, the year of postmodernism's rebranding. Perhaps not coincidentally, 1973 was also the year when the *Ouvroir de Littérature Potentielle,* or OuLiPo, the group of Parisian experimentalists whose name is synonymous with procedural writing, emerged from the obscurity of its coterie origins to greater public visibility and even celebrity. In 1973, the first OuLiPo manifesto, drafted by François LeLionnais as early as 1962, was belatedly published. Even more importantly, Italo Calvino and Harry Mathews were inducted as new members, the first newcomers to the circle since Georges Perec's induction in 1967 (Becker, 2012, 32).

Both Calvino, an Italian, and the American Mathews had been using preestablished procedures in their writing before their induction; indeed, it was their proceduralist practice that brought them to the OuLiPo's attention in the first place. Calvino had applied a subtle system to determine the alternation of sections in *Invisible Cities* (1972), but a few years previously he had used a bolder procedure in *The Castle of Crossed Destinies* (1969), laying out a deck of tarot fortune-telling cards and discovering in their images a proliferating series of narratives, and then doing it all over again with a different deck, the "luck of the draw" determining the very shape of the stories (McHale, 1987, 28–9). Mathews, too, had already used procedures, at least to some extent, in composing his first two novels, *The Conversions* (1962) and *Tlooth* (1966), and he would use them again to write *The Sinking of the Odradek Stadium* (1975).

Nevertheless, joining OuLiPo marked a turning point in both Calvino's and Mathews' careers. It was as an Oulipian that Calvino published his most widely admired novel, *If on a Winter's Night a Traveler* (1979). Celebrated for its use of second-person narrative and its pastiches of novels in various popular genres – all of them left teasingly unfinished – *If on a Winter's Night* also, though less obviously, applies a complex Oulipian apparatus to govern the unfolding of the story *between* the pastiche chapters (see Calvino, 1995, for an abundance of details). While Mathews' fiction would never achieve the degree of recognition that Calvino's did, he nevertheless produced an Oulipian classic with crossover potential in *Cigarettes* (1987). While it appears to be a realistic novel of upper-middle-class manners, distinguished by the oddity of some of its plot twists and the unpredictable (but not unbelievable) personality changes its characters undergo, *Cigarettes* was evidently generated by means of a covert system, similar perhaps to the *algorithm* for combining and recombining a fixed set of the elements that Mathews described to his Oulipo colleagues sometime in the mid-seventies and formulated in print in 1981 (Mathews, 1986; see McHale, 2000b). Our uneasy suspicion that some sort of generating apparatus was used, in Mathews' case as in Calvino's, opens up a disorienting ontological gap or disparity between the storyworld's appearance and its reality, as though the text concealed a "secret history" about which we can only speculate.

More even than Calvino, however, and much more than the relatively obscure Mathews, it was Georges Perec who brought international celebrity to the OuLiPo through his 1978 novel *La Vie mode d'emploi* (*Life a User's*

Manual). Perec had already in 1969 published what is arguably the definitive Oulipian novel, *La Disparition* (translated into English as *A Void*), a text governed by a single global constraint: none of the words in it contains the letter *e*, the most frequent vowel in the French language (as it is in the English language). If *La Disparition* is a tour de force, *La Vie* is something else, a tangled collection of stories ramifying outward into the world, but all rooted in the rooms of a single Parisian apartment block. Narratively compelling, these stories nevertheless depend for their existence on a whole series of procedural constraints to which they are subject, including a sort of master constraint, a chess problem known as the "knight's tour," that governs their order (Perloff, 1991, 139–145). A machine for generating narrative, *La Vie* converges with the narrative-friendly poetics of magical realism and Avant-Pop, countering the anti-narrative tendencies of other postmodern avant-gardes (see "Alice").

If the OuLiPo represents one model of proceduralism, it is certainly not the only one. In fact, procedural practice seems ubiquitous in the period 1973–90, not all of it modeled on Oulipian proceduralism, but sometimes deriving from alternative tendencies (such as Burroughs's cut-ups or the found poetry of Ginsberg and others; see Chapter 2), sometimes prompted by the potential of new technological resources. Thus, for example, Walter Abish uses a simple alphabetical system to constrain word choice – and therefore world-building – in his novel *Alphabetical Africa* (1974), while Christine Brooke-Rose denies herself the use of any verbs in the indicative mood in constructing the novel *Amalgamemnon* (1984), thereby restricting her narrative to hypothesis, speculation and conditionality. John Barth uses the actual shapes of the letters in the title of his epistolary novel *LETTERS* (1979), superimposed on a calendar, to determine its sequence. James Merrill uses the Ouija board, which functions for him like a primitive writing machine, to generate the raw text from which he shapes *The Changing Light at Sandover* (1976–82) (see McHale, 2004b, 39–49), while Raymond Federman uses the technical constraints of an electric typewriter to shape, quite literally, the squares of print that compose *The Voice in the Closet* (1979) (see McHale, 2000b). The novels in Gilbert Sorrentino's *A Pack of Lies* trilogy (1985, 1987, 1989) are each subject to complex procedures and constraints (see Mackey, 1997; Conte, 2002); so, too, are some of Peter Greenaway's films of this period, including *A Zed and Two Noughts* (1985) and *Drowning by Numbers* (1988). Some of Sophie Calle's artworks of the seventies and eighties involved fixed procedures, including those in which she followed strangers and documented their activities (1979, 1981), and one in which she hired a private detective to follow *her* and report on her *own* activities (1981). A number of her art procedures reappear, attributed to a fictional character, in Paul Auster's 1992 novel *Leviathan* (see Calle, 2007). Related to the writing-machine types of proceduralism, though in a different cultural sphere and a different medium of expression, is the emergence of *sampling* and *mixing* as aesthetic practices in hip-hop music, first implemented through the use of analog technology – turntables – then later on, in the eighties, by digital means, with the advent of MIDI sampling technology (see Rose, 1994; Potter, 1995; McHale, 2004b, 192–9).

Here, again, popular art and the avant-garde converge and cross. Radiating outward from its birthplace in the Bronx in the late seventies, hip-hop sampling converges with the compositional techniques of avant-garde poets like Bruce Andrews. Andrews, recognizing not only the aesthetic potential of musical sampling but also its potential as a vehicle for political critique, remediates and repurposes hip-hop in long prose-poetry sequences such as "Confidence Trick" (written 1981, published 1987; McHale, 2004b, 162–203):

> Talk *is* cheap – We jump up lobotomized post syn-fuels; propaganda amputee kills Doc; in God we trust insect coins – (The information kit is free) – Getting this optative just enjoy what are our; electro-wave your meltdown brain army revved up – Freedom by any means necessary, but almost involuntary UFO brandname without any sentiment – Cultural transmission christ statue; women in the middle income – Multiple humor stands bad with congas at the convent gate, my TV police on chairs, you qualify vet, KGB bid to slay pope; yellow spot. (Andrews, 1987, 168)

Andrews belongs to a like-minded group of avant-gardists, the L=A=N=G=U=A=G=E poets, who couple procedural practices with radical political critique, using a range of procedures – including sampling, in Andrews' case – to expose and counter the ideological premises and power disparities encoded in language. Emerging from the anti-war, feminist, and gay-liberationist subcultures of the late sixties and early seventies (Huntsperger, 2010, 5–6), the L=A=N=G=U=A=G=E group flourished on both the East and West Coasts of North America, and eventually developed affiliations with avant-gardists in the United Kingdom and elsewhere. Comparisons with OuLiPo, though inevitable, yield more differences than similarities. Though both groups develop and apply predetermined procedures in composition, the OuLiPo writers rarely display any overt political or critical purpose; running in more subterranean channels, their politics reflect the collective experiences of a different nation and generation (see Becker, 2012, 313–4). The L=A=N=G=U=A=G=E writers, by contrast, are explicit in their critique of late-capitalism and its cultural consequences.

Which does not mean that the politics of L=A=N=G=U=A=G=E writing is always self-evident; quite the contrary – it is often elusive. A textbook case of political mistaken identity is Jameson's reading of "China," a short poem by the West Coast L=A=N=G=U=A=G=E poet, Bob Perelman (Jameson, 1991, 28–30). Jameson exhibits "China" as symptomatic of what he regards as postmodernism's "schizophrenic" disjointedness. However, Jameson also acknowledges that Perelman's poem has a "structural secret." In fact, it is a procedural poem, based on found material – the illustrations in a primer for Chinese-speaking elementary-school pupils, which Perelman, unable to read the Chinese captions, has recaptioned:

> We live on the third world from the sun. Number three. Nobody tells us what to do.
> The people who taught us to count were being very kind.
> It's always time to leave.
> If it rains, you either have your umbrella or you don't.
> The wind blows your hat off.   (Perelman, 1981, 60)

– and so on, for another twenty-two lines. Jameson goes so far as to concede that "China" is "in some curious and secret way a political poem" (1991, 29). Perelman himself would argue (1996, 63–4) – and others have argued on his behalf (Hartley, 1989, 42–52; McHale, 2004b, 162–7; Huntsperger, 2010, 84, 126–7) – that his poem is not a *symptom* of late-capitalist schizophrenia at all, but rather a *diagnosis* of it, perhaps even an attempt at a remedy.

However different their purposes, the L=A=N=G=U=A=G=E poets are at least as prolific as the OuLiPo group in inventing and applying procedures. The sampling of found materials occurs frequently among the L=A=N=G=U=A=G=E writers, not only in Andrews's poems (such as the one from which I quoted previously) but in those of Charles Bernstein and many others. A related practice involves *writing through* or *writing over* texts by other writers, as in Acker's writing-over of Gibson's *Neuromancer* (also quoted earlier) and in many poems by Barrett Watten, Susan Howe, and others (McHale, 2004b, 204–49). A number of L=A=N=G=U=A=G=E compositions seek to exhaust the possibilities of a limited, preestablished vocabulary, a restricted subset of words or constructions selected more or less arbitrarily out of the total stock of the language (Watten, 2003, 1–44). Especially ingenious and resourceful in his invention of procedures is the West Coast L=A=N=G=U=A=G=E poet Ron Silliman. Silliman's *Tjanting* (1980), for instance, is based on the Fibonacci series of numbers (1, 1, 2, 3, 5, 8, 13, 21, and so on, each number being the sum of the previous two): its first paragraph has one sentence; the second, also one; the third, two; the fourth, three, the fifth, five, the sixth, eight, and so on (Huntsperger, 2010, 97–130). The notes at the end of his 1,000-page poem *The Alphabet* (published 2008, but written mainly in the eighties and early nineties) reveal some of the "structural secrets" behind the composition of each section: "Jones" (1987) records what he noticed by looking at the ground "every day for a year," "Skies" (1980–81) what he noticed by looking at the sky, also "every day for a year"; "Non" (1987–89) observes the rule, "The instant you feel comfortable with a stanzaic form, abandon it"; "Paradise" (1984) was written over the course of a single year, each paragraph at "one sitting"; "You" (1995) also over the course of a year, "One paragraph a day, one section a week"; and so on (Silliman, 2008, 1057–62).

An especially conspicuous instance of procedural practice is Lyn Hejinian's book-length prose poem *My Life* (1978, 1986), whose role in the breakthrough of L=A=N=G=U=A=G=E writing to a wider public is comparable to that of Perec's *Life a User's Manual* in the case of OuLiPo. As its title suggests, Hejinian's text is evidently a memoir, and each of its sentences certainly seems to refer to the experiences of a girl and later a young woman growing up in the America of Hejinian's generation. However, the sentences do not cohere among themselves, falling into no apparent order, and there is none of the continuous narrative one expects from a conventional memoir. Like Perelman's "China," *My Life* turns out to be another text with a "structural secret": Hejinian has produced one chapter for each of the 37 years of her age when she composed *My Life*, each chapter comprising exactly 37 sentences, though neither the chapters nor the sentences follow the chronological order of her life (Perloff, 1991, 162–70). When Hejinian updated the text at age 45, she added eight completely new chapters, and interpolated eight new sentences in each of the original chapters. The experience is hers, but mediated, as in "China," by a procedure. *My Life* experiments not just with form but with a *world*, which the text both does and does not construct, or constructs and deconstructs, produces and erases.

Like other poets of the L=A=N=G=U=A=G=E group, Hejinian both evokes and resists the narrativity that is implied in "life-writing." Procedural practices such as hers accommodate the narrative impulse, while at the same time countering it. Such ambivalence toward narrativity, running like a powerful current throughout L=A=N=G=U=A=G=E writing, can be detected even in writers who do not typically practice proceduralism, such as Leslie Scalapino, Hejinian's friend and sometime collaborator. Her trilogy of long prose poems from the very end of the peak period (1990–91), modeled on comic books and other serial forms, seems to vacillate between embracing and rejecting narrative. Reflecting a similar vacillation in the visual arts of the period, Scalapino titles one of these poems *The Return of Painting*.

7. Pictures and the Return of Painting

Andreas Huyssen opens his 1984 essay "Mapping the Postmodern," seminal for "postmodernism theory" (see section 2), by reporting on his experience of visiting *Documenta 7*, an influential survey of new art, in Kassel, Germany, in 1982. He expresses disappointment at what he perceives to be a retreat from "irony, reflexiveness . . . self-doubt" and "critical consciousness" in the art of *Documenta 7*, coupled with the restoration of an ideology of art that is anything but avant-garde: "The museum as temple, the artist as prophet, the work as relic and cult object, the halo restored" (Huyssen, 1986, 180, 179). Where is the critical demystification of art as practiced by the avant-garde of the previous two decades? In its place Huyssen detects a revival of art's "aura," that quality of almost magical specialness and insulation from the practical world that, according to the modernist-era theorist Walter Benjamin, ought to have eroded away under the impact of photography and other modes of mechanical reproduction. Huyssen mentions only obliquely and in passing one of the main features of *Documenta 7*, namely its showcasing of the new figurative painting, especially German "Neoexpressionism," but the return of painting seems to confirm Huyssen's critique. If any art form is associated with the "auratic" in art, it is painting. "A painting is not just an object: it has aura again," proclaims Sandro Chia (quoted in Godfrey, 1986, 69), one of the Italian "Transavantgarde" painters who exhibited alongside the Germans at *Documenta 7*. When painting returns, so does art's aura (see Rose, 2002 [1980], 396–7).

   Why was Huyssen so surprised and disappointed to see the artistic ideology of aura return in *Documenta 7*? Because so much of the art of the late sixties and seventies had worked so hard to extirpate it, and with it the very *objecthood* of art – "the work as relic and cult object," as Huyssen put it. Artists in the interval between postmodernism's "big bang" in 1966 and its rebranding around 1973 engaged in a collective project of what Lucy Lippard, in an important book covering exactly that period (Lippard, 1997 [1973]), termed the "dematerializaton of art." Following in the tradition of earlier avant-gardes such as Dada and Fluxus, art practices of that period yielded artworks that were increasingly *not* objects but performances, sites, words or ideas – conceptual art (Smith, 2011, 35–6). "Conceptual art, for me," writes Lippard, "means work in which the idea is paramount and the material form is secondary, lightweight, ephemeral, cheap, unpretentious and/or 'dematerialized'" (Lippard, 1997, vii). Characteristic examples include Joseph Kosuth's "One and Three Chairs" (1965), which juxtaposed a real chair with a photograph of a chair and a verbal description of one (see Prinz, 2012, 326–7); Sol LeWitt's written instructions for the production of murals to be executed by someone else; and Vito Acconci's "Following Piece" (1969), in which he literally followed strangers around on the street until they went indoors. Conceptual art practices always implicitly reflected on and critiqued the art institution itself and sometimes did so explicitly. They could also be adapted as vehicles of political expression, especially, from the seventies on, of feminist politics (e.g., Mary Kelley's "Post-Partum Document," 1973–79), and in the eighties of AIDS activism (see Foster et al., 2011, 649–55; Molesworth, 2012). Allied with conceptualism were other art practices of the same era, including performance and installation art (e.g., Josef Beuys), body art (e.g., Dennis Oppenheim, Carolee Schneeman), and site-specific and earth art (e.g., Michael Heizer, Robert Smithson; the latter died in 1973 in a plane crash, while surveying from the air sites for a projected earth-work).

Diverse as these practices were in means and materials, they were nevertheless united in what they collectively *rejected*: the illusions of representation, the traditional means of easel painting and sculpture, and the production of *objects* designed to be bought and sold in an art market. Conceptualism and other allied "dematerialized" practices, including performance and installation art, remained a force in the art world throughout the "peak" era of postmodernism and beyond, down to the present, as witness the careers of Laurie Anderson, Ann Hamilton, Sophie Calle, and many others.

Kosuth speaks for many of his conceptualist colleagues when in 1969 he writes, "If you make paintings you are already accepting (not questioning) the nature of art" (Kosuth, 1999, 163). Nevertheless, in the mid-seventies conceptualism provoked a vigorous counter-reaction in the form, precisely, of a return of easel painting to art-world prominence. Conceptualism evidently failed to satisfy a certain appetite for images, at least among art-world professionals and collectors. This appetite was first catered to, somewhat unconvincingly, by Photorealist painters during the late sixties and early seventies, then more decisively by non-photography-based figurative painting in the seventies and eighties – so-called Neoexpressionism (Smith, 2011, 46–65). One can trace the upward trajectory of this tendency through a series of exhibitions, most of them with "new" in their titles, from "New Image Painting" at the Whitney Museum, New York, 1978, through "A New Spirit in

Painting," London, 1981, on to the *Documenta 7* show in 1982 that so disappointed Huyssen. The painters brought together under the "Neoexpressionist" rubric were an aesthetically heterogeneous group, not all of them evidently related to the others, except for marketing purposes. They included the Germans Rainer Fetting, Jörg Immendorf, Anselm Kiefer, Helmut Middendorf, and A. R. Penck, but also Georg Baselitz and Markus Lüpertz, who, having been around the art world for a decade or more already, were hardly "new," as well as Gerhard Richter and Sigmar Polke, who were not expressionists at all, "neo" or otherwise. The group also included the Italians Chia, Francesco Clemente, and Enzo Cucchi, and the Americans Eric Fishl, Robert Longo, David Salle, and Julian Schnabel, but also Susan Rothenberg, really an abstract painter, despite her incorporation of animal imagery in her paintings. The art market makes strange bedfellows.

Charles Jencks, for one, sees the return to figuration in the paintings of Chia, Salle, Fischl, Longo, and others as a characteristically postmodern phenomenon, treating it as another manifestation of the double-coding (see section 2) that he also identifies in postmodern architecture and literature. Other contemporary observers, while recognizing that Neoexpressionist painting constituted *a* postmodernism in the visual arts, denied that it was the *only* postmodernism – indeed, denounced it as precisely the *wrong* postmodernism. In particular, the critics and theorists associated with the journal *October* (founded in 1976), including Benjamin Buchloh, Douglas Crimp, Hal Foster, Rosalind Krauss, and Craig Owens, regarded the return to painting as reactionary, retrograde, and entirely market-driven, and even associated it with the incipient authoritarianism of the Reagan/Thatcher years. The *October* group distinguished between two different image-based postmodern practices: on the one hand, the conservative postmodernism of the return to painting; on the other, a critical and deconstructive practice involving the appropriation of preexisting mass-media or art-historical imagery (see Foster et al., 2011, 627; Molesworth, 2012, 21). The first they associated with what Jameson called *pastiche*, the a-historical and literally pointless recycling of familiar models, while the second, deconstructive kind was much closer to Lyotard's sense of postmodernism as the persistence of an intransigently radical and critical avant-garde (Melville, 2004, 90; see section 2).

The *October* critics' model for the second, critical and deconstructive use of images, was the work exhibited in the 1977 "Pictures" exhibition at Artists Space, curated by one of their own number, Douglas Crimp (see Eklund, 2009). Typical examples of the art of the "Pictures" group included Sherrie Levine's controversial rephotographing of classic modernist-era art photographs; Cindy Sherman's series of "Untitled Film Stills" (1977–80), in which Sherman posed herself in roles and situations all too familiar from mass-media representations of women; and Richard Prince's rephotograph-ing and re-contextualizing of advertising images, most famously the "Marlboro Man" of cigarette ads. The "Pictures" artists, like their literary contemporary Kathy Acker, practiced an art of *appropriation*, of the "theft" and repurposing of images.

However, the barrier that the *October* critics erected between the two postmodernisms – a retrograde return to painting on one side, a deconstruc-tive practice involving "pictures" on the other – was never airtight. Longo, for instance, who appeared in the "Pictures" show, migrated to the painting camp, as did Salle, who studied at the California Institute of the Arts under the conceptualist John Baldessari and alongside several "Pictures" artists, and who associated with the "Pictures" group. Basing their drawn and painted images on photographs, Longo and Salle both practiced an appropriative art very much in the spirit of their "Pictures" associates. Conversely, the appro-priative art of the "Pictures" group itself can be seen as "driven by concerns about painting," and even, somewhat paradoxically, as *belonging to* the prac-tice of painting, despite its photographic medium (Melville, 2004, 92).

Salle's practice seems to teeter right on the divide between "pictures" and Neoexpressionist painting, and thus to involve *both* postmodernisms (see, e.g., Jameson, 1991, 175–7; Eklund, 2009, 211–7). In a typical mid-eighties paint-ing such as "Colony" (1986; see Figure 2), he combines photography-based

Figure 2. David Salle, *Colony* (1986). Acrylic and oil on canvas. 94 in. × 136 in. (238.8 cm × 345.4 cm).
© David Salle/License by VAGA, New York, NY.

images with art-historical pastiches, juxtaposing them *non sequitur* fashion, but also *layering* them one on top of the other, sometimes overpainting and obscuring the underlying layers but sometimes allowing them to be seen *through* the upper layers. The bottom image here, painted in *grisaille* (shades of the same color), apparently based on a photograph, is that of a young woman, eyes closed, breasts bared – typically for Salle, who was widely criticized for his apparently sexist use of female nudes – evidently pressing up against something like the underside of a glass coffee table. Over this image are superimposed two other figurative images, a disembodied eye (echoing the closed eyelids of the woman) and a decapitated head (appropriated from the French Romantic painter Théodore Géricault, as it turns out), as well as two nonfigurative zones of color; on top of one of these zones, in turn, is superimposed some kind of genre scene of village musicians, outlined in blue, from which a blue streak extends, cutting across the young woman's arm to connect up with a puddle of blue paint on the left. Finally, literally inset into the painting's surface is *another* painting, an amateur's Venetian scene, probably scavenged from a thrift-store or garage-sale. Multiple styles of painting, multiple sources of imagery, multiple planes, even multiple painted surfaces, jockey for our attention.

Is this a representational picture? That is, does it produce an illusion of space populated by figures? Yes and no: while "Colony" is obviously figurative, its figures occupy not a single integrated space but disjunct, uncoordinated spaces, floating above or apart from each other. As Barbara Rose writes (though she has abstract paintings in mind), "If an illusion of space is evoked, it is simultaneously rescinded" (Rose, 2002, 402). Is it a narrative picture? Does it tell a story? Yes and no: while its elements seem charged with narrative potential, no overall narrative sequence emerges. Some of the Neoexpressionist painters embraced narrative, including, conspicuously, Salle's friend Fischl, but Salle himself resisted narrative readings of his paintings: "There's no narrative" (quoted in Sandler, 1996, 236).

This "yes and no" – illusionist and not-illusionist, narrative and not-narrative – seems strongly reminiscent of double-coding in Jencks's sense. In its complexity of planes, levels and kinds of image, "Colony" also seems akin to postmodernist literary texts – to Pynchon's *Gravity's Rainbow*, for instance, with its multiplicity of juxtaposed genres, registers, styles and kinds of representation (documentary, fantastic, melodramatic, cartoonish), its layering of ontological levels (dream, hallucination, fantasy, other worlds), and its capacity to "flicker" between reality and unreality ("Of course it happened. Of course it didn't happen"; Pynchon, 1973, 667). Moreover, Pynchon's use of movies throughout his novel, both as a model

for episodes and character types and as a separate ontological level, inter-
posed between the reader and the novel's storyworld – as though we were
reading the recounting of a *film* called *Gravity's Rainbow* – seems to find an
equivalent in the cinematic or, better, televisual quality of Salle's paintings.
Can a work such as "Colony" perhaps be grasped as a representation of the
quintessentially postmodern experience of *channel-surfing*?

Predictably, Salle resists this analogy with television, too, as he does
the possibility of narrativization (Sandler, 1996, 239). Nevertheless, his paintings seem to be a site for the mingling of high and low culture, of art history
and the mass media, as are those of other painters of the same mid-eighties
moment, such as Robert Yarber, a much lower-visibility painter than Salle, but
for that very reason perhaps even more characteristic of the era. Yarber's mid-
eighties paintings are explicitly modeled on wide-screen Technicolor movies,
in their colors, their iconography, and even their scale (Shaman, 1989), and his
spaces, typically resort hotel rooms, often incorporate television screens. His
images of ambiguously flying, floating or falling bodies (see "Angels") manifestly resonate with postmodernist writing, and for that matter with writing
about postmodernism. Yarber's painting "Regard and Abandon" (1985; see
Figure 3) is reproduced on the cover of Ronald Sukenick's novel *Blown Away*
(1986), a postmodern retelling of Shakespeare's *The Tempest* (see "Prospero's
Books"), while his painting "The Strip" (1986), which perhaps alludes to the
postmodern aesthetic of Venturi's *Learning from Las Vegas* (see section 1),
appears on the cover of my own *Constructing Postmodernism* (1992).

Figure 3. Robert Yarber, *Regard and Abandon* (1985). Pastel on paper.
39½ in. × 55½ in. (100 cm × 141 cm).
Courtesy of Sonnabend Gallery, New York. Photo: Jon Abbott.

If Yarber's overall aesthetic is cinematic, his figures are strikingly *cartoonish* – caricatural, blocky, big-footed – a feature they share with figures in paintings by other postmodern painters, including Philip Guston (an important forerunner), the German Immendorf, the Italian Chia, even the American Elizabeth Murray (see Varnedoe and Gopnik, 1990, 409–12). Here is another symptom of the leakage of low culture into high art. That leakage seemed momentarily, in the early eighties, to have grown into a torrent as the levees that had previously protected the art world from the imagery of the "street" seemed to have collapsed with the upsurge of graffiti art, associated with the crossover of hip-hop culture to a wider public, and first seen spray-painted, guerrilla fashion, on urban walls and the sides of New York subway trains (see Cooper and Chalfant, 1984; Varnedoe and Gopnik, 1990, 376–82). Ultimately, however, the levees were restored, and only a few graffiti artists were actually absorbed into the art world. Two who were, as it turns out, were actually art-school trained: Keith Haring, who began his career drawing on unused advertising spaces on subway platforms, and Kenny Scharf, whose complex cartoon compositions echoed subway spray-painters.

The only true "street" artist to be fully embraced by the art world – too fully, perhaps, for his own good – was Jean-Michel Basquiat. By no means a "primitive," but with meager formal training, he began as a graffitist, using the tag "Samo" (short for "same old shit"), and eventually graduated to easel painting, developing a distinctive figurative iconography and incorporating words in many of his paintings. An example is "To Repel Ghosts" (see Figure 4), one of several paintings of his with that title. This version features fields of color, drippy passages, and layered images: a cartoon ghost super-imposed upon a skull, a complex *momento mori*. The words of the title are repeated, but some of them are crossed out, placed under erasure. Typically for Basquiat, they are also copyrighted, or at least the conventional copyright sign, ©, is brushed in beside them – perhaps by way of reflecting on the art world and its preoccupation with possession, attribution, and originality.

This painting, too, has been reproduced on a book cover, in this case that of Kevin Young's book-length poem by the same name, *To Repel Ghosts* (2001), a fragmented verse biography of Basquiat that shifts back and forth between his life and evocations of his paintings, incorporating many of Basquiat's titles and some of the words he used in his paintings. Young's poem, coming late in the history of Basquiat's posthumous celebrity – he died tragically young, in 1988 – proposes a counter-mythology, pushing back against the mythologiz-ing of Basquiat as doomed genius by, among others, his fellow painter Julian Schnabel. Himself an incorrigible *self*-mythologizer, Schnabel crossed over to

Figure 4. Jean-Michel Basquiat, *To Repel Ghosts*.
© The Estate of Jean-Michel Basquiat/ADAGP, Paris/ARS, New York 2014.

film with his bio-pic about Basquiat (1996), and then stayed to make a career in cinema (*Before Night Falls*, 2000; *The Diving Bell and the Butterfly*, 2007; etc.). Others of his generation of artists also crossed over to moviemaking – Sherman and Salle with small-scale independent films, Longo with a Hollywood SF action picture, *Johnny Mnemonic* (1995), based on a cyberpunk story by William Gibson – confirming, as if further confirmation were needed, the cinematic, mass-mediated quality of *both* "pictures" and the return of painting.

8. Downtown, or, the Capital of Postmodernism

Special conditions had to prevail for an artist like Basquiat to thrive as he did – to cross over from street culture to art-world celebrity, from tagging walls to collaborating with Andy Warhol – and those conditions could really only arise in the kind of urban space we call, for short, "Downtown." Not only Basquiat, but many of the other visual artists of both the "Pictures Generation" and the Neoexpressionist movement alike, lived in New York City's Downtown at some point in their careers and were sustained by Downtown galleries, support systems and personal relationships. Indeed, not just visual art but also many other cultural developments of the peak period of postmodernism, 1973–1990, are associated with this particular type of urban space. The breeding ground of the punk and New Wave subcultures in music, fashion, and graphic design, Downtown in this period was also a hothouse for alternative forms of dance, performance, and writing, as well as visual art. It was a zone of contact where artists of diverse backgrounds, differing in aesthetic principles and practice, working in different media, could interact and collaborate, where high and low culture mingled, high theory cross-pollinated with avant-garde practice, and art-world careers were incubated.

Downtown was a place, but also a cultural model, what the Russian theorist Bakhtin might have called a *chronotope*, a particular, recurrent configuration of time and space. The Downtown model can be realized anywhere, in any city where alternative artistic activity, more or less independent of the official institutions of culture and art-world commerce, achieves a certain critical mass, and where artists live in close proximity to each other. London in this period, for instance, had the equivalent of a "Downtown" scene, more dispersed than New York's, centered in Chelsea, where the anarchist entrepreneurs Malcolm McLaren and Vivienne Westwood helped create the conditions for punk music (McLaren managed the Sex Pistols) and the fashion and graphic styles associated with it (Marcus, 1989, 27–33; Strongman, 2007, 65–100). Berlin, too, had an equivalent scene, which would come fully into its own only after the city's reunification in 1989–90. Nevertheless, the Downtown model is particularly identified in this period with several neighborhoods of Lower Manhattan – different neighborhoods at different times: first, SoHo (the neighborhood immediately *so*uth of *Ho*uston Street), from the mid-sixties through the early eighties; then, a little later, from the seventies on, the East Village and the Lower East Side, as well as Tribeca (the *tri*angle *be*low *Ca*nal Street) and still later New York's Chelsea (Kostelanetz, 2003, 223).

In one sense, then, New York's Downtown is representative of urban alternative-art communities everywhere. In another sense, however, it is unique, a special case: the world capital of postmodernism during its peak period. In addition to the work of visual artists like Basquiat, its characteristic products included the appropriation-based writing of Kathy Acker, beginning with her *Black Tarantula* trilogy of 1974–75 and continuing through to *Empire of the Senseless* (1988) and beyond; the opera/spectacle *Einstein on the Beach* (1975), a collaboration among the avant-garde theater director Robert Wilson, the minimalist composer Philip Glass, and the postmodern dancer and choreographer Lucinda Childs; the punk-rock album *Horses* (1975) by the poet Patti Smith and her band, with an iconic cover image of the singer by the photographer (and her former lover) Robert Mapplethorpe; Art Spiegelman's and Françoise Mouly's magazine *RAW* (1980–86), showcasing graphic narrative art and preparing an audience for Spiegelman's own *Maus* (1986, 1991); the mixed-media performances of Laurie Anderson, and the recordings and films that spun off from them, including her unlikely hit single *O Superman* (1981); the eclectic music of the jazz saxophonist and composer John Zorn, including his recordings *The Big Gundown* (1985), *Spillane* (1987), and *Naked City* (1989), recycling movie-music and genre-film conventions in a style combining free jazz, punk, and ambient urban noise; Sonic Youth's *Daydream Nation* (1988), an ambitious post-punk, noise-rock recording, their last before signing with a major label, with paintings by Gerhard Richter on the cover and lyrics that allude to the cyberpunk fictions of William Gibson; and Nan Goldin's photographs of friends and lovers from the Downtown world, arranged as slideshows and projected to music in clubs and galleries throughout the eighties under the title, *The Ballad of Sexual Dependency*. Most of the tendencies of peak-era postmodernism that I have documented in this chapter are reflected in these works. They mingle pop culture and avant-garde aesthetics, in the manner of Avant-Pop, and in a few cases (Glass, Spiegelman, Patti Smith, Laurie Anderson) mark the artists' crossover to mainstream acceptance. They often involve appropriation, recycling, and other artificial procedures, and they violently juxtapose styles, genres and levels of reality, sometimes (as in *Empire of the Senseless, Einstein on the Beach, Daydream Nation*, and some of Laurie Anderson's texts) spilling over into the alternative worlds of science fiction. If few are expressly informed by postmodern "theory" – except for Acker's writings, if Robert Siegle is right about this (Siegle, 1989, 47–123) – all of them can be framed after the fact and illuminated by the kind of theory that Lotringer's *Semiotext(e)* book series purveyed to Downtown artists from the early eighties on.

New York's Downtown was also postmodern in being a product of neo-liberal economic policy. Artists' SoHo (as Richard Kostelanetz calls it) emerged in the wake of the de-industrialization of Lower Manhattan, when formerly commercial and light-industrial loft spaces were left vacant, real-estate prices tumbled, and the city relaxed zoning restrictions to allow artists to convert lofts to studios (Kostelanetz, 2003, 31–2). Impoverished artists turned their studios into combined living/working spaces, and the SoHo scene was born. The Downtown scene in the East Village and the Lower East Side is a somewhat different case, since these are residential neighborhoods, home to African-American, Puerto Rican, and immigrant working-class communities that bore the brunt of the deterioration of city services and infrastructure during the New York fiscal crisis of the seventies, when the city literally went bankrupt (Harvey, 2005, 44–8). Artists who took advantage of low rents in these neighborhoods and created an art-world scene in these communities' midst, have been seen by some as agents of gentrification, even as "shock troops for real-estate developers" (Stansbaugh, 2007, 54; see Deutsche and Ryan, 1984). Once artists have "pioneered" an unfashionable neighborhood and made it hip, according to this scenario, uptown gallerists soon follow, then retailers and restaurateurs, and before long the neighborhood is flooded with upscale interlopers, rents skyrocket, and the original residents are displaced – and along with them many of the artist-pioneers, no longer able to afford the rents. In this sense, the Downtown scene is not only a product of neoliberal economics, but also its agent and accomplice, however inadvertently. While there is certainly some painful truth in this scenario, it is also the case that the artists who created and sustained the Downtown scene during the seventies and eighties, a particularly difficult period in New York's social history, shared many of the same dangers and hardships with long-term resident communities, enduring not only urban blight and successive waves of the drug plague, with its associated violence, but also the AIDS epidemic.

Hardship forces artists to be resourceful. Downtown conditions were mild compared to the immiseration of the African-American communities of the South Bronx during the same period, where extreme deprivation created the conditions for an explosion of cultural expression which continues to resonate down to the present: graffiti art, breakdancing, rap, all the components of hip-hop culture emerge from this crucible (Berman, 2007, 25–8). Contemporaneous Downtown artistic expression, while not subject to such crushing pressures, nevertheless reflected the particular constraints and conditions under which it was produced. Thus, for example, SoHo artists, able to take advantage of the loft spaces of their studios and the galleries that showed or staged their work, tended to produce more "spacious" works – performance, dance, installations, larger-scale paintings – by comparison with the East Village artists who lived, worked and exhibited in much more constricted spaces (Kostelanetz, 2003, 211–2). Here smaller-scale, photographically based work flourished instead, as well as writing (Siegle, 1988; Stosuy, 2006).

"I believe that downtown writing is *postmodern,*" Siegle writes (1989, 395), but if so, it is not postmodern in the same way as the characteristic megafictions of Pynchon, Coover, Barth, Fuentes, Rushdie, and other postmodernists. While the latters' ambitions were manifestly "major," their aspirations monumental, and most of them enjoyed the luxury of commercial publication and distribution, the Downtown writing of Acker, Constance DeJong, Lynne Tillman, Theresa Cha, and the others whom Siegle documents was defiantly "minor" – oppositional, in-your-face, ephemeral by design, speaking from the margins, a minimalist alternative to the megafictionists' maximalism. Moreover, their texts were initially produced and distributed almost clandestinely, well outside the usual commercial publishing channels; the Downtown fiction magazine *Between C & D,* for instance, was printed on fanfold paper by a dot-matrix printer, and distributed in plastic ziplock bags (Siegle, 1989, 312–3). Only belatedly did Downtown writers find some commercial success, as Acker, for instance, did from 1984 on, when her books began to be published by Grove Press.

The hardships that Downtown artists endured in pursuit of artistic autonomy and community were stylized and glamorized in cyberpunk science-fiction. In effect, the Downtown scene contributes the *punk* component of *cyberpunk.* Downtown is the model for the dangerous, anarchic space of the immiserated future cities of the cyberpunks – the Sprawl of Gibson's early stories and first trilogy (1984–88), the Orbitals of Bruce Sterling's *Schismatrix* (1985), the Freezone of John Shirley's *Eclipse* (1987) – which both complements and contradicts the bloodless virtual reality of cyberspace. Half-criminals, half-artists, the lone-wolf hacker-heroes of these cyberpunk fictions move freely between the two realms, negotiating the divide between urban slum and "consensual hallucination," much as the real-world artists of the Downtown scene themselves did. However, few of the cyberpunk writers seem actually to have spent much time Downtown (as far as I can tell), so the Downtown model must have been mediated to them by science-fiction precursors who did, such as Samuel Delany, whose novels *Dhalgren* (1975) and *Trouble on Triton* (originally titled *Triton,* 1976) displace Downtown to distant worlds or parallel dimensions. The cyberpunks could also have glimpsed Downtown in the background of Ridley Scott's film *Blade Runner* (1982), nominally set in Los Angeles, or scaled up to the size of the whole of Manhattan in John Carpenter's *Escape from New York* (1981).

However, neither of these movies captures the science-fiction potential of Downtown as fully as the obscure cult film *Liquid Sky* (1982). A kind of Downtown parody of Spielberg's blockbuster, *Close Encounters of the Third Kind* (1977), the film observes the New Wave milieu – its music, fashion, décor, drug culture, and sexual mores – from a literally alienated point of view: that of the film's Russian émigré makers, Slava Tsukerman and Nina Kerova, but also, interior to the film's storyworld, that of an extraterrestrial who arrives in a comically miniature flying-saucer to vampirically consume the endorphins released by Downtowners in the midst of orgasms or drug rushes. Amateurishly acted, but visually and sonically startling, *Liquid Sky* pictures Downtown as an enclave of heightened and stylized reality folded within normal, everyday Manhattan, an "inner space" where extraterrestrials are hardly more alien than the locals. (The London equivalent might be Hanif Kureishi's film *Sammy and Rosie Get Laid* [1987], a magical-realist retelling of Shakespeare's *King Lear* against the backdrop of a riot-torn, near-apocalyptic London.)

In other words, the world of *Liquid Sky* (or of *Sammy and Rosie*) is a *heterotopia*: an "other space," in Michel Foucault's sense (1967/1984), or a "zone," in my own sense of that term (McHale, 1987, 43–58). A heterotopia is a type of space folded within the urban fabric, integrated but also separate, a "counter-site." Examples of heterotopia, according to Foucault, include prisons, psychiatric hospitals, cemeteries, theatres, gardens, museums and libraries, fairgrounds, and brothels. Charles Jencks, looking back over the thirty or more years of commercial development and gentrification that have intervened since Foucault's initial analysis, adds college campuses, theme parks, megamalls, and mixed-use skyscrapers (Jencks, 2011, 119–29) – cities-within-the-city, akin to the Westin Bonaventure Hotel that Fredric Jameson famously characterized, early in the development of postmodernism theory, as typical of a certain kind of postmodern architecture (Jameson, 1990, 38–45). To this list we can now add "urban artist colonies," which is how Kostelanetz characterizes SoHo (Kostelanetz, 2003, 7), and by extension Downtown more generally. Discontinuous with the city that surrounds it, Downtown also *mirrors* that city, on a smaller scale; it is a *mise en abyme* of the city, and perhaps, beyond that, of the postmodern world in general, in something like the same way that (according to another of Jameson's famous architectural analyses) Frank Gehry's house in Santa Monica mirrors or maps postmodernity (Jameson, 1991, 127–9).

A picture of Downtown as heterotopia, *Liquid Sky* is also a premonitory history of the end of Downtown, anticipating (as early as 1982) the eventual winding down of the scene, which corresponds rather closely with the end of peak postmodernism around 1989–90. After the waning of Downtown as the site of postmodernism – with the cooling of the art market, increasing gentrification, and the irremediable losses to drugs (Basquiat), AIDS (Mapplethorpe, Haring, David Wojnarowicz, many others) and violence

(Theresa Cha) – the postmodern heterotopia would gradually migrate from real cities to the virtual realm of cyberspace.

PROSPERO'S BOOKS

1. Enchanted Islands

Did Shakespeare anticipate postmodernism? Of course not – no more than he did, say, psychoanalysis, or science fiction, or modernism itself, even though, through a trick of historical perspective, it sometimes seems as though he anticipated *all* these twentieth-century cultural phenomena (see Chapter 1). It is only because of the way Freud and Joyce (among others) read *Hamlet*, for instance, that Shakespeare appears to have anticipated psychoanalysis and modernism. By the same token, it is only because of the way postmodernists have read *The Tempest* that Shakespeare appears to have anticipated postmodernism (and science fiction, too).

Our capacity to read our own cultural moment back into Shakespeare, and then to claim to have *found* it there, folded up *inside* Shakespeare's plays, waiting to be unfolded, is attributable in part to the extraordinary *openness* of the plays – their openness to interpretation and reinterpretation, to revision, repurposing, adaptation, and appropriation. "Shakespearean texts are by nature open," Stephen Orgel reminds us (1987, 12), but *The Tempest* exceptionally so, even by Shakespearean standards. *The Tempest*'s special openness to appropriation and repurposing is borne out by its peculiar performance history in the period between 1667 and 1838, when, unlike any other Shakespeare play, it held the stage continuously. It did so, however, under a different title –*The Enchanted Island* – and in a version radically overhauled by John Dryden and William Davenant, and with abundant song and dance numbers, mostly supplied by Thomas Shadwell in 1674 (Orgel, 1987; Roach, 2000; Dobson, 2001). As far as the "long eighteenth century" was concerned, there *was* no *Tempest* except this retooled and repurposed one. So it only seems appropriate that when, in winter 2012, the Metropolitan Opera sought to revive the eighteenth-century practice of operatic *pasticcio* – that is, an opera pieced together from material borrowed from various composers – it was *The Tempest* that provided the plot scaffolding. Inevitably, the title was Dryden's and Davenant's: *The Enchanted Island*.

By the time of the Met's *Enchanted Island*, *The Tempest* had already for several decades been treated as, in effect, a postmodernist property. Its susceptibility to postmodernist reading and repurposing is ultimately traceable to certain features of the play itself. To begin with, Shakespeare's*Tempest* is a work of *metatheater*, in which a powerful central figure, Prospero, autocrat and magician, behaves like a theatrical director, literally stage-managing the events of the play and producing a series of theatrical illusions, including a play-within-the-play in the form of a masque for the betrothal of his daughter, Miranda. This playwright/illusionist has long been read as Shakespeare's surrogate, a portrait of the artist as an old man, and his renunciation of magic as Shakespeare's farewell to the theater – an attractive if historically dubious reading (though see Bruster, 2001 for a version that is more historically responsible).

The Prospero-centered version of the play, with its metatheatricality, illusionism, and foregrounded world-making and -unmaking, may be the one that postmodernists favor, but, Shakespeare being Shakespeare, it is far from the only possible version of the play. Prospero's play – the one he plans, produces, casts, stages, and then consigns to nothingness – is not necessarily identical with *The Tempest* as such; his is only *one* of the plays in *The Tempest*, though apparently the authoritative one. Nevertheless, there is room, if we choose to acknowledge it, for *other* plays, centered on *other* characters' experiences, perspectives, interests, and desires (see Barker and Hulme, 1985). There is, as it were, some *play* in this play, and while Prospero speaks with indubitable authority (and literally gets the last word), it is nevertheless the case, as has long been noticed, that some of the finest poetry in the play, and many of its most memorable lines, are assigned to his subordinates: his daughter Miranda ("O brave new world . . ."), his servant Ariel ("Full fathom five thy father lies . . ."), and above all his slave Caliban ("The isle is full of noises . . .", and much else besides). It is as though Shakespeare had, right from the outset, and somewhat contrary to the autocratic structure of his play's world, *distributed* linguistic power, democratizing it.

Revisionist adaptations and appropriations seize on the opportunities presented by this "play" in the play, and reconceive *The Tempest* as *someone else's* play – not Prospero's but instead Caliban's, or Miranda's, or even the shipwrecked castaways' play. In the second half of the twentieth century, several of these potential "other" plays have been unfolded from the *Tempest* matrix, yielding one of several *alternative Tempests*: Caliban's play has yielded a post-colonial alternative; Miranda's play, a feminist alternative; the castaways' play, a science-fiction alternative. Nor have the Prospero-centered versions of the play remained unaffected. In the aftermath of all this revisionism, even Prospero's *Tempest* cannot help but be colored by the oppositional, resistant appropriations of recent decades (Zabus, 2002, 177–9). These alternative versions of *The Tempest* have arrived in successive waves, with the postcolonial revision emerging in the fifties and arguably cresting in the seventies (see Nixon, 1987, 20), followed by a feminist wave in the seventies and eighties. The science-fiction wave arises earlier, in the modernist era, and the postmodernist version in the sixties, but these versions, too, crest during what we might think of as the "long eighties," from about 1977 (the year of John Fowles's revision of *The Magus*) to about 1992 (the year of Marina Warner's *Indigo*) – in other words, during the peak phase of postmodernism.

2. Caliban's Play

Whatever else Shakespeare's *Tempest* may be, it is hard now *not* to see it as a reflection on English imperialism in the West Indies and Virginia (and perhaps in Ireland too), displaced to a Mediterranean island. That interpretation, so self-evident to us, actually emerges quite late in the history of the play's reception. In academic criticism, it enjoyed very little currency before 1976, when Stephen Greenblatt placed it on the critical agenda with his landmark essay "Learning to Curse," in the process helping to consolidate so-called "New Historicism," one of the manifestations of the turn toward "theory" in Anglophone criticism (see section 2). The situation was different elsewhere, outside the Anglophone academy, in the nations of the newly emergent postcolonial world, where writers and critics had already for at least two decades been reading *The Tempest* as an apology for imperialism. More than that, they had been reading it *against the grain*, recognizing the way the play to some degree compromises or undermines its own imperialist ideology by granting eloquent voice to the colonized Other, in the figure of Caliban. They read it, in other words, as a colonialist text that leaves room for *post*colonial possibilities, and in doing so they discovered Caliban's play folded up inside *The Tempest* (see, among others, Lie and D'Haen, 1997; Vaughan, 1998; Cartelli, 1999; Hulme and Sherman, 2000; Zabus, 2002; Goldberg, 2004).

Intellectuals in Latin America, the Caribbean and Africa taught themselves to read *The Tempest* as, in effect, an anti-colonialist allegory, with Prospero as the figure of the European imperialist and Caliban as the figure of indigenous resistance. In fact, the earliest version of this allegorical appropriation, José Enrique Rodó's, from the turn of the twentieth century, was somewhat different, with Ariel standing for Latin American aspirations, while Caliban was associated with the capitalist and imperialist United States. By the sixties and seventies, however, it was Caliban who came to represent the struggle against colonialism in essays, poems, plays, and novels by, among others, the Barbadians George Lamming and Edward Kamau Brathwaite, the Martiniquan Aimé Césaire, the Cuban Roberto Fernandez Retamar, and the Sierra Leonean Lemuel Johnson. *The Tempest*, writes Rob Nixon, "came to serve as a Trojan horse, whereby cultures barred from the citadel of 'universal' Western values could win entry and assail those global pretensions from within" (Nixon, 1987, 206).

Postcolonial versions such as Césaire's play *Une tempête* (1960) or Lamming's novel *Water with Berries* (1971) rank among the most powerful of all the versions of Caliban's play, and they are certainly the most consequential as far as cultural history is concerned. Nevertheless, they are not the *only* versions. Whenever the objective is to upend the hierarchy of values and persons implied by Shakespeare's play – to challenge Prospero and his values *from below*, as it were, or even to dethrone him – then Caliban's play becomes the preferred option. Thus, we find all kinds of ironic, antithetical, perverse, against-the-grain, but not necessarily postcolonial revisions that recast *The Tempest* as Caliban's play. It is hard to imagine a clearer example of this than W. H. Auden's *The Sea and the Mirror* (1944), a cycle of poems in which Auden gives each of the main characters of Shakespeare's dramatis personae the chance to reflect in verse on his or her role in the play. Each of them, that is, except Caliban, for whom Auden composes instead a prose address to the audience, many times longer than the speeches he supplies for the other characters, in a style that pastiches Henry James's. It is Caliban who reflects on the aesthetics of the play, as though he, not Prospero, were the illusionist, master of ceremonies and author-surrogate – in effect, as though the play were really his.

More complex, and more fully postmodern, are John Banville's rewriting of *The Tempest* as Caliban's play in his novel *Ghosts* (1993), and Richard Powers' version in *Galatea 2.2* (1995). In the latter, a fictional character named Richard Powers, a novelist suffering writer's block, returns to a large Midwestern research university and becomes involved in the experimental development of an artificial intelligence. Powers' role is to train this AI, called Helen, to pass a qualifying exam in literature. If the output Helen generates is indistinguishable from that produced by a flesh-and-blood master's candidate, then Helen will have satisfied the criterion of the so-called Turing Test. She will have "passed" in the other sense of the term: passed *as human*. Obviously both a metafiction and a science fiction, *Galatea 2.2* is also a version of Caliban's play, because the text set by Helen's examiner are Caliban's lines from *The Tempest*: "Be not afeard: the isle is full of noises,/Sounds and sweet airs, that give delight, and hurt not" (III.ii.130–1). Helen identifies so completely with the slave and monster that she not only refuses to cooperate further, aborting the test, but withdraws into silence. Not exactly a postcolonial subject, Helen nevertheless *humanizes* herself through an act of resistance, as do many of the properly postcolonial Calibans.

3. The Women's Play

Why are there so few female Calibans? Helen the AI is one, arguably, though in a rather special sense. Suniti Namjoshi makes her Caliban female in a cycle of poems called "Snapshots of Caliban" (1984). However, in general, Caliban-centered versions, especially postcolonial ones, tend to exclude women from the play's emancipatory politics. Rob Nixon explains this in terms of the assumption shared by early postcolonial writers that "heroic revolt" was "a preeminently male province" (Nixon, 1987, 205). Worse, women in many versions of Caliban's play are not only overlooked but subordinated (Murphy, 2001, 52), and in some cases even made the object of displaced anti-colonial violence, as in Lamming's diasporic novel *Water with Berries* (see Nair, 1996, 66–71).

There is precedent for this exclusion of women in Shakespeare's *Tempest* itself, where only one woman actually appears – Miranda, Prospero's dutiful daughter, who is married off to Prince Ferdinand to restore the family's dynastic fortunes. In fact, three other women are mentioned, though they never appear: the witch Sycorax, Caliban's mother, original proprietor of the island, but dead long before the action begins; Claribel, King Alonso's daughter, whose offstage wedding to the King of Tunis has just been celebrated; and Prospero's nameless wife, Miranda's mother, also long dead, about whom we learn almost nothing. Slight as it is, the trace presence of these women allows for the possibility of a different alternative *Tempest*, a feminist rather than postcolonial one: not Caliban's play but Miranda's play, or perhaps Sycorax's or Claribel's; let's call it the women's play.

Almost no one, except the American poet H. D. (Hilda Doolittle), in a cycle of poems from her volume *By Avon River* (1949), has ventured to write Claribel's play. However, many women writers and intellectuals, especially in the United States (see Showalter, 1991), have appropriated Miranda as a figure for their aspirations, "writing back" against the patriarchal assumptions underlying Shakespeare's play. Many others have similarly appropriated Sycorax, a female magus and potentially (despite his libeling of her) Prospero's rival and double. Almost all of these versions of the women's play also enter into critical dialogue with, or even push back against, Caliban's play. This is the case, for instance, with Toni Morrison's *Tar Baby* (1981). A contemporary romance novel set largely on a Caribbean island and involving the troubled relationship between a refined and expensively educated woman of color, Jadine, and Son, an African-American fugitive, *Tar Baby* "signifies" on postcolonial *Tempests*, in Henry Louis Gates's sense of the term (1988). That is, it improvises ironically and critically on the materials of another, precursor text, mainly, in this case, Césaire's *Une tempête*, but also other postcolonial versions of Caliban's play, and of course Shakespeare's *Tempest* as well.

Pushing back even more vigorously against the unreflective masculinism of postcolonial *Tempests*, Marina Warner in her novel *Indigo, or, Mapping the Waters* (1992) juxtaposes two versions of the women's play. A double narrative, *Indigo* interweaves two stories: the history of the Caribbean island of Liamuiga at the time of its first encounter with Europeans at the beginning of the seventeenth century, rendered from the point of view of an indigenous wise woman called Sycorax, and the story of Miranda, a twentieth-century descendant of the island's English colonizers, now living in London. Thus, Warner actually rewrites *Tempest* twice over, once as Sycorax's play, once as Miranda's, in versions that partly mirror and partly counterpoint one another.

The ultimate feminist revision of *The Tempest*, one might think, would be one that turned the play's patriarchy completely on its head, changing the gender of Prospero himself. In fact, the director Julie Taymor did just that in her 2010 film of *The Tempest*, casting Helen Mirren as Prospera – with disappointingly meager consequences for the gender dynamics of the play. For a genuine example of radical regendering, one would need to look instead at Gloria Naylor's novel *Mama Day* (1988), which (like Morrison's *Tar Baby*) "signifies" vigorously on *The Tempest* (Andreas, 1999). Transferred to a sea island just off the Georgia/South Carolina coast, Naylor's is a magical realist version (see section 3) which, like Warner's, is dominated by a traditional wise-woman. Naylor, however, complicates the system of identifications by naming her wise-woman Miranda, and by displacing her Sycorax-figure to a dimly-remembered past, where she figures as the semi-legendary foremother of the island's present-day black inhabitants. Naylor's Miranda in fact absorbs the functions of Shakespeare's Prospero (though there is also a male false Prospero on the island). Here, then, we have Miranda in the role of Prospero, the resourceful daughter displacing the autocratic father – literally, Miranda's play in place of Prospero's.

4. The Shipwreck Play

The world of Shakespeare's *Tempest* is viewed from the perspective of Prospero's island, and from that perspective the shipwrecked castaways are interlopers, outsiders, off-islanders. However, in the same way that inverting the play's master/subordinate hierarchy allows for the possibility of imagining Caliban's or Miranda's plays as alternatives to Prospero's play, so, too, does shifting the perspective to the off-islanders enable us to imagine another alternative; let's call it the shipwreck play.

Among the group of shipwrecked courtiers and their underlings one might think that Prince Ferdinand would emerge as the likeliest candidate for a starring role in an alternative version of his own; he is, after all, Miranda's love interest. Perhaps the most distinguished literary work to treat Ferdinand as a key figure is Eliot's *The Waste Land*, where (we are informed in one of Eliot's endnotes) he "is not wholly distinct" from the Phoenician Sailor, a major "character" of the poem. Moreover, a few versions of *The Tempest* do reconfigure the play as a sort of *Bildungsroman* or "sentimental education" of the young aspirant to Miranda's hand – John Fowles' *The Magus* (1966; 1977) is an example. Most of the Ferdinand-centered versions, including Angela Carter's *The Infernal Desire Machines of Dr. Hoffman* (1972) and Richard Rush's film *The Stunt Man* (1980), based on Paul Brodeur's novel of the same name (1970), are darkly ironic exercises in manipulation, betrayal and disillusion. None, however, is darker than Fowles's earlier version, *The Collector* (1963), where Ferdinand (real name: Frederick Clegg) is a sexually obsessed kidnapper who confines Miranda in a basement cell.

In any case, Ferdinand's story is only rarely separated out from the larger collective story of the castaways. That story, traces of which can be detected throughout Shakespeare's play, is a traveler's tale of adventure and mishap, involving disorienting first encounters with alien beings, utopian fantasies of fresh beginnings, and a confrontation with a mysterious, ambiguous authority-figure who wields knowledge as power. In other words, seen from the castaways' perspective, *The Tempest* contains many of the building-blocks of what would much later be called science-fiction: space travel, aliens, utopia, a mad scientist.

The Tempest's potential to serve as a template for science fiction had already been recognized in landmark modernist-era texts such as H.G. Wells's *The Island of Dr. Moreau* (1896) and Aldous Huxley's *Brave New World* (1932). However, it is only during the postmodern decades, when science fiction completes its migration from the cultural side-channels to the mainstream, and allies itself with postmodernism, that *The Tempest* begins to appear in retrospect as a foundational text for science fiction and postmodernism alike. The trajectory that ends in cyberpunk science fiction of the eighties, coinciding with the peak moment of postmodernism, begins in 1956 with a seminal film adaptation, *Forbidden Planet,* directed by Fred Wilcox.

Forbidden Planet, an unapologetic pop-culture remake of *The Tempest*, reconfigures the castaway party as the crew of a United Planets starship who, landing on planet Altair-IV, discover survivors of an earlier starship wreck: Dr. Morbius and his nubile daughter Altaira, served by a robot factotum inevitably named Robbie. The identifications are straightforward and unproblematic: Morbius (played by Walter Pidgeon) corresponds to Prospero; Altaira (Anne Francis) is Miranda; Robby the Robot is Ariel; and the starship captain, Adams (Leslie Nielsen), who falls for Altaira, is the Ferdinand figure. It is from the outsiders' viewpoint of the starship party that we view Morbius, and from that perspective he is profoundly mysterious. That mystery becomes a literal murder-mystery as crewmen begin to die horribly at the hands (or claws and fangs) of an invisible marauding monster. The monster proves to be nothing less than a projection of Morbius' unconscious mind, released by his experimentation with the mind-enhancing technology left behind on Altair-IV by a long-vanished race of aliens, called the Krell. This monster, here identified, in the pop-Freudian discourse of the day, as the id-monster, all too clearly maps onto Shakespeare's Caliban (recall Prospero: "this thing of darkness I/ Acknowledge mine," V.i.275–6; Morbius might have said the same); while the vanished Krell play the role of Caliban's mother, the witch Sycorax.

It would be hard to overestimate the influence of *Forbidden Planet* on popular science fiction of subsequent decades. The original *Star Trek* series, which premiered ten years later (see Chapter 2), borrows extensively from *Forbidden Planet*, including visual elements such as the design of the starship bridge and even the style of Star Fleet uniforms, not to mention such recurrent plot motifs as the womanizing captain, the mysterious and powerful older male protector and his younger female ward, advanced alien technologies misunderstood and abused by their latter-day inheritors, and so on. All of these motifs, many of them ultimately derived from *The Tempest,* radiating out from *Stark Trek,* subsequently enter the repertoire of popular science-fiction film and television. So, too, by a slightly different route of transmission, does the id-monster of *Forbidden Planet,* so memorably rendered by Disney animators, which surely influenced Ridley Scott's *Alien* (1979) and its sequels, and through them many other SF horror films and series, down through ABC television's *Lost* (2004–2010) and beyond.

In effect, elements of *The Tempest* became incorporated in the DNA of popular science fiction through the mediation of *Forbidden Planet.* But the shipwreck play's potential was not exhausted by its striking ubiquity in popular movies and on television. It also served as a template for more ambitious literary science fictions during the postmodern era, first in the sixties and seventies, during the period of science fiction's so-called New Wave, then again in the eighties and early nineties, during its cyberpunk phase.

No figure is more iconic of New Wave science fiction, at least in its British version, than J.G. Ballard, whose novel *Crash* (1973) crossed over to become a key text of postmodernism as well (see section 1). Ballard, as it happens, seems to have been preoccupied with *The Tempest* throughout his career, from at least as early as *The Drought,* also called *The Burning World* (1965), one of his tetralogy of end-of-the-world novels, until at least as late as his short story "Dream Cargoes" (1991). The pivotal version, however, is *Concrete Island* (1973), from the period of *Crash.* Robert Maitland, an architect, crashes his car on a patch of waste ground hemmed in by motorway embankments, overpasses, and chain-link fencing. Because of his injuries, and the topography of the "island," he can neither escape nor attract attention to his plight. Eventually he discovers that he is sharing this concrete island with two other inhabitants, a brain-damaged tramp named Proctor and a drop-out named Jane Sheppard, who turns tricks for a living.

It is not immediately clear why this novel should be regarded as science fiction at all, since it is set in the contemporary world, ca. 1973, and displays none of the futuristic or extraterrestrial motifs one expects of SF. In a sense, it is because we recognize *Concrete Island* to be a version of the shipwreck play that we are disposed to regard it as SF, rather than the other way around. Jane, a "sprit," is transparently an Ariel figure, while Proctor corresponds to Caliban. Maitland himself, of course, plays the Prospero role, but a Prospero newly shipwrecked, and without Miranda. The harder we look, however, the less settled these identifications appear, until the entire system of correspondences comes to seem fluid and changeable. Proctor, the Caliban figure is also an ex-trapeze artist, that is, an aerialist (Ariel-ist?), and Jane reports that he was already living on the waste ground before the motorways were constructed, so that "When they built the motorway they sealed him in" (Ballard, 1985, 98) – language evoking Ariel sealed in the "cloven pine" by Sycorax (I.ii.274–81). Jane corresponds to Ariel, but Maitland also likens her to a "down-at-heel witch" (Ballard, 1985, 84) – in other words, a Sycorax figure. Moreover, *The Tempest* is not the only relevant template here; others include *Robinson Crusoe*, itself a revision of *The Tempest* (Dobson, 2001, 249), as well as several more recent shipwrecked castaway narratives, all competing for possession, as it were, of this same narrative material. Generically unstable, Ballard's novel realigns itself first one way and then another, according to which template seems uppermost at any given moment. This is, of course, just the sort of instability one has learned to expect from postmodern science fiction.

A comparable instability characterizes Michael Swanwick's cyberpunk novel *Stations of the Tide* (1991), though it only manifests itself very late in the text – literally on its last pages. Swanwick's protagonist is a nameless functionary known only as "the bureaucrat," whose job is to enforce an embargo on the export of high technology to planets judged not yet ready to absorb it. Viewers of *Star Trek* will readily recognize this motif as the Prime Directive, that is, the Star Fleet prohibition on interfering in indigenous cultures' development. The planet to which the bureaucrat's mission takes him is named Miranda; its three moons are Prospero, Caliban, and Ariel; a rebellion in its recent past was led by an artificial-intelligence program named Trinculo (after the insubordinate jester in *The Tempest*). Planet Miranda, it transpires, is on the verge of undergoing a "sea-change/Into something rich and strange" (I.ii.404–5): it is about to experience the melting of its ice cap, a cataclysm that occurs regularly every two hundred years, inundating a large part of its land surface and triggering the metamorphosis of most of its indigenous flora and fauna from terrestrial to aquatic forms.

What else could this be, if not a version of *The Tempest*, specifically a version of the shipwreck play? Playing the role of the shipwrecked courtiers of *The Tempest*, the bureaucrat comes to Miranda seeking a local magician named Gregorian, who is suspected of stealing off-world technology. This Gregorian harbors strong resentments against the interstellar bureaucracy, one of whose number, it transpires, is secretly his father. Clearly, Gregorian is this novel's aggrieved Prospero figure. He briefly distracts the bureaucrat from his mission by sending a beautiful witch to seduce him – a version of Miranda, shall we say?

So we proceed through the novel, identifying various correspondences with *The Tempest*, until its closing pages, when, in an abrupt ironic reversal, the entire system rotates 180 degrees, and we discover that all our identifications have been mistaken. Gregorian, it turns out, is not a true magician at all but a con-man – not a Prospero figure but Caliban, as we should have guessed when we encountered his mother, an aged, bedridden hag, a Sycorax figure. It is the bureaucrat who possesses technological magic immeasurably more powerful than anything he or anyone else has displayed so far, most of it embodied in his briefcase, a resourceful artificial intelligence who addresses him as "boss." In the novel's closing pages the bureaucrat sets his briefcase free, as Prospero does Ariel – a gesture that identifies the briefcase with Ariel and confirms the bureaucrat's own identification with Prospero. The whole novel wheels around, and though it remains a version of *The Tempest*, it now reveals itself to have been all along a different version than we thought: not the shipwreck play, but Prospero's play.

5. Prospero's Books

The traditional and presumably "authorized" version of *The Tempest* – the one centered on Prospero, a benign patriarch and artist figure who uses magic to achieve reconciliation and restoration – has never disappeared; indeed, we have glimpsed several versions of that Prospero-centered play already. In the face of all the pressure from alternative, revisionist, against-the-grain *Tempests*, to persist in orienting one's version around the traditional patriarchal Prospero seems like a retrograde gesture. Nevertheless, John Fowles does just that in *The Magus* (1966, 1977), despite adopting the point-of-view of the Ferdinand figure, and so does Iris Murdoch in *The Sea, the Sea* (1978), though she subjects her Prospero figure to irony, exposing him as a false magus and substituting a true one at the end of the novel.

Most egregious of all the unreconstructed Prospero-centered versions is Paul Mazursky's 1982 film *Tempest*, in which Shakespeare's play is updated as the story of a powerful male's mid-life crisis. Phillip Dimitrius (played by John Cassavetes), a successful big-city architect (like Ballard's Maitland), walks out on his career and his wife of many years, Antonia (Gena Rowlands), and, taking his teenage daughter Miranda with him, runs away to Greece, where he picks up a much younger drifter (Susan Sarandon) and settles on a barren island to live the good life. Reaffirming patriarchy and (neo)colonialism, Mazursky puts Miranda's and Caliban's plays in their place: Miranda (Molly Ringwald) is a cliché teenager, while the Greek islander Kalibanos (Raul Julia) is a comic Third-Worlder, sycophantic toward Americans and a scavenger of pop culture. It seems clear that director Mazursky himself identifies with the Prospero figure, as witness his casting of another film *auteur*, Cassavetes, as the architect Dimitrius (Zabus, 2002, 254–5).

But Prospero's play need not be as retrograde as Fowles's, Murdoch's and Mazursky's versions seem to be. A counter-example is *Philadelphia Fire* (1990) by the African-American novelist John Edgar Wideman, set in a troubled late-eighties Philadelphia, in the aftermath of the police massacre of the black separatist MOVE commune in 1985. A black Philadelphian, Cudjoe, returns from self-imposed exile on a Greek island to direct a production of *The Tempest* with a cast of West Philly schoolkids. Which *Tempest* version will this be? Maybe Caliban's, given the fraught contemporary background of struggle and resistance; maybe Miranda's, since the production showcases a preadolescent actress; but in any case Cudjoe's – that is, Prospero's.

As Cudjoe returns to Philadelphia to direct his play, so Prospero returns as artist figure and world-maker in postmodernist *Tempests*. However, postmodernist Prospero is not the traditional patriarch, and the world he makes is not a stable and centered one, but rather a provisional arrangement, flickering in and out of existence, subject to erasure. Indeed, this Prospero does not so much *make* his island-world as attempt to manage, not entirely successfully, the confrontations among a *plurality* of worlds (see Greene, 2000, 138–9). He is an author, no doubt, but his authority is only partial, just as his magic is only "partial magic" (see Borges, 1952). If he is the architect of his world, like Ballard's Maitland and Mazursky's Dimitrius, building and rebuilding it freely, he is also himself an inhabitant of that world and subject to its mutability and fragility (see Zabus, 2002, 177–8). This weak magician and his vulnerable world, like Caliban's resistance or Miranda's feminism, are already present implicitly as a potential in Shakespeare's play, glimpsed in the moment when Prospero realizes that "the great globe" itself and everything in it are as "baseless" and "insubstantial" as the wedding masque that he has summoned into existence and then consigned to nothingness (IV.i.148–60).

The definitive postmodernist Prospero is the one in Robert Coover's short story, "The Magic Poker," from his seminal collection *Pricksongs & Descants* (1969). Like many of the other recent versions of Prospero's play, Coover's *Tempest* is an updated one, set on an island in a lake in the Upper Midwest, where a deserted holiday home stands, visited by two sisters. Like those other versions, too, Coover identifies with Prospero – or rather, the "author" of the story does. This author-figure is revealed to us in the act of inventing the story's world:

> I wander the island, inventing it. I make a sun for it, and trees – pines and birch and dogwood and firs – and cause the water to lap the pebbles of its abandoned shores. This, and more: I deposit shadows and dampness, spin webs, and scatter ruins . . . I impose a hot midday silence, a profound and heavy stillness. But anything can happen. (Coover, 1969, 20)

The ontological tension of the story lies right there, between the uncontrollable accidentalism of "anything can happen" and the author's evident power to *make* things happens, arbitrarily, at his own whim. He brings the sisters to the island; has them spied on by caretaker's degenerate son, a Caliban-figure; invents a handsome stranger for them to encounter (Ferdinand?); and has them find a rusted fireplace poker in the grass (Prospero's staff?). He retells these episodes multiple times, with variations, some mutually incompatible, in multiple modes: fairy tale, verisimilar realism, gothic, grotesque slapstick. The author himself never materializes as a character; this is Prospero as an offstage manipulator, stage manager, and world-maker, but also the author as solipsist, projecting a private world. Acknowledging the paradoxes of world-making, he admits to a loss of confidence, and ultimately effaces himself – and the reader with him:

> I am disappearing. You have no doubt noticed . . . . But before we drift apart to a distance beyond the reach of confessions . . . , listen: it's just as I feared, my invented island is really taking its place in world geography . . . . I look on a map: yes, there's Rainy Lake, there's Jackfish Island. Who invented this map? Well, I must have surely . . . . Yes, and perhaps tomorrow I will invent Chicago and Jesus Christ and the history of the moon. Just as I have invented you, dear reader, while lying here in the afternoon sun, bedded deeply in the bluegreen grass like an old iron poker. . . . (Coover, 1969, 40; my ellipses)

An exemplary metafiction, reflecting on the making of fiction *in* fiction, as well as its unmaking and erasure, "The Magic Poker" sets the standard for later post-modernist *Tempests*, culminating in two of the most characteristic works of peak postmodernism and the long eighties: the novel *Blown Away* (1986) by the American surfictionist Ronald Sukenick, and *Prospero's Books* (1991) by the maverick British filmmaker Peter Greenaway. Each of them is, like Coover's story, thoroughly metafictonal (or meta-cinematic, in Greenaway's case), but each is also, as Coover's text is not, a profound reflection on the media ecology in which they find themselves at the peak of the postmodern era. *Blown Away*, a novel about the making of movies, *remediates* film in prose, while *Prospero's Books*, a movie about books (as its title announces), remediates books on film. They are, in this respect, and perhaps others too, mirror images of each other.

Sukenick updates *The Tempest's* play-within-a-play structure, but also post-modernizes the conventional "Hollywood novel" (of which Brodeur's *The Stunt Man*, mentioned earlier, is an example). *Blown Away*, the novel, tells the story of the making of a film also called *Blown Away*, a B-movie version of *The Tempest*, updated to contemporary Los Angeles – in other words, a movie not unlike Mazursky's *Tempest*, though with a smaller budget. The film *Blown Away* functions as *mise-en-abyme* of the novel *Blown Away*, the events of the film doubling or mirroring those of the novel itself. Or rather, it *would* have functioned as *mise-en-abyme* if its production weren't interrupted so many times, and if there weren't so many competing alternative versions of *Blown Away* jostling for attention. Apart from the movie *Blown Away* itself, in production as the novel unfolds, there is also the scriptwriter Victor Plotz's prose "prenovelization" of the film, as well as his "renovelization" of it, that is, his own insider's narrative of the making of the movie. There are also script conferences, speculative and fantasy versions, tabloid gossip, and so on. Versions proliferate, interfere and merge, finally collapsing into infinite regress at a conference between the scriptwriter Plotz and director Rod Drackenstein, when the script begins to duplicate the very scene of the script conference itself (Sukenick, 1986, 159).

To the plurality of *Tempest* versions corresponds a plurality of Prospero figures. The psychic Boris Ccrab plays Prospero to starlet Clover Bottom's Miranda; he even quotes (in fact, deliberately misquotes) Prospero's "We are such stuff as dreams are made on" speech (IV.i.148–60; Sukenick, 1986, 29). Director Drackenstein also plays Prospero to Clover Bottom's Miranda but, to complicate matters, his own daughter is also named Miranda; moreover, Drackenstein himself actually plays the role of Prospero (renamed "Propper") in front of the camera in *Blown Away*, the movie he is making. As the Prospero surrogates multiply, the characters who fill these roles disintegrate and mingle: Ccrab, with two c's, splits into a pair of one-c Crabs, one of whom insinuates himself into Drackenstein's personality, literally taking possession of Drackenstein. The effect of this dispersal of Prospero figures across multiple selves is to dilute and defuse Prospero's mastery. Thus, Sukenick uses Prospero's play, in its metafictional version, as a tool to subvert the received version of Prospero's play, the version we find, say, in Mazursky's *Tempest*, with its masterful, heterosexual, stage manager Prospero. Sukenick turns the magus's play against the magus.

Unlike Sukenick's and most other recent versions, Greenaway's film does not update *The Tempest*, but keeps it in the seventeenth century, producing a lush visual simulacrum of a Renaissance world, and retaining Shakespeare's language intact. He also retains the original's metatheatricality, installing Prospero at the center of the play as stage manager, artist figure, and world-maker. He even seems to have embraced the canonical reading of Prospero as Shakespeare's surrogate, but he extends this traditional identification, perhaps to the breaking point, by conflating Shakespeare, author of *Tempest*, with Prospero, stage manager of events, and both in turn with John Gielgud, the great Shakespearean actor cast as Prospero. Prospero here is not only lord of the island and master manipulator, he is literally the author of the play *The Tempest*. Gielgud as Prospero is shown writing the play; moreover, Gielgud voices over the lines of *all* the characters (until the last scene, where finally they are allowed to speak for themselves). The entire substance of the play is understood to be Prospero's fiction, embodying his fantasies of revenge, irresistible power, and restoration to his dukedom.

Moreover, the world of *Prospero's Books* – its objects, people, spaces, and so forth – is derived from the stock of imagery to be found in a Renaissance scholar's imagination, the visual representations with which he would have surrounded himself, and the books he would have read – hence *Prospero's Books*. From beginning to end, the screen is crowded, to the point of claustrophobia, with neoclassical architectural forms, emblematic objects, allegorical processions, mythological characters, and animated scenes from paintings and book illustra-tions. It is as if the decorated title pages of seventeenth-century printed books were to pop up into 3-D, and the characters in them to come alive and step out into the world. It is within this world, literally the world of Prospero's imagination, that the events of this *Tempest* transpire. The effect is to relocate the entire play *inside* Prospero's mind. This is the motif of Prospero as solipsist that we already identified in Coover's "Magic Poker," and it is the ultimate metafictional gesture of placing the world under erasure. One could hardly conceive of a version that was more thoroughly Prospero's play.

6. Masques of Postmodernism

Another way of characterizing what Greenaway does in *Prospero's Books* is to say that he takes the masque of goddesses that Prospero stages in Act 4, scene 1 to celebrate his daughter's betrothal, and *generalizes* it, making it coextensive with the whole of *The Tempest*.

Like other plays-with-the-play in the Shakespearean canon, the wedding masque in *The Tempest* is a partial *mise-en-abyme* of the play as a whole. In this case, the inset play doesn't mirror the outer play's plot (as does "The Murder of Gonzago" in *Hamlet*, for instance), but instead mirrors the very fact of the outer play's *having been staged* – its status as *theater*. Prospero is the producer and director of the play-within-the-play, as he is of the events of *The Tempest* generally; he *stages* them both. The masque, mirroring the play as a whole, lays bare Prospero's role as master manipulator of the outer play's events. Greenaway enhances the mirroring or doubling relation between the masque and the play by making the play itself *more masque-like*. Where other versions make a point of distinguishing the masque world of the play-within-the-play as sharply as possible from the play's "real world," Greenaway does the opposite, deliberately conflating the two worlds: *The Tempest* becomes *all-over* masque, *wall-to-wall* masque. The allegorical and mythological characters, architectural sets, and special effects that belong to the masque spill over into Prospero's real world, swamping the entire film.

In breaking down the barriers between real world and masque world, *Prospero's Books* aligns itself with a general tendency in postmodernism toward the revival and/or reinvention of masque aesthetics (see Chapter 1). This is true as well of other postmodernist versions of *The Tempest*, such as Fowles's *The Magus*, where the Prospero figure Conchis stages theatrical scenes for the edification of young Nicholas Urfe that blur the boundary between theater and reality, or Russell Hoban's masquelike libretto, *Some Episodes in the History of Miranda and Caliban* (1992).

Evidently postmodernists found many features of the court masque congenial to postmodernist poetics: the plurality of worlds; the intrusion of beings from one world into another, or the spectacular transformation of a world; the mingling on the same plane of characters of different ontological status (historical, fictional, mythological, allegorical); motifs of masking and unmasking, illusion and the laying bare of illusion; and the like. Such features are all to be found in Shakespeare's *Tempest*, as they are in Greenaway's *Prospero's Books* and other postmodernist *Tempests*. They are even to be found in Derek Jarman's film of *The Tempest* (1979), in many ways the *least* masquelike of all the postmodernist *Tempests*.

Going visually to the opposite extreme of Greenaway's lushness, Jarman's is an intentionally "poor" *Tempest*, deliberately stripped down, set in a dilapidated country house, its characters dressed up in second-hand thrift-shop finery, its magic muted. In view of the film's austere aesthetic, it is hard to see where the resources for a masque would come from, either in the world of this *Tempest* or in the filmmakers' minuscule budget. And indeed, the masque seems to have been dismembered and recycled, some of its key speeches, such as the goddesses' blessing of Miranda and Ferdinand, being displaced to earlier scenes and placed in the mouths of other characters. However, just before the end, the masque DNA reasserts itself after all, and we get a spectacularly campy performance by the shipwrecked sailors in their white duck uniforms, dancing a hornpipe to the music of Gheorghe Zamfir's panpipes, followed by a final surprise: a black goddess enters (the blues diva Elisabeth Welch, in fact) and sings, what else, "Stormy Weather." The effect is simultaneously revisionist, lyrical, deliriously queer, and completely postmodern.

Chapter 4

Interregnum, 1989–2001

1. Between

In the same essay in which he pinpointed an onset date for postmodernism (see Chapter 2), Raymond Federman also identified its endpoint. Postmodernism "changed tense" from past to present, he wrote, on the same date that Samuel Beckett did: December 22, 1989, the day Beckett died (Federman, 1993, 105; see Chapter 1). That date, like the onset date of October 1, 1966, while proposed in a spirit of play, nevertheless has multiple cultural resonances. With the breaching of the Berlin Wall the month before, marking the symbolic if not quite the actual end of the Cold War, global postmodern culture seemed, maybe not to "change tense" exactly, but at least to undergo a decisive reorientation. But a reorientation toward what?

Cumulatively, the geopolitical events of the period 1989–93, comprising not only the fall of Wall and the dissolution of the Soviet Union and its empire, but also the bloody suppression of the democracy movement at Beijing's Tiananmen Square, the release of Nelson Mandela, and the beginning of the end of apartheid, certainly seemed to herald the end of something and the onset of something else. The U.S. administration of George Bush the elder thought it heralded a New World Order in which America, as the sole remaining superpower, would inevitably take the global lead, as it did in the First Gulf War ("Operation Desert Storm") in 1991. However, American triumphalism did not last long, and as the decade advanced it proved more difficult to create an international consensus to address geopolitical crises such as the Yugoslav civil war of 1991–95 (Chollet and Goldgeier, 2008).

Christian Moraru (2011) sees the 1989–93 threshold differently. He thinks that the breakdown of the Cold War deadlock between the superpowers made possible a new kind of cosmopolitanism in the cultural sphere, which he proposes to call *cosmodernism*. Moraru's cosmodernism is something like the "cultural logic of late globalization" (Moraru, 2011, 39), as long as we understand *globalization* here not as a euphemism for the global triumph of neoliberal economics (see Chapter 3), or as one-size-fits-all Americanization, but as including all the forms of dialogue and interaction among cultures that our hypernetworked condition now makes possible. Cosmodernism implies multilateral rather than unilateral globalization, a situation in which the cultures of the world's regions exchange texts and ideas (or "memes") among themselves outside the center/periphery structure of either the old imperial colonialism or Western-centric cultural neocolonialism.

Moraru's account of the "cosmodern turn" around the year 1989 is no doubt too optimistic, even euphoric, for complete comfort. It is, for one thing, a little too compatible with Francis Fukuyama's controversial claim, first made just before the pivotal events of 1989 and then reiterated in 1992, that history had actually *ended* with the triumph of the Western idea and the collapse of capitalist democracy's sole rival. However, history kept doggedly refusing to end, in Yugoslavia and elsewhere, until it finally came roaring back with a vengeance in the terror attacks on New York and Washington, D.C. on September 11, 2001.

The decisive return of history on 9/11, after its supposed expiration around 1989, prompts a different approach to the culture of the nineties. According to Phillip Wegner, the "long nineties," the phase between the symbolic turning-points of 1989 and 2001, represents a kind of interregnum, a "place between two deaths":

> the 1990s are the strange space between an ending (of the Cold War) and a beginning (of our post–September 11 world) . . . . This place, located as it is between the Real Event and its symbolic repetition, is strictly speaking "non-historical," and such an "empty place" is experienced in its lived reality . . . in a Janus-faced fashion. On the one hand, it feels like a moment of "terrifying monsters," of hauntings by a living dead past. Yet it is also experienced as a moment of "sublime beauty," of openness and instability, of experimentation and opportunity, of conflict and insecurity – a place, in other words, wherein history might move in a number of very different directions. (Wegner, 2009, 24)

There is abundant evidence in the nineties, as we shall see, of the "openness and instability," the "experimentation and opportunity," the "conflict and insecurity," and the potential multidirectionality of history of which Wegner speaks. Others have had similar insights into the nature of this cultural phase. Samuel Cohen characterizes the nineties as an "interwar decade," a "time between wars" (Cohen, 2009, 4, 6), while Andrew Hoberek uses the term "lull" (which he borrows from the arts curator Minsoo Kang) to describe the decade (Hoberek, 2007). It seems as though Fukuyama was reacting to a genuinely felt transition when he announced the end of history, but he used the wrong metaphor for it. Nineteen eighty-nine didn't mark the end of history; it didn't even mark the end of postmodernism. What it ushered in was an *in-between* phase of culture – an interregnum.

How to understand and articulate the twelve-year interregnum in global affairs between 1989 and 2001 troubled even seasoned policymakers such as Bill Clinton's secretary of state Madeline Albright, who is reported as saying, "You couldn't keep talking about the post–Cold War world. It was an era that was hard to explain to people. It was like being set loose on the ocean and there wasn't really any charted course" (Chollet and Goldgeier, 2008, 69–70). During this strange interlude, the dualistic or manichaean world-view of the Cold War era was temporarily suspended, replaced by a vision of multi-polarity, or even *a*-polarity, that was at once baffling, risky, and rich with possibilities, with implications and knock-on consequences extending far beyond geopolitics. The condition of "being set loose on the ocean" expresses itself not only at the policy level, but also through the cultural production of the nineties interregnum, especially in the years immediately after the fall of the Wall.

An episode of multi-polarity not only in world affairs, but also in culture and the arts, the early nineties were the years of multiculturalism, yet also of the backlash against it in the so-called "culture wars," when the global confrontations of the Cold War were in effect turned inward upon culture itself (Cohen, 2009, 8–9). The culture wars were waged with particular ferocity over issues of gender and sexuality (Rodgers, 2011, 145). Typical skirmishes included challenges on the floor of the U.S. Senate (1989) to federal funding for controversial artworks such as Andrés Serrano's *Piss Christ*; the prosecution of a Cincinnati museum director (1990) for exhibiting flagrantly homosexual photographs by Robert Mapplethorpe; and the scandals occasioned by exhibitions of the *Sensation* show of Young British Artists, first in London (1997), then in New York (1999–2000) (Oxoby, 2003, 221–3). Early nineties culture was also characterized by the proliferation and flowering of various subcultural and paracultural alternatives such as New Age spirituality, "independent" film and "alternative" rock (Oxoby, 2003, 165–7, 193–4), including the reprise of the seventies punk aesthetic in the brief heyday of Seattle's grunge-rock scene (Clover, 2009, 73–89). The years right around 1989 also marked the high point of the political phase of hiphop culture and rap music ("conscious rap"), and the beginning of the dominance of gangsta rap in popular culture, occasioning further episodes of culture war (Clover, 2009, 25–50).

In the course of the nineties, all of these cultural phenomena – "indie" film, "alt" rock, gangsta rap – initially countercultural in orientation, were eventually co-opted by the corporate culture industry. This was also the fate of online culture which, in the early nineties, enjoyed a short-lived but heady utopian and communitarian phase. The World Wide Web, making use of the Internet's infrastructure, itself emerges during the threshold years of 1989–90, becoming generally available to Internet users in the early nineties, only to be swept up in the frenzied commercialization of cyberspace that drove the cycle of boom and bust in the new Internet-based dot-com industry (see section 3). "Boom and bust," indeed, was a hallmark of the nineties economy, fueled by new technologies (personal computing, the Internet, mobile telephony) that promised limitless growth and prompted "irrational exuberance" (as the chairman of the U.S. Federal Reserve once called it) among stock-market investors.

"In such volatile moments," Joshua Clover writes, "with one dominant toppling and another not yet consolidated, the field flies open, or at least so it feels" (Clover, 2009, 41). This volatility, the feeling of fields flying open, or of what the performance-artist Laurie Anderson (1991, 90–1) called "gravity failure," pervades culture in the interregnum, both high and low, from TV programming and online commerce to avant-garde art. The most apt emblem of nineties lightness was the popular iconography of the *angel*, a hallmark of an era of in-betweenness, volatility, multidirectionality, and a bubble economy (see "Angels in America").

2. Late

One might, if one wished, consider the nineties the phase of *late postmodernism*, as Jeremy Green does (Green, 2005). What seems indefensible is the claim that nineties culture had somehow already passed beyond post-modernism to some kind of "post-postmodernism." Impatience with post-modernism, and eagerness to get "beyond" it somehow, is pervasive in the early nineties, but impatience and expressions of discontent are not the same thing as actually breaking through to the "post-post," as the novelist David Foster Wallace's career in the nineties seems poignantly to demonstrate (see section 4). Indeed, it may be that the very *resistance* to postmodernism in the nineties can be seen as merely one of the late forms that postmodernism itself takes (Hoberek, 2007, 237).

Far from ending or subsiding about 1989, postmodernism seemed, if anything, to come into its own in the nineties. Postmodern modes of expression seemed particularly well adapted to capture the decade's volatility and multi-directionality. To put it the other way around, it almost seemed as though what postmodernism had been anticipating and preparing for all along were nineties conditions, and especially the new technologies of the decade, which seemed perfectly to complement its own aesthetics. The wars of the decade are one example. If the Vietnam War of the sixties and early seventies qualifies as the first postmodern war, in the sense of being the first *televised* war, then the 1991 Gulf War ought to be regarded as the first war to be *fully* postmodern, since it was not only televised but *staged* for television, as the postmodern theorist Jean Baudrillard controversially argued in *The Gulf War Did Not Take Place* (1995). Postmodern in a different sense, the Yugoslav civil war seemed to blow a hole in the world of postwar Europe, allowing a monstrous alternative reality to enter – a scenario literalized by the British playwright Sarah Kane in her play *Blasted*, which provoked public revulsion for its over-the-top sexual violence when it premiered in 1995, but upon its revival in 2001 was recognized as a work of visionary realism.

Multiplication of alternative realities, of course, had always been a hallmark of postmodernist fiction, but during the nineties its capacity to multiply worlds seemed particularly attuned to contemporary culture, especially online culture, with its proliferation of sites and windows – alternative worlds, worlds within worlds. In effect, postmodernist poetics became, through convergence with contemporary culture, a form of *realism*, faithfully capturing the multi-world quality of nineties experience.

Ontological plurality and alternativity can be traced right across the decade through a sequence of postmodern historical novels (Cohen, 2009), prolonging and extending the genre of historiographic metafiction that was so characteristic of the peak period (see Chapter 3). At the beginning of the decade, William Gibson and Bruce Sterling, cofounders of cyberpunk in the eighties, collaborated on a novel of alternative history, *The Difference Engine* (1990), that reenvisioned the nineteenth century, in the process consolidating (if not quite inaugurating; others had already done that) a new genre, *steampunk*, a sort of retro-futurism, whose later examples include Phillip Pullman's alternative-world trilogy *His Dark Materials* (1995–2000), Alan Moore's and Kevin O'Neill's series of graphic novels, *The League of Extraordinary Gentlemen* (beginning in 1999), and Dexter Palmer's *The Dream of Perpetual Motion* (2010; a version of *The Tempest,* incidentally). As deeply researched as any realistic historical novel, Thomas Pynchon's long-awaited major novel of the nineties, *Mason & Dixon* (1997), evidently under way since before the appearance of *Gravity's Rainbow* in 1973, multiplies alternative, hypothetical and subjunctive histories, in the plural, producing worlds under erasure, despite its firm historical grounding (McHale, 2000a, 43–62). Throughout the "long nineties," writers of speculative fiction entertained thought-experiments involving future or alternative world orders *without America* – a sort of skeptical reply to American triumphalism in the aftermath of the Soviet Union's collapse. Speculation especially shifted to the possibility of a world dominated by China, as in the British science fiction novelist David Wingrove's *Chung Kuo* cycle of novels (1990–97), or one divided between China and Islam, as in Kim Stanley Robinson's alternative history of a world without Europeans, *The Years of Rice and Salt* (2002) (see section 7).

New technologies not only multiplied realties in ways that seemed compatible with postmodern poetics, but also made everyday reality routinely paradoxical in ways that the postmodern arts were well equipped to explore. An example is mobile-phone technology. The upsurge in cellular-telephone use throughout the nineties, beginning with a scattering of early adopters at the start of the decade and ending in the near-ubiquity of mobile phones by the turn of the millennium (Agar, 2003; Oxoby, 2003, 21–2; Mercer, 2006, 119–34; Ling and Donner, 2009, 4–10), transformed everyday communication. Its very everydayness, however, obscured cell-phone technology's capacity for uncanny effects of *bilocation* – being in two places at once. The uncanniness of mobile telephony was dramatized in David Lynch's postmodern film *Lost Highway* (1997; Agar, 2003, 145), as well in one of the most characteristic tv series of the nineties, *The X-Files* (1993–2002), where cellphone communication often seems to *separate* the partners, FBI agents Scully and Muldar, instead of bringing them together in their pursuit of the elusive truth that they know to be "out there" (see "Angels in America"). As much as personal computing or the Internet, cellphone technology was integral to nineties culture, from the peripatetic rave scene of London's M25 ring-road (the "orbital") in the early nineties (Agar, 2003, 162–3; Clover, 2009, 53–70) to the haunting cellphone communications from the stricken World Trade Center Towers and the hijacked flights during the terror attacks of 9/11, which brought the interregnum to its catastrophic close (Agar, 2003, 149; Ling and Donner, 2009, 132–3).

3. Virtuality, or, All That Is Solid Melts into Air

Francis Fukuyama thought he glimpsed the end of history as early as the summer of 1989, just ahead of the world-transforming events of 1989–91 (Rodgers, 2011, 245–6). The book-length elaboration of his end-of-history argument appeared in 1992, the same year that another "end" was announced: that of books themselves. The end of books would be predicted repeatedly throughout the nineties – prematurely, as indeed Fukuyama's prediction of the end of history would also prove to be – but this particular announcement carried special weight, appearing as it did in the *New York Times Book Review*, and coming from the postmodern novelist Robert Coover, himself the author by that point of at least ten books.

Coover took pains to distinguish the putative end of books (about which he was, in any case, ambivalent) from tediously familiar anticipations of the "death of the novel," a cliché since at least the sixties. In fact, Coover's essay on "The End of Books," as well as the omnibus review he published in the same literary supplement a year later (1993), celebrated the *health* of narrative fiction. If wider access to computer technology and networked connectivity threatened the codex book, which had historically been the novel's main medium, it also provided opportunities for narrative fiction – especially for the kind of postmodern fiction that Coover himself practiced.

The new form for which Coover was advocating, in effect anointing it as the print novel's successor, was fiction that was *born digital,* designed to exploit the capacity of computers to store, retrieve, and connect blocks of information: hypertext fiction. Theorized as early as the sixties, but emerging as a practical reality only in the eighties, hypertext allowed textual or other informational media to be distributed in discrete units (which eventually came to be called *lexias*, a term borrowed from Roland Barthes) and joined by electronic links. This node-and-link structure in turn allowed users to thread multiple pathways through a text, thus investing the user with new freedom to construct sequences as he or she saw fit. Hypertextual organization could also be achieved in print texts, of course: Nabokov's *Pale Fire* (1962) achieves it one way, through annotation, Cortázar's *Hopscotch* (published in English translation in the watershed year 1966) another way, through its alternative chapter orders, Milorad Pavić's *Dictionary of the Khazars* (1984) yet another, through internal cross-referencing. Coover's own fiction, notably a number of the stories in *Pricksongs and Descants* (1969) – "The Babysitter," "The Elevator," "Quenby and Ola, Swede and Carl," "The Magic Poker" (a rewrite of *The Tempest;* see "Prospero's Books") – anticipates hypertext by producing multiple, mutually contradictory narrative sequences that compete with each other for a toehold in the story's "real world." Thus, the babysitter in the story by that title is murdered, yet also survives to run away with the husband; the corpse in the bathtub is both hers and that of the baby she is supposed to be looking after; and so on.

Print narratives such as these, literalizing the branching structure that Borges imagined in his story "The Garden of Forking Paths," anticipate the kind of organization that comes naturally to computer-mediated fictions that exploit the nodes-and-links resources of hypertext. Postmodern fiction, one might say, aspires to the condition of hypertext, while conversely hypertext realizes in its very structure the poetics of postmodern fiction (Eskelinen, 2012, 192). Composed using the Storyspace software developed by the novelist Michael Joyce and the theorist Jay David Bolter, together with John B. Smith, and distributed on CD-ROM by Eastgate Systems, the canonically classic hypertext fictions of the form's "golden age" (roughly 1987–95) all realize in their various ways typical postmodern devices. For instance, Joyce's own seminal novel, *afternoon* (1987), reflecting the forking-paths structure native to hypertext, features mutually contradictory sequences and events under erasure (*sous rature*; Aarseth, 1997, 76–96; Bell, 2010, 28–66). Stuart Moulthrop's *Victory Garden* (1991), another forking-paths narrative, adds a historical and political dimension. Using the resources of hypertext to capture the simulacral quality of the 1991 Gulf War (theorized by Baudrillard; see section 2), it reinvents in the digital context the print genre of historiographic metafiction (Bell, 2010, 67–106; see Chapter 3). Shelley Jackson's *Patchwork Girl* (1995) realizes a different dimension of postmodern poetics, making hypertext the vehicle of the kinds of stylistic pastiche, appropriation and self-construction that one finds, for instance, in the print fiction of Kathy Acker (Landow, 1997, 198–205; Bell, 2010, 107–49; see Chapter 3).

Marie-Laure Ryan writes of the "natural and elective affinities of electronic writing for postmodern aesthetics" (1999, 103). Hypertext and postmodernism are, in some sense, made for each other. Another way to express their affinity is to say that hypertext realizes or embodies the theory of which postmodern aesthetics is itself an expression. Such claims were rife in the first wave of hypertext theory and practice in the early nineties (e.g., Bolter, 1991; Landow, 1992). "Critical theory promises to theorize hypertext," writes George Landow, Robert Coover's colleague at Brown University, "and hypertext promises to embody and thereby test aspects of theory" (1992, 3). He is thinking of aspects of poststructuralist theory developed by Derrida, Foucault, Barthes, Deleuze and Guattari, and others since the sixties (see Chapter 3), including ideas of limitless intertextuality, multivocality, the decentering of the subject, and especially the displacement of the author's authority by the reader's (the so-called "death of the author"; Poster, 1999; Ryan, 1999, 100–2). "An almost embarrassingly literal embodiment" of such ideas (Landow, 1992, 34), hypertext gives "theory" substance; it is "theory" by other means. If "theory" was indeed dying by the end of the eighties, as some people asserted, more or less gleefully (see Chapter 3), then hypertext seems to have afforded it a kind of posthumous existence, an afterlife or Second Life®.

Bold claims about hypertext and its affinity for both postmodern aesthetics and poststructuralist theory underwent drastic reevaluation in the course of nineties. For one thing, it became clearer in retrospect that not all of the classic hypertext fictions of the first wave shared a common postmodern poetics. Joyce's *afternoon*, in particular, came to look less like a postmodernist fiction and more like a modernist one – a classic epistemological puzzle rather than an anatomy of world-making (Aarseth, 1997, 89–90; Landow, 1997, 179; Ciccoricco, 2007, 472). In any event, by the end of the decade the entire genre of hypertext fiction had begun to seem obsolete, and Coover, who in 1992 and 1993 had celebrated its emergence, by 1999 was announcing its passing (Ciccoricco, 2007, 2). As for the broader claim that hypertext realized or embodied "theory," here the repudiation was even harsher. The conflation of hypertext with poststructuralist theory came to look ill-informed at best, sheer wish-fulfilment fantasy at worst, especially the claim that hypertext "liberated" the reader, turning the latter into a kind of surrogate author (Aarseth, 1997, 58, 83–5, 165, 170–1; Ciccoricco, 2007, 8, 58, 64; Bell, 2010, 11–2; Eskelinen, 2012, 6).

What happened in the interim to invalidate, or at least mitigate, those bold early claims for hypertext? To see what happened, just compare the 1992 edition of Landow's *Hypertext* with the revised edition, *Hypertext 2.0*, that appeared five years later in 1997. The index to the 1992 edition conspicuously lacks entries for "HTML" ("Hyper Text Mark-up Language"), "Internet" or "World Wide Web," all of which appear in the 1997 edition. In other words, if in 1992 a book about hypertext could afford to overlook the Internet and the Web, within five years this was no longer possible. In the interval, the Web had started to become the inescapable fact of life online that it has been ever since.

The Internet itself, in the sense of the networked electronic infrastructure that enables the online exchange of information, had already existed for some time by 1992, first as a project of the U.S. Defense Department's Advanced Research Projects Agency, then, from 1990, as an independent entity. The World Wide Web, the most popular and ubiquitous of the services making use of that infrastructure, dates from the very same threshold years as the onset of the interregnum period itself, 1989–90. Proposed by Tim Berners-Lee in 1989 at CERN (the Conseil Européen pour la Recherche Nucléaire) in Switzerland and launched in 1990, the Web only became navigable with the release of the first Web browsers, Mosaic in 1993, then shortly thereafter Netscape Navigator, which soon dominated the market (Gillies and Cailliau, 2000, 236, 257–8).

Landow can be forgiven, then, for overlooking a feature of the digital landscape that had not yet made its presence felt in 1992, but by 1997 it was impossible to overlook. If the World Wide Web represents, as Gillies and Cailliau put it, "the marriage of hypertext and the Internet" (2000, 201), then Landow and other first-generation hypertext theorists ought to have felt vindicated in their early advocacy of hypertext, which was now becoming ubiquitous. Its ubiquity, however, was purchased at a price – literally. Initially reserved for use by researchers and academics, then expanded to provide vehicles for ad hoc communities of like-minded users through chat rooms, Listservs, and other online enclaves, the Internet, beginning in 1991 and more decisively from 1994, swerved into e-commerce (Gillies and Cailliau, 2000, 265). The Web became generally available to Internet users just in time to succumb to the frenzy of commodification and monetization of cyberspace that drove the dot-com boom of the nineties (see section 5). The liberatory and even utopian potential that first-generation theorists attributed to hypertext was overwhelmed by the commercial imperatives of the market. Revealingly, among the new material that Landow introduced into the revised *2.0* edition of his 1992 book were several pages reflecting on the challenges of online pornography and gambling (1997, 296–300), two of the kinds of commercial offering that had come to dominate the Web, and continue to do so to this day.

By the mid-nineties, hypertext fiction itself had migrated onto the Web, rendering distribution via CD-ROM largely obsolete; Moulthrop's *Hegirascope* (1995) is exemplary of this development (Ciccoricco, 2007, 124; Ciccoricco, 2012, 472–3). More importantly, however, the entire digital-media ecology had changed by the mid-nineties, and not only because of ever-expanding access to the Web. Hypertext was now competing for cultural space (and market share) with a whole range of other digital forms of art and entertainment. For forms that shared the quality of requiring significant interaction on the reader's part, above and beyond interpretation, Espen Aarseth in 1997 (the same year as Landow's *Hypertext 2.0*) proposed the umbrella category of *cybertext*, grouping under that umbrella not only hypertext fictions but also text-based adventure games, interactive fictions (Montfort, 2004; Hayles and Montfort, 2012), and massively multiuser online role-playing games. Alongside these text-based cybertexts, and far outstripping them in popularity and ubiquity (though not yet in cultural prestige), were graphics-based games (Wolf, 2001; Ensslin, 2012). Beginning as arcade games in the seventies, shifting over to home consoles and handheld devices in the eighties, then expanding onto personal computers and the Web in the nineties, video games had by the middle of the decade diversified into a multitude of genres – adventure-games (e.g., *Myst*, 1993), combat games (e.g., *Mortal Kombat*, 1992), first-person-shooter games (e.g.,

Doom, 1993), simulation games (e.g., *Sim City*, 1989; *The Sims*, 2000), multiplayer online role-playing games (*Ultima Online*, 1997), interactive movies (e.g., *Johnny Mnemonic* [1995], based on Robert Longo's film of William Gibson's short story; see Chapter 3), and so on. Violence in video games, especially of the combat and first-person-shooter types, provoked waves of "moral panic," but no amount of public disapprobation seemed capable of slowing the proliferation of video gaming into every niche of popular culture, or its integration with other media platforms in transmedia franchises (e.g., *Star Wars* or *The Matrix* trilogy, which spilled across film, television, books, and comics, as well as video games; Jenkins, 2004, 12; Pearce, 2004, 153; Eskelinen, 2012, 335).

By the turn of the millennium, the video-game medium had arguably become culturally dominant (Ciccoricco, 2007, 9), displacing television, the culturally dominant medium of the peak-postmodern decades, which had itself in turn displaced cinema, the medium native to modernism. As of the second decade of the new millennium, video games are perhaps themselves already being displaced by social media (Facebook, YouTube, Twitter, etc.). In any case, video gaming's cultural dominance, however short-lived, has created rich opportunities for artistic appropriation and manipulation, in the spirit of audiovisual remixes and mashups (Newman, 2008), for instance Cory Arcangel's *Super Mario Clouds* (2002), a video collage comprising characteristic cloudscapes appropriated from the popular Nintendo game.

The cultural consequences of the successive reconfigurations of the media landscape over the course of the nineties, through the emergence of hypertext, the development of the World Wide Web, and the proliferation of video gaming, have been profound. If hypertext did not embody poststructuralist theory as fully as the first wave of theorists imagined it did, it might be argued that the Web and its technological vehicles – including the handheld devices that would eventually develop into our contemporary smartphones – are in fact increasingly realizing the "ironic myth" of the cyborg presciently proposed by Donna Haraway in the mid-eighties (Aarseth, 1997, 54–5; Tomasula, 2012, 493–96). As our minds and bodies become increasingly integrated with our electronic prostheses, we approach ever closer to the cyborg condition theorized by Haraway and imagined by cyberpunk science fiction writers (see Chapter 3) – for better or worse.

The proliferation of digitally-mediated forms of art and entertainment has accelerated and intensified the infiltration of "paramount reality" (to use Berger and Luckmann's term; see Chapter 2) by alternative realities: simulations (as in *The Sims*), science-fiction and fantasy worlds, virtual realities such as Second Life[*]. Decades ago, Borges in his essay "Partial Magic in the

Quixote," and even more compellingly in his short story, "Tlön, Uqbar, Orbis Tertius," had speculated about the risk of an inversion of ontological hierarchy, where virtual or simulated second life bleeds into the first life of the everyday, contaminating it and eventually even displacing it. In a sense, this palace revolution in which the virtual overthrows the real has been underway throughout the postmodern decades, but more than ever since the onset of digital Web culture. Anxiety about the invasion of paramount reality by alternative realities has become widespread; for instance, it colors the major science fictions of the second-generation cyberpunk writer Neal Stephenson, from *Snow Crash* (1992) through *The Diamond Age* (1995) to *REAMDE* (2011).

If the infiltration of reality by the virtual is one ontological consequence of Web culture, another potential consequence is the dissolution or volatilization of material reality itself, at least in our collective imagination. It sometimes seems as though all the services and institutions on which we depend – commerce, journalism, education, health care, professional and personal communication, entertainment (it goes without saying), even sex – have migrated online, shedding their materiality for the ephemerality of electron streams and pixels. Characteristically, we speak dismissively nowadays of "bricks-and-mortar" structures, meaning stodgy, material-based institutions rendered obsolete by the Internet – real-world sites made redundant by Web sites. "All that is solid melts into air," Marx and Engels said of the volatilizing effect of capitalism, a phrase that Marshall Berman applied to the experience of modernity (1982), but that might with even greater propriety be applied to the experience of postmodernity, especially digitized postmodernity. This volatilization is contagious, spreading from the online world to the real-world economy, where it contributed its own effervescence to the short-lived "bubble" economy of the nineties (Ryan 1999, 94). Already in 1992, Coover had observed that hypertext fiction could induce in the reader a sense of weightlessness, "that dreamy gravityless lost-in-space feeling of the early sci-fi films." He could not then have imagined how pervasive that sense of postmodern antigravity would become once the Internet had begun to achieve parity with the real world (see section 5).

4. After *Gravity*, or, Anxieties of Influence

Raymond Federman's essay about the end of postmodernism, with which I began this chapter, originated in a lecture delivered in Stuttgart in 1991 at a symposium provocatively titled, "The End of Postmodernism." "It is hard, perhaps impossible," wrote the symposium's convener, Heide Ziegler, in her introduction to the conference proceedings,

> to say when an era has reached, or will reach, its end, especially if that era happens to define one's contemporary environment. Perhaps we have come to clamor for the end of postmodernism because we feel increasingly uncertain about its beginnings and thus our own stance within it. Or, unhappy with postmodernism's ambiguities, we feel the urge for a new beginning and new directions. Or, worst of all, we despair of ever getting out from under postmodernism and thus ironically proclaim its end in the hopes of seeing it arrive. (Ziegler, 1993, 5)

Interestingly, the five participants in the "End of Postmodernism" symposium, all distinguished novelists or critics, mostly declined to proclaim postmodernism over, ironically or otherwise. The novelist and critic Malcolm Bradbury hedged – "I do not know whether Postmodernism is at an end or not," he wrote, "but I know something is" (Bradbury, 1993, 85) – while the novelist John Barth actually projected the endpoint of the postmodernism into the future: "2000 seems an appropriate target date for winding up Postmodernism as a cultural and aesthetic dominant" (Barth, 1995, 309).

As it happens, Federman also contributed to another collection of essays similar in spirit to the Ziegler symposium proceedings, *In Memoriam to Postmodernism* (1995). Here the editors, Mark Amerika and Lance Olsen, actually have a candidate in mind for postmodernism's replacement, namely Avant-Pop, the avant-garde practice of appropriating and repurposing pop-culture materials. They try to distinguish Avant-Pop from postmodernism and to argue that, by the early nineties, the former had displaced the latter, constituting a "post-post-modernism." Here, too, however, the contributors mainly hedge or dissent outright from the editors' claims about Avant-Pop, for good reason: Avant-Pop is manifestly a postmodern practice, a version of what Charles Jencks called double-coding, forming *part* of postmodernism, rather than an alternative to it, or its successor (see Chapter 3).

Appearing nearly contemporaneously, the Ziegler symposium and the Amerika and Olsen collection reflect an early nineties impatience with postmodernism, a desire to break free of it, but they seem powerless actually to achieve the break itself. The same impatience to break through to some form of "post-postmodernism," and the same powerlessness to do so, can be glimpsed elsewhere in the literary world of the late eighties and early nineties among the younger generation of writers (Burn, 2008; McLaughlin, 2008 and 2012). The novelist Jonathan Franzen, for instance, in controversial essays published in the mid-nineties and early 2000's, sought to distance himself from the aesthetics of postmodernist megafictions such as those of Gaddis and Pynchon, advocating a more reader-friendly realist mode of fiction, less difficult, less intimidating in size and scope, more popular. Ironically, his novel *The Corrections* (1991), which reflected this reorientation, involved him in a very public conflict with the TV talk-show host Oprah Winfrey, who invited him to appear on her televised Book Club and then, when he expressed misgivings about the kind of popularity such an appearance implied, inhospitably *dis*invited him (Green, 2005, 97–116). Whether or not Franzen's novel was itself postmodern, the spectacle of his contretemps with pop culture certainly was.

The most influential expression of impatience with postmodernism is the much-cited essay "E Unibus Pluram" (1993) by Franzen's friend and rival, David Foster Wallace. It is the affinities between postmodernism and popular culture that trouble Wallace – precisely the affinities that Olsen, Amerika, and McCaffery celebrate. Postmodernism has failed to maintain its ironic distance from pop culture, especially from television; in fact, television has absorbed the lessons of postmodernism and become self-reflective and ironic itself, beginning (according to Wallace) around 1974, the year of the Watergate hearings (Wallace, 1997, 36) – the same historical moment that Killen identified as postmodernism's onset, and that I contend was actually its moment of *rebranding* (see Chapter 3). Henceforth, postmodernist self-reflection is compromised, preempted by television's self-reflectiveness: "it is now *television* that takes elements of the *postmodern* – the involution, the absurdity, the sardonic fatigue, the iconoclasm and rebellion – and bends them to the ends of spectation and consumption" (Wallace, 1997, 64). Postmodernists of Wallace's own generation, such as Mark Leyner, try to "resolve the problem by celebrating it" (Wallace, 1997, 76), "reabsorb[ing] the very features TV has itself absorbed from postmodern art" (Wallace, 1997, 81), but this is a capitulation, not a solution, and Wallace can only hope for the emergence of a post-ironic backlash against the tainted ironies of postmodernism (Wallace, 1997, 81–2)

Wallace's dissatisfaction with postmodernism barely camouflages what the theorist Harold Bloom would have called his "anxiety of influence." Haunted by feelings of belatedness, of being preempted and overshadowed by his postmodern precursors (Scott, 2000), Wallace struggled to escape from their shadow. He expressed his oedipal resentment of his literary fathers in fictions such as, the novella "Westward the Course of Empire Takes Its Way," "written in the margins of John Barth's 'Lost in the Funhouse'" as the disclaimer on the copyright page puts it (*The Girl with Curious Hair* [1989]). If Barth is Wallace's "primary fictional father"

(Boswell, 2003, 9), another source of anxiety was Pynchon, whose *The Crying of Lot 49* (1966) Wallace rewrote in his first novel, *The Broom of the System* (1987). Wallace claimed not to have read Pynchon's novel until *after* he had published his own (Boswell, 2003, 215 n. 18), but whether or not this is so, he certainly seems to have heard something about it – enough, at any rate, to be able to model his own heroine's situation on Oedpia Maas's. As for Wallace's 1,000-page meganovel of the nineties, *Infinite Jest* (1996), here the presence of his postmodern precursors is ubiquitous (LeClair, 1996, 30–36). For instance, at the catastrophic climax of a complicated simulation game played on the tennis court at Ennisfield Academy, the game computer's hard drive, monitor and modem are accidently catapulted into the air; in slow motion, the "hardware that's now at the top of its rainbow's arc" (Wallace, 1996, 34) descends right onto the unfortunate referee. That "rainbow's arc" is gravity's rainbow – the parabolic flight path traced by V-2 rockets in Pynchon's seminal postmodernist novel of 1973.

As hard as he struggled to evade the influence of his postmodern precursors, Wallace seemed stuck in repetition. His case, which took a tragic turn with his suicide in 2008, suggests that nineties writing was not yet "post-postmodern," as much as writers such as himself and Franzen might have wished it were. Nineties writers seemed condemned to the status of second-generation postmodernists, acutely aware of their first-generation precursors and afflicted to various degrees with anxiety of influence. It did not help that many of the key figures of peak-period postmodern fiction continued to be productive throughout the nineties – oppressively so, perhaps, from the point of view of a second-generation writer. Pynchon, Gass, and Coover all published long-awaited novels that had been promised for years, even decades. Barth, Eco, DeLillo, Fuentes, Alasdair Gray, Morrison, and Rushdie all continued to publish actively. The only major postmodernists who were no longer publishing new books, or so it seemed, were those few who had died prematurely – Georges Perec, Italo Calvino, Angela Carter – and even in their cases posthumous translation and repackaging continued apace.

Moreover, major postmodernist novels of the peak period left their mark on many of the most ambitious novels of the nineties. Wallace's *Broom* and *Infinite Jest* are far from the only novels that exhibit a debt to Pynchon. A whole series of "Pynchonesque" novels can be traced, most of them indebted to *Gravity's Rainbow,* some to *The Crying of Lot 49* as well, from William T. Vollmann's *You Bright and Risen Angels* (1987) and Steve Erickson's *Tours of the Black Clock* (1989) through Richard Powers's *The Gold-Bug Variations* (1991), Neil Stephenson's *Cryptonomicon* (1999),

Colson Whitehead's *The Intuitionist* (1999), and Michael Chabon's *The Amazing Adventures of Kavalier and Clay* (2000). A comparable genealogy of magical-realist fiction connects Rushdie with Karen Tei Yamashita's *Through the Arc of the Rainforest* (1990), Zadie Smith's *White Teeth* (2000), Hari Kunzru's *The Impressionist* (2003), and other second-generation novels. Martin Amis's *Time's Arrow* (1990) is written in the shadow of Kurt Vonnegut's *Slaughterhouse-Five* (1969), Mark Z. Danielewski's *House of Leaves* (2000) in that of Barth's "Lost in the Funhouse" and Nabokov's *Pale Fire*, and so on.

Just as nineties meganovelists write in the shadow of Pynchon and other peak-period postmodernists, and nineties magical realists write in the shadow of Rushdie, so nineties science fiction struggles in various way with the legacy of cyberpunk (see Chapter 3). As in the case of mainstream postmodern fiction, here too the key figures of the peak period, far from slacking off, continued to produce prolifically: William Gibson himself, for instance, published his second trilogy between 1993 and 1999, and jointly with Bruce Sterling helped spin off the new subgenre of *steampunk* (see section 2). A second generation of cyberpunk writers emerged (Kelly and Kessel, 2007; Murphy and Vint, 2010), beginning with Neal Stephenson (*Snow Crash*, 1992), and by the end of the decade, after a false start, the cyberpunk genre finally crossed over to mass-market popularity with the success of the Wachowski siblings' film *The Matrix* (1999).

The same sort of impatience with peak-period postmodernism that characterizes mainstream fiction and post-cyberpunk science fiction can also be detected on the avant-garde poetry scene, where the pervasiveness of L=A=N=G=U=A=G=E poetry as a model (see Chapter 3) provoked some younger poets to explore the possibilities of "post-Language" poetry (Wallace and Marks, 2002). However, younger avant-gardists who emerged in the nineties in the wake of L=A=N=G=U=A=G=E poetry, such as Peter Gizzi, Myung Mi Kim, Tan Lin, Jennifer Moxley, Harryette Mullen, Juliana Spahr, Brian Kim Stefans, and others, seem mostly to continue and extend the practices of their first-generation forerunners, including procedural writing and found-poetry practices (Bernstein, 2012; Epstein, 2012). A characteristic figure of the younger generation, Kenneth Goldsmith (see Chapter 5), achieved a certain degree of notoriety with his book *Day* (2003), in which he laboriously transcribed everything he found in one day's issue of the *New York Times*, all the words, including running heads, the words in advertisements, market information, obituaries, the weather forecast – everything. The day he chose was Friday, September 1, 2000 – the year in which John Barth foresaw the end of postmodernism.

5. Anti-Gravity

Suspended between worlds, the nineties were a decade in metaphorical free-fall. At the movies during the year 1991 one could have seen multiple images of bodies in free-fall, ambiguously defying gravity or succumbing to it, flying or falling. For instance, in Wim Wender's science-fiction film of that year, *Until the End of the World*, a sort of global road movie set on the threshold of the millennium, in 1999, two characters flying over the Australian outback in a single-engine plane are overtaken by the electromagnetic pulse from a nuclear explosion. Their plane loses power, and they glide down in dream-like stillness to a safe landing in the desert. That same year, in Ridley Scott's *Thelma and Louise*, a feminist revision of the road-move genre, the two women of the title, partners in crime on the run from the police, with no options left, power their Chevrolet convertible over the edge of the Grand Canyon, to certain death. However, our last image of them is a freeze frame – Thelma and Louise in midair in the convertible, perpetually suspended, ambiguously flying or falling.

The aspiration to weightlessness, in the face of the inevitability of gravity, had been a leitmotif of postmodernism since at least Warhol's "Silver Clouds" (see Chapter 2) and Pynchon's *Gravity's Rainbow* (1973), but the figure of the free-falling body only fully came into its own in the nineties. Italo Calvino seemed to anticipate this nineties condition of weightlessness when, in a lecture he prepared in 1985 but did not live to deliver, he advocated "Lightness" as one of the literary values appropriate to the coming millennium (Calvino, 1988). Tracing, in effect, the genealogy of a certain strain in post-modernism, Calvino finds figures of lightness throughout literary history, from Lucretius in the ancient world through Shakespeare in early modern times (e.g., *The Tempest*; see "Prospero's Books") down to Kafka in the twentieth century. Figures such as Kafka's "Bucket-Rider," who flies around town astride an empty coal scuttle, or Don Quixote when he drives his lance through the windmill's vane and is hoisted aloft, Calvino calls "visual images[s] of lightness," attributing to them "emblematic value" (Calvino, 1988, 18). Had he lived long enough, he might have characterized in these same terms the cinematic images of 1991: the powerless airplane descending to the desert floor in *Until the End of the World*, Thelma and Louise suspended in their convertible.

Lightness, in Calvino's account, is a positive quality, but as he himself acknowledges, it can be viewed otherwise, as negative or even "unbearable," as in Milan Kundera's novel *The Unbearable Lightness of Being* (1984). Jameson, too, refers negatively, or at least ambivalently, to the postmodern motifs of "flotation" or "weightlessness," and what he calls "a kind of anti-gravity of the postmodern" (Jameson 1991, 100–1). Presumably, the postmodern sense of lightness or antigravity derives ultimately from the experience of consumer culture, where solidity and gravity are leached away from the material world and replaced by weightless simulacra (Lears, 1983). A characteristic expression of consumerist "lightness of being," on the very eve of the nineties, is the memorable music video for a song by Tom Petty and the Heartbreakers, "Free Fallin'" (1989), which shows the singer himself descending an escalator into the sunlit commercial spaces of a vast indoor shopping mall, intercut with images of skateboarders performing gravity-defying stunts in slow motion.

The experience of the weightlessness of consumerism, evoked so strikingly by "Free Fallin'," was certainly reinforced and amplified by the ungrounded effervescence of the bubble economy of the nineties. The new technologies of personal computing, the Internet, and cellular telephones, all sustained by an expanding telecommunications infrastructure, promised a "New Economy," and encouraged what Alan Greenspan, chairman of the U.S. Federal Reserve, famously characterized as "irrational exuberance" in the U.S. stock market (Hughes and MacDonald, 2004, 12). Fortunes were invested in Internet-based dot-com companies that earned no profits and were literally worthless (Lowenstein, 2004, 220–1). A cascade of bankruptcies and corruption scandals, beginning in 2000–2001, spelled the end of the dot-com boom, and when the bubble finally burst "investors, not unlike the familiar cartoon character, saw that they had been running on air" (Lowenstein, 2004, 157–8).

Running on air: the phrase evokes Marx and Engels' memorable observation that, under the volatilizing effects of capitalism, "All that is solid melts into air" (see Berman, 1982). When all that is solid melts, and the economy discovers it has been running on air, then culture itself becomes volatile and light – or *lite*, to use the spelling that Ellen Friedman and Corinne Squire (1998) appropriate from the commercial realm, where *lite beer* is low in calories (and tasteless), *lite music* is generic and inoffensive, and so on. Friedman and Squire ascribe the quality of *liteness* to a range of nineties phenomena: New Age belief, the cult of celebrity, TV "infotainment" and "reality" programming, radio call-in shows, the Internet and online "life" generally, shopping malls (as in Tom Petty's "Free Fallin'"), Disney World and other artificial pseudo-communities, even the hypermediated Persian Gulf War of 1991 (which Baudrillard viewed as entirely simulacral, claiming, provocatively, that it "did not take place"; Baudrillard, 1995). In all such phenomena, we have the sense that reality is evaporating or leaking away, to be replaced by something not-quite-real, something *lighter* than reality: *lite* reality. So, we have New Age beliefs instead of "real" religion, talk-shows instead of "real" conversation about serious topics, celebrities instead of "real" achievement, the Internet, shopping malls, and Disney World instead of "real" communities, even simulacral war instead of the real thing. Nevertheless, Friedman and Squire, though critical, are not entirely negative toward *lite* culture, identifying in it certain redeeming qualities or potentialities. Cultural *liteness* can provide strategies for resisting or outflanking discourses of authority; it offers opportunities for cultural "others" to join the conversation in mainstream mass-culture venues; it empowers consumers to become, if only to a limited degree, producers themselves; it encourages improvisation and self-invention; and it is *pleasurable*. If Friedman and Squire are right, there might actually be some measure of freedom in free-fall.

If the ultimate referent of the free-fall figure is consumer culture and the bubble economy of the nineties, then where does the image itself, this emblematic icon, come from? Calvino's genealogy gives us an abundance of sources, not least of all Cyrano de Bergerac's story of his flight to the moon, one of the forerunners of science fiction. In the second half of the twentieth century, it is no doubt mainly aeronautics and space flight that supplied the imagery of free-falling bodies: sky-divers in free-fall, astronauts bobbing around in the cabins of their spacecraft or at the end of tethers during extra-vehicular activities, or bounding across the moon's surface in lunar gravity. This repertoire of images was fixed in the contemporary imagination once and for all by Stanley Kubrick's film *2001: A Space Odyssey* (1968), with its arresting special-effects sequences of people and things floating or tumbling in zero gravity. The same imagery can be found, for instance, at the close of Wenders' *Until the End of the World*, when the heroine (who previously had experienced free-fall in the powerless airplane) is glimpsed onboard an orbiting space-station, floating weightlessly – a motif revisited again, with 3-D enhancement, in Alfonso Cuarón's *Gravity* (2013).

Our vicarious experience of one kind of weightlessness, that of outer space, has been reinforced more recently by the more direct, hands-on experience of a different kind, the weightlessness of cyberspace, where we imagine ourselves to be traveling, frictionless and disembodied, through the virtual spaces on the "other side" of the monitor screen. Presciently, Calvino already identified this as one of the sources of postmodern lightness as early as his 1985 lecture, written only a year or so after William Gibson coined the term "cyberspace" and established the conventions that would come to govern its representation and eventually its (virtual) reality. Lightness of one kind or another persists as a motif of science fiction throughout the nineties and beyond. For instance, the mile-high cities that the British science-fiction writer David Wingrove imagines for a future earth in his novel *Chung Kuo* (1990), the first volume of a series by the same name, are fabricated from a super-strong material so lightweight that the wind would blow everything away if the cities weren't securely moored (see section 7). In the last volume of another important series of the nineties, Kim Stanley Robinson's Mars trilogy (1993–6), human settlers on a transformed Red Planet enjoy self-powered flight in the weaker Martian gravity – but they also sometimes fall to their deaths.

The figure of lightness or antigravity in nineties postmodernism is almost always ambivalent: both liberating and not-quite-real; both exhilarating and anxiety producing; both flying and falling. Only rarely, typically in popular-culture products, is free-fall unambiguously positive and exhilarating. One example is the MTV video for Sheryl Crow's "All I Wanna Do" (1993), the breakthrough hit from her debut album, and a 1995 Grammy Award-winner, where the singer is seen busking on a streetcorner, and passersby who leave money for her literally lose their gravity, bobbing up into the sky like hot-air balloons, an emblem of "irrational exuberance." Similarly unambiguous in its embrace of the pleasures of levitation is the enormously popular series of novels about the education of the young sorcerer Harry Potter (1997–2007) by the British writer J. K. Rowling. Surely one of the (many) reasons for the series' success with young readers (and adults, too) is the airborne game of Quidditch played at Hogwarts School. Markedly different in kind, though equally unambiguous, is the spiritual exhilaration that some evangelical or fundamentalist communities anticipate at the moment of Rapture, when the saved remnant of humanity will be caught up into heaven, leaving the rest of us behind to struggle with the Tribulations prophesied for the era leading up to the end of the world. The Rapture and its earthbound aftermath are the subject of the *Left Behind* series (1995–2007) of Christian-apocalyptic thrillers by Tim LaHaye and Jerry B. Jenkins. (Roughly contemporaneous with the *Harry Potter* series, *Left Behind*, like *Potter*, has spun off products on multiple media platforms, including movies, graphic novels and video games.) A different version of the Rapture, perhaps, is found in Tony Kushner's two-part drama of the AIDS epidemic, *Angels in America* (1990, 1992), when the character Harper describes her dream-vision of the souls of AIDS victims floating upward into the atmosphere, "like skydivers in reverse, limbs all akimbo, wheeling and spinning" (Kushner, 1995, 275), to repair the damaged ozone layer.

Generally, however, ambivalence, rather than unalloyed exhilaration, is the hallmark of levitation in the nineties. Already from the mid-eighties on, the postmodernist figurative painter Robert Yarber had depicted a series of embracing couples or sometimes individual figures leaping, falling or flying from hotel balconies against a background of garish technicolor sunsets or neon-lit cityscapes. In a characteristic Yarber canvas of this period, such as "Regard and Abandon" (1985), it is not clear whether the airborne couple, locked in an embrace, are lighter-than-air figures of erotic exhilaration or doomed lovers falling to their death in a suicide pact – or both at once (see Chapter 3, Figure 3). Here and in other paintings, such as *Sleeping Couple* (1984), *Sign-Off* (1984), or *The Tender and the Damned* (1985) (see "Angels in America," Figure 5), Yarber's figures seem massive, literally statuesque, yet they also appear weightless. Ultimately ambiguous, the meaning of all these airborne figures is left "up in the air," indeterminate, suspending the viewer in an interpretative free-fall parallel to the free-fall experience of the figures *in* the paintings themselves.

Lightness and gravity, indeterminacy and meaning mingle in other cultural products of nineties postmodernism. Ambivalent imagery of weightlessness, free-fall and flight figure in literary fictions of the decade, such as Paul Auster's *Moon Palace* (1989), *Leviathan* (1992), and *Mr. Vertigo* (1994), Karen Tei Yamashita's *Through the Arc of the Rain Forest* (1990), Thomas Pynchon's *Mason & Dixon* (1997), Anne Carson's verse-novel *Autobiography of Red* (1998), Colson Whitehead's *The Intuitionist* (1999), Mark Z. Danielewski's *House of Leaves* (2000), and many others. In the epilogue of *Angels in America*, Kushner has his hero Prior, who has been hounded by angels throughout the play, reflect wryly on their weightless quality. Sitting on the rim of the Bethesda Fountain of New York's Central Park, with its angel statue, Prior explains:

> I like them [angels] best when they're statuary .... They are made of the heaviest things on earth, stone and iron, they weigh tons but they're winged, they are engines and instruments of flight. (Kushner, 1995, 279)

Heavy and literally statuesque, like the figures in Yarber's paintings, but also light, in both senses of the term, the angels of *Angels in America* are danger-ously threatening figures of the apocalypse but also, at the same time, figures of healing and reassurance. Similarly ambivalent or indeterminate is the motif of lightness in the songs and performances of Laurie Anderson. Bridging the gap between the avant-garde and popular culture, between performance art and rock concert, Anderson is an important figure in the dissemination of the antigravity motif across cultural spheres (see Chapter 3). Her preoccupation with flying, falling, and floating, already a feature of eighties pieces such as "Walking and Falling" (from *Big Science*, 1982), intensifies in her early nineties performance *Empty Places* (premiered 1989), which includes the number "More Strange Angels" (in which, despite the title, no angels actually appear):

> You know what I've always liked
> about Superman,
> it's that his alter ego
> was a newspaperman.
> No matter where Superman was,
> there was always a phone booth
> and Clark Kent could call it in.
> "Hello. Kent here. Yeah … listen,
> there's been a gravity failure.
> You heard me! Gravity failure!
> And uh, things have just started floating up.
> Yeah, well of course Superman was there.
> I can see him from here." (Anderson 1991, 90–91)

Anderson's association of Superman/Clark Kent with antigravity – from which he can rescue people thanks to his own capacity to fly – reminds us that moviemakers throughout the century have sought to perfect the cinematic illusion of flight. "You'll believe a man can fly!" ran the advance advertising for the 1978 film version of *Superman* – but of course no-one did, so unpersuasive were that movie's special effects. Not until the nineties did filmmakers begin to achieve more plausibly realistic effects of lightness. Levitation and antigravity recur throughout nineties cinema. The decade's aspiration to defy gravity helps explain the fascination with *Crouching Tiger, Hidden Dragon*, directed by Ang Lee (2000), which introduced moviegoers worldwide to Chinese cinematic conventions of levitation and flight. However, it is only through the development of computer-generated imagery (CGI) that realistic superhero flight finally becomes attainable in movies. CGI technology begins to impact moviemaking from the late eighties on (Venkatasawmy, 2013), though, perhaps ironically, some of its earliest achievements actually focused on simulating *weight* and *mass* (not entirely convincingly, in fact): the dinosaurs of Steven Spielberg's blockbuster *Jurassic Park* (1993), the luxury ocean liner of an even bigger blockbuster, James Cameron's *Titanic* (1997). Chinese cinematic techniques of levitation converge with the technology of CGI right at the end of the decade, in 1999 (the year imagined by Wim Wenders as the end of world), in the Wachowski siblings' *The Matrix*, which juxtaposes the lightness of simulated reality with the gravity of the "desert of the real" (to use a phrase that the Wachowskis lifted from Baudrillard). *The Matrix* reflects the belated crossover of cyberpunk into mass entertainment (see Chapter 3), as well as the final triumph of antigravity in the movies.

But the high point of the lightness motif in nineties culture, arguably, is achieved at the climax of Richard Powers' novel *Plowing the Dark* (2000). Two narratives alternate in Powers' novel: one, the story of a research project in Seattle during the heady early days of virtual reality, 1989–91; the other, the story of an American hostage held for five years in Beirut during the Lebanese civil war, 1986–91. The two stories, apparently unrelated, actually share the theme of virtual reality, for it is not only the Seattle research team that experiments with virtually real spaces, but so does Taimur Martin, the Beirut hostage – except that the virtual reality into which he retreats during his long incarceration lies inside his mind. Then startlingly, just before the novel's end, the firewall between the two narratives is uncannily breached. Adie Karpol, the heroine of the Seattle story, goes cruising in the virtual reality she has helped design, a simulacrum of Hagia Sophia basilica. Her experience is one of lightness of being, frictionless navigation, the antigravity of the postmodern – until she falls:

> She booted up the cathedral and stepped back in. She leaned into the nave's great hollow, feeling herself move despite her better sense. . . . She let herself rise into the hemisphere apse, then farther up, all the way into the uppermost dome. . . .
>
> She spun her body in the invented volume, the large ballet of an astronaut repairing failed equipment far off in the infinite vacuum. The God's-eye view: in the simulation, but not of it. And deep beneath her, where there should have been stillness, something moved.
>
> . . .She fell like a startled fledgling, back into the world's snare. The mad thing swam into focus: a man, staring up at her fall. . . . (Powers, 2001, 399; my ellipses)

The man, of course, is Taimur Martin, deep in his own fantasy world, which somehow has come to coincide with the virtual reality space of Adie's Hagia Sophia. Taimur, whose story is narrated throughout in the second person, experiences the same moment this way:

> Strange flickers led you deeper into the light, until you stood dead center, under the stone crown. Then you heard it, above your head: a noise that passed all understanding. You looked up at the sound, and saw the thing that would save you. A hundred feet above, in the awful dome, an angel dropped out of the air. An angel whose face filled not with good news but with all the horror of her coming impact. A creature dropping from out of the sky, its bewilderment outstripping your own. That angel terror lay

> beyond decoding. It left you no choice but to live long enough to learn what it needed from you. (Powers, 2001, 414).

The free-falling figure of Adie, aloft in the virtual reality she has helped design, crashes through an ontological barrier into another reality, a subjective one, Taimur's. Worlds collide, and the ontological shock of that collision feels like an encounter with an angel. (See "Angels in America.")

It seems impossible, from a twenty-first-century perspective, not to see in these free-falling figures – from the figures in Yarber's paintings through Thelma and Louise to *The Matrix* and the falling angel of *Plowing the Dark* – an uncanny anticipation of the "falling man" photograph that became, briefly, an icon of the terrorist attacks of September 11, 2001. The image of a man falling headfirst to his death from the North Tower of the World Trade Center, caught inadvertently by the news-service photographer Richard Drew, was seen everywhere during the hours right after the attack, and then, as if by some mysterious consensus, all but disappeared from the archive of that day's images (see Junod, 2003). Like the return of the Freudian repressed, it only resurfaces much later, but transposed into narrative form in literary fictions such as Don DeLillo's *Falling Man* (2007), Ronald Sukenick's posthumous novel *Last Fall* (2005), and especially Jonathan Safran Foer's *Extremely Loud & Incredibly Close* (2005), in which the direction of the fatal fall is literally reversed, becoming an image of flight. "If [the falling man] were not falling, he might very well be flying," writes Tom Junod. In the falling-man photo, the antigravity of the postmodern nineties – the *liteness* of its culture, the effervescence of its bubble economy, the speed and volatility of its online life – succumbs to the gravity of the 9/11 world.

6. Arts of Suspension

Far from being limited to popular culture, the attribute of *liteness* identified by Friedman and Squire characterizes even the fine art of the interregnum period. "High art lite," Julian Stallabrass calls it, defining it mordantly as "an art that looks like but is not quite art, that acts as a substitute for art" (Stallabrass,1999, 2). He has in mind the so-called "Young British Artists," or YBAs, including Damien Hirst, Tracey Emin, Sarah Lucas, Jake and Dinos Chapman, Chris Ofili, and others, who emerged at the end of the eighties in the aftermath of the cooling of the art market in 1987–89, and whose reputations were amplified by shrewd self-publicists such as Hirst and by the marketing savvy of Charles Saatchi (of the Saatchi and Saatchi advertising agency), a major collector of YBA art. The ascent of the YBAs to prominence coincided with an interregnum in British political life, the years of John Major's premiership, 1992–98, a period of drift sandwiched between "two confident, nationalist and demagogic governments" (Stallabrass, 1999, 128), those of Mrs. Thatcher in the eighties and Tony Blair around the turn of the millennium.

Stallabrass characterizes "high art lite" as two-faced, simultaneously oriented "outwards to wider audiences and media notoriety" and "inwards to the art world" (Stallabrass, 1999, 62). It is, in this respect, canonically postmodern, replicating the double-coded quality that Jencks identified in the peak-period postmodernism of the seventies and eighties (see Chapter 3). An example is Hirst's *The Physical Impossibility of Death in the Mind of Someone Living* (1991), perhaps the most recognizable and iconic of all the YBA works: a tank of formaldehyde containing the body of a full-grown tiger shark. Designed to be sensational and scandalous, it evokes mass-media imagery, especially the shark of Steven Spielberg's blockbuster film *Jaws* (1975), while at the same time addressing an art-world audience that recognizes its relationship to earlier decades' art movements – minimalism, conceptualism – and perhaps even places it in rivalrous dialogue with contemporaries such as Jeff Koons, whose *Equilibrium Series* (from 1985) suspended basketballs in tanks, or Andrés Serrano's *Piss Christ* (1987), the photograph of a crucifix floating in a tank of what was said to be the artist's own urine. Predictably, *Piss Christ* provoked a scandal in 1989, when questions were asked on the floor of the U.S. Senate about National Endowment for the Arts funding for works such as Serrano's, much as, a decade later, the *Sensation* show of YBA art from the Saatchi collection would provoke scandals first at the Royal Academy of Art in London (1997), then at the Brooklyn Museum of Art in New York (1999–2000).

If Hirst's *The Physical Impossibility of Death*, like precursor works by Koons and Serrano, exemplifies "high art lite" in Stallabrass's sense, it is also *literally* suspensive: the shark (like Koons's basketballs and Serrano's crucifix) literally *floats*. An icon of YBA art, *The Physical Impossibility of Death* is also a visual image or emblem of lightness or levity, in something like Calvino's sense, or of *liteness* in Friedman's and Squire's.

It is tempting to nominate "high art lite" as the dominant period style of the nineties, in the same way that the return of figuration, in its radical "Pictures" and conservative Neoexpressionist modes, dominated the eighties (see Chapter 3). However, as Terry Smith argues, what actually characterizes high art since the eighties is the *absence* of any dominant style; in fact, he would say that no style has really been dominant since the era of minimalism and conceptualism, around 1970 (Smith, 2009, 245). Contemporary art, Hal Foster writes in a similar vein, "floats free" of categories and conceptual definitions (Foster, 2009, 3). Somewhat paradoxically, however, it is precisely this very "floating-free" quality that defines some of the most characteristic artworks of the decade, and not just the "high art lite" of YBAs such as Hirst.

Take, for example, Matthew Barney's ambitious *Cremaster* cycle of five films, produced out of order (*Cremaster 4* came first, then *1*, *5*, *2*, and *3*, in that order) between 1994 and 2002. Collectively, Barney's cycle is a major work of interregnum postmodernism, comparable, say, to *Gravity's Rainbow* in the peak period, or to Kushner's *Angels in America* at the beginning of the nineties. *Cremaster* aspires to the condition of *Gesamtkunstwerk*, a "total work of art," combining cinema with performance (the films record Barney himself undergoing various strenuous athletic ordeals), sculpture (Barney regards the cycle as essentially sculptural, and a number of actual sculptures have been spun off from his performances; see Spector, 2003, 83–9; Smith, 2009, 100), even music and dance. As with many other comparably heterogeneous postmodernist works, Barney's cycle is clearly affiliated with the *masque* tradition (see Chapter 1 and "Prospero's Books").

The *Cremaster* cycle exhibits many of the hallmarks of postmodernism. High and low cultural sources and materials mingle – arcane symbolism and college sports, art-world in-jokes and punk-rock mosh-pits, conceptualism and gangster-movies – in a typically Avant-Pop way (Smith, 2009, 100). Barney himself is something of a crossover figure, as confirmed by his high-profile marriage to the eccentric and aesthetically ambitious Icelandic pop singer Björk. The films' worlds are ontologically complex and contradictory, crowded with characters belonging to different, incompatible orders of being: mythological and fantastic creatures (satyrs, giants, a zombie, a half-woman half-cheetah), real-world figures (the escape artist Houdini, the murderer Gary Gilmore), celebrity actors whose real identities bleed through into their fictional roles (the writer Norman Mailer, the sculptor Richard Serra, the iconic movie star Ursula Andress). The cycle ranges over multiple levels of reality, a structure captured in miniature in the section called *The Order* (folded into the middle of *Cremaster 3*), in which Barney literally scales five levels of the Guggenheim Museum's rotunda, encountering a different world, and a different challenge, on each level, as in a video game. *The Order*, in other words, is a *mise-en-abyme* of the entire cycle – another typically postmodern feature (see Chapter 3).

However, of all its postmodern features, the one that is most integral to the cycle is ontological *hesitation*. Characters fluctuate between states, hovering between literal and allegorical, character and personification; entire worlds hesitate between objective existence and dream or hallucination (Spector, 2003, 19, 23–4). This hesitation structure reflects the cycle's underlying biological theme of sexual undifferentiation. Through allegory and symbolism, *Cremaster* dramatizes the sexually undifferentiated condition of the human embryo in its first two trimesters and maps the process whereby sexual identity emerges *in utero*; indeed, the cycle's very title, *Cremaster*, refers to the muscle that controls the descent of the testicles in the male. Like certain characteristically postmodern works (but markedly unlike others; see "Alice"), *Cremaster* is driven by narrative (Smith, 2009, 99), and what it narrates is the *grand récit* of sexual identity and ultimate differentiation. However, that narrative of sexual difference is continually being deferred, interrupted by ancillary quests and contests, forays into history and myth, a pile-up of incidents, many of them laboriously drawn out. The very proliferation of narratives impedes narrativity, leaving the embryonic organism (the ultimate "hero" of the cycle) suspended between identities until the moment in the last installment, *Cremaster 5* (1997), when the descent of the testicles is finally celebrated.

Emblematic of the cycle's condition of hesitation and suspension is the scenario of *Cremaster 1* (the beginning of the cycle, but the second installment in order of production, made in 1995, after *Cremaster 4*). Here, two Goodyear blimps float above a football stadium; onboard, the character Goodyear – played, in a gender switch, by a hyper-feminine actress – directs by remote control the precision-dance configurations of a squad of cheerleaders on the field below. Heavy though the theme of sexual undifferentiation might be, here it is depicted with undeniable levity: a pair of lighter-than-air craft, figuring undescended testicles!

Barney is preoccupied with in-betweenness on the level of the individual organism and of the species generally, but not on the level of historical experience. Someone who does address the historical condition of in-betweenness in the nineties is William Kentridge, whose series of nine *Drawings for Projection*, 1989–2003 (expanded to ten in 2011), overlaps with Barney's cycle and coincides rather precisely with the interregnum period in his native country, South Africa. Kentridge's animated films reflect, sometimes directly, sometimes less so, the unraveling of the apartheid regime and the emergence of a new post-apartheid South Africa, from the freeing of Nelson Mandela in 1990, through the first universal elections in 1994, to the work of the Truth and Reconciliation Commission in the period 1995–2000. This was the era of what has been called "transitional justice" in South Africa (Rothberg, 2012), bridging the gulf between a delegitimized old regime and a new, nonracial one just coming into being. The South African novelist Nadine

Gordimer, anticipating this era, spoke of the experience of "living in the interregnum," when "the old is dying, and new cannot be born," citing the Italian Marxist Antonio Gramsci (quoted by Rothberg, 2012, 3–4). This is the experience that Kentridge captures in his *Drawings for Projection*.

He does so, first of all, narratively, if obliquely, through the story of a romantic triangle among three white South Africans, the entrepreneur Soho Eckstein, his wife, and his alter ego, the artist-figure and exile Felix Teitlebaum, all played out against a background of bleak industrial wastelands and mass political demonstrations. More crucially, however, Kentridge reflects the interregnum experience through his technique of stop-action animation, which entails using a movie camera to film, a few frames at a time, a charcoal drawing (occasionally enhanced with pastels) that Kentridge alters between "takes," thereby producing a deliberately crude illusion of motion when the film is subsequently projected. At a period when commercial animated movies were introducing hyper-realistic computer-generated imagery, Kentridge's low-tech method of drawing for projection imposed severe formal limitations that he turned to advantage. In particular, it is all but impossible to fully erase a charcoal mark on paper, so as the image changes from frame to frame, its former states persist as ghostly traces, producing an effect of palimpsest (layering of images) or of drawing *sous rature*, under erasure – a flickering reality, both there and not there. The world of Kentridge's narratives is surrounded by the aura of its successive states, as when newspapers flutter in a breeze (a recurrent effect) and all their successive positions can still be seen, half-erased, or when a body morphs into a landscape and the body's contours remain visible (Rothberg, 2012, 10–2). In short, Kentridge's technique involves suspension and hesitation, projecting a world in which the old, only half-erased, persists alongside, behind, and inside the new. What better method to capture the experience of living through an interregnum era of transitional justice?

The U.S. sculptor and installation artist Sarah Sze shares Kentridge's low-tech sensibility, as well as his aesthetics of suspension, though she works in three dimensions instead of two. Her work invites, not narrativization, but *inventory* (Norden, 2007, 9), a typically postmodern form of (non-) organization (see "Introduction"). Sze began by assembling accumulations of low, mundane, even abject mass-produced consumer items – toys, push-pins, drinking straws, Q-tips, birthday candles, hard candies, dollar-store and souvenir-shop tchotchkes of all kinds – and marshaling them into patterns and formations. Low in their cultural associations, these accumulations also tended to remain low to the ground, hugging corners, lining up on ledges and shelves, filling storage spaces. Sze's pieces might have "*aspired* to rise" (Danto,

2007, 6), but they didn't actually do so until the late nineties when, given the opportunity to exhibit installations at several major museums and biennials, Sze literally took off. Her pieces, no longer low-lying, became airborne, spiraling upward to the ceiling, climbing walls, even poking through dividers into adjacent spaces. One of them, appropriately entitled (after a Flannery O'Connor story) *Everything That Rises Must Converge* (1999), installed at the Fondation Cartier in Paris, "rises like a whirlwind, crisscrossing the upper part of the space like the aerial apparatus of wires and ropes that acrobats use.... It is as if she had deconstructed the lacy architecture of the Eiffel Tower to create a fragile cat's cradle of flying parts that indeed converge to form a structure as delicate as a spiderweb" (Danto, 2007, 6). A main structural element of many of these "elegantly implausible suspensions" (Norden, 2007, 9) is ladders fabricated from matchsticks laborious glued together. One could imagine a doll or action figure climbing such ladders; alternatively, changing scale, one could think of these spiraling matchstick ladders as models of microscopic DNA molecules (Rushkoff, 2002, 49). Change of scale is integral to Sze's work; indeed, in some of the same works where toy-scale matchstick ladders appear, one also finds real, full-scale aluminum stepladders (e.g., in *Seamless* at the Carnegie International, Pittsburgh, from the same year, 1999). Ladders at any scale, as Danto reminds us, are "light, consisting after all mostly of emptiness united by rungs" (Danto, 2007, 6–7).

Sze's breakthrough installations of the late nineties are, thus, suspensive in several senses. Made of flimsy, lightweight, airy materials (matchsticks on one scale, aluminum stepladders on another), they probe or spiral into the air. Lowly, abject and ephemeral in their cultural associations, they amount almost to "sculpture under erasure," resembling in this respect Kentridge's drawing under erasure. Finally, they keep us hesitating or vacillating between scales – full-size, toy-size, microscopic – leaving us suspended.

Everything rises in Sarah Sze's installations of the late nineties, everything flickers in Kentridge's *Drawings for Projection*, and everything hesitates in Barney's *Cremaster* cycle, but this does not make "high art lite" the dominant period style of the decade. No style dominated, and counter-examples could easily be cited – for instance, Rachel Whiteread's materialization of negative space. Whiteread, associated in the press with the Young British Artists (despite sharing little in common with them), developed a practice of creating casts of empty spaces – the spaces under schoolroom chairs (1994–5), the space of a room (*Ghost*, 1990), finally the interior spaces of an entire demolished working-class house (*House*, 1993), which provoked controversy for its implied critique of gentrification (see Chapter 3). Contrary to Kentridge or Sze, who place materials under erasure, Whiteread materializes the immaterial, turning emptiness into solid blocks of stuff – resin, plaster, concrete. Clearly, not all of the major artworks of the nineties were light, or *lite*; some, such as Whiteread's, were weighty.

7. Planet China

Since its peak period in the 1970s–80s, postmodernism had been associated with a kind of trivial globalism, the globalism of eclectic consumption enabled by transnational corporations and the swift dissemination of cultural fads. Recall Lyotard:

> Eclecticism is the degree zero of contemporary general culture: you listen to reggae; you watch a western; you eat McDonald's at midday and local cuisine at night; you wear Paris perfume in Tokyo and dress retro in Hong Kong . . . . (Lyotard, 1993, 8; see "Introduction").

Such global eclecticism of consumption was a privilege of the Western industrialized world. Arguably, however, in the course of the interregnum of the nineties postmodernism became transnational in less one-sidedly "Western-centric" ways, and merely consumerist globalism was superseded by a something approaching global postmodern culture.

In one sense, the transnational dissemination of postmodernism is simply a consequence of what appeared to be the global triumph of the neoliberal economic order after the collapse of the Soviet block in 1989–90, sweeping postmodernism (its cultural counterpart) along in its wake (Harvey, 2005; see Chapter 3). However, there are other, less economically determined dimensions of the expansion of postmodernism's global scope in the nineties. If the collapse of the Soviet Union confirmed the success of neoliberalism, it also facilitated the emergence of a new kind of transnationalism, one no longer predicated on the division of the planet into three "worlds" – First ("free"), Second (Communist), and Third (underdeveloped/developing) – tensely confronting one another across unbridgeable chasms of difference. What the post-1989 "cosmodern turn" (Moraru, 2009) seemed to promise was neither cosmopolitanism in the old, outdated sense, implying Western privilege and leisure travel, nor globalization in the sense of universal Americanization, but rather the potential for genuine dialogues among cultures.

Cosmodernism is one dimension of post-1989 global culture; "planetarity" is another. Reflecting an ever-widening recognition of our sharing a finite and vulnerable world, the emergent "sense of planet," or of "planetarity," complemented and to some degree served as an alternative to neoliberal economic globalization (Spivak, 2003, 71–102; Heise, 2008). A planetary perspective had been potentially available already for several decades, since at least the early seventies, when widely circulated photographs of our "Blue Planet" viewed from outer space became an emblem of planetary finitude and global solidarity (Heise, 2006). However, the breakdown of Cold War polarization, accompanied by a heightened awareness of acute environmental threats – the risk of nuclear accident, exhaustion of fossil fuels, damage to the ozone layer, and the prospect of global climate change, among others – made the planetary perspective more compelling than ever in the nineties.

Postmodern culture had always been global in scope, if only in the limited sense of including, almost from the outset, at least one culture located on the opposite side of the globe from postmodernism's Western (Euro-American) "heartland"– that of Japan. Japan projected a powerful, worldwide cultural presence throughout the peak era of postmodernism, especially in popular culture, where its electronic consumer goods and product design, the visual styles of its *manga* (graphic-novel) and *anime* (animated-cartoon) genres, and above all its ubiquitous video games and devices (produced by Nintendo, Sega, Sony, and others), flooded the marketplace (see section 3). Complex feedback loops developed between the Western (especially American) and Japanese versions of postmodernism (Tatsumi, 2006). A conspicuous example is the novelist Haruki Murakami, whose novels of the eighties and nineties (from *A Wild Sheep-Chase* [1982] and *Hardboiled Wonderland and the End of the World* [1985] to *The Wind-Up Bird Chronicle* [1995] and beyond) sounded to many like Japanese translations of postmodern American fiction, while Western translations of Murakami's own novels in turned influenced Western postmodernists, and so on, around the feedback loop from West to East and back again (Tatsumi, 2013). Entangled in a similar feedback loop is Araki Yasusada, a Japanese postmodernist poet and Hiroshima survivor, whose notebooks were translated into English in the mid-nineties by Kent Johnson and others, appearing in book form under the title *Doubled Flowering* (1997). Scandalously, it eventually emerged that no such person as "Araki Yasusada" ever existed, and that his poetry, entirely fabricated, was either a hoax perpetrated on the poetry establishment by Kent Johnson or (the alternative interpretation that I favor) a serious postmodern reflection on identity, authenticity, and cross-cultural (mis)apprehension (McHale, 2003 and 2012b).

Japanese economic prowess during postmodernism's peak period provoked anxiety in the West, stimulating imaginative speculation about a future world order dominated by Japan. Such a world order had already been imagined by Philip K. Dick as early as 1962 in his celebrated novel of alternative history, *The Man in the High Castle*, but a preoccupation with the future cultural dominance of Japan only came fully into its own in the cyberpunk fiction of the eighties. Glimpsed in Ridley Scott's highly influential science fiction film *Blade Runner* (1982), the model of a "Japanized" future emerged definitively in William Gibson's "Sprawl" trilogy of the eighties. Anxiety reached a paranoid climax in the episode of "Japan bashing" in American culture, reflected most toxically in Michael Crichton's bestselling thriller *Rising Sun* (1992), adapted in 1993 as a commercially successful film starring Wesley Snipes and Sean Connery.

Crichton's paranoid vision of Japanese criminal conspiracy was a little belated: by 1992, Japan was already deep into the economic crisis that followed in the wake of the bursting of its real-estate bubble beginning in 1990, which would make the nineties a "lost decade" for the Japanese economy. Japan's cultural presence in global popular culture never waned – if anything, its "market share" only grew during the nineties, as reflected for instance in Gibson's second cyberpunk trilogy (the "Bridge" trilogy, 1993, 1996, 1999), which was still Japan-oriented – but Japan no longer seemed poised on the cultural cutting edge.

The place that Japan relinquished on the cutting edge of global postmodernism in the nineties came to be occupied by China. One of the great transformations of the nineties was the reemergence of China on the global stage, not only as an economic and geopolitical powerhouse but also as a cultural presence. During the onset phase of postmodernism in the West, and into the peak phase, China was isolated and inwardly oriented, convulsed by the Cultural Revolution that Mao Zedong initiated in 1966. However, this did not prevent Western intellectuals and artists from imagining a postmodern China tailored to their own needs. A particularly egregious case of "Chinese dreams" was the fascination with Maoism on the part of the circle of writers and theorists associated with the Parisian avant-garde journal *Tel Quel* in the late sixties and early seventies, climaxing in a pilgrimage to China by a group of Telquelians (including Julia Kristeva, Philippe Sollers and Roland Barthes) in spring 1974 (Hayot, 2007). Typical, too, though less faddish and more self-critical, is the L=A=N=G=U=A=G=E writer Bob Perelman's poem "China" (1981), which Jameson identified as characteristically postmodern (see Chapter 3) and which at least acknowledges, in its enigmatic and oblique way, that imagining China presents a *problem*. Similar in spirit is John Adams's historical opera in the minimalist style (see Chapter 3), *Nixon in*

China (1987), which dramatizes, with unstable irony, abundant absurdity and an undercurrent of violence, the American president's 1972 visit to Mao's China.

The China of 1972 or of 1974 (when the Telquelians went there) had not yet been exposed to Western postmodernism, but that situation had changed by 1987, the year of Adams's opera. Dating from the "New Period" of 1978–89, China's "discovery" of postmodernism was a process in which a crucial catalyzing role was played by Fredric Jameson, whose 1985 lectures in Beijing and Shenzhen introduced Chinese academics and intellectuals to the concept of postmodernism (Liu, 2004, 111; Wang, 2010, 127). Chinese academic discourse of postmodern theory stimulated translation of Western postmodern literary "classics" by Barth, Beckett, Borges, Calvino, Márquez, Pynchon, Robbe-Grillet, and others, which in turn stimulated development of an indigenous postmodern fiction (Wang, 1997, 2010 and 2013; Liu, 2004, 102–26; Fokkema, 2008). Coincidentally, in the same year as Jameson's seminal lectures, 1985, the American Pop artist Robert Rauschenberg brought a globe-trotting show of his postmodern visual art to Beijing, stimulating an upsurge among local Chinese artists of avant-garde projects incorporating "found" materials and objects (Andrews, 2008, 33). The postmodern avant-garde moment in Chinese literature and visual art was short-lived, brought to an abrupt and premature end by the violent suppression of the popular democracy moment at Tiananmen Square in June 1989 – the same year as the other events that, in the Soviet bloc and elsewhere, signaled the onset of the interregnum phase of postmodernism.

Ends, even violent and bloody ones, can also be new beginnings (as we have seen elsewhere). Despite the Tiananmen crackdown, even in part because of it, by the later nineties the process of cultural postmodernization had advanced to the point where China was re-exporting postmodernism to the West, mainly in the form of visual art, which enjoyed an international vogue. If one consequence of the suppression of the democracy movement was to stifle avant-garde practice at home, or redirect it into different channels, another consequence was to drive Chinese avant-garde artists into exile abroad, to France (Huang Yong Ping), North America (Gu Wenda, Xu Bing), or Japan (Cao Guo-Qiang). (The most conspicuous of the dissident artists, Ai Weiwei, had actually lived in the United States throughout most of the New Period and the Tiananmen Square crisis, only returning to China in 1993.) The expatriation of the avant-gardists led, in turn, paradoxically enough, to heightened awareness of, and appreciation for, contemporary Chinese arts in the Western artworld. A series of high-visibility exhibitions of work by Chinese artists in exile throughout the nineties, culminating in the

1999 Venice Biennale (where Huang Yong Ping represented France and Cao Guo-Qiang received the prestigious Golden Lion award), coupled with the activity of a handful of Western collectors (including the Swiss Uli Sigg and the Belgians Guy and Myriam Ullens; Smith, 2011, 165–6), created a platform for Chinese art in the West. When, in the course of the nineties, the exiles began to return to China, as some did, they had already gained a foothold in the Western art market, where contemporary Chinese art boomed.

The vogue for contemporary Chinese art in the Western artworld is one symptom of China's integration into global postmodernism, but hardly the only one. For another symptom of China's planetary cultural reach, we might revisit Western speculative fiction where, in the course of the nineties, fascination with a "Japan-centric" future (typical of the cyberpunks of the eighties) gave way to a different thought experiment, one involving speculation about an alternative global order based on Chinese cultural dominance – a "China-centric" future. Among the most ambitious and provocative of the China-centric models of globalization was the British science-fiction writer David Wingrove's cycle of eight immense novels appearing under the collective title of *Chung Kuo* (1990–97). Wingrove imagines a future Earth entirely covered by seven continent-spanning mega-cities, each governed by one of seven ethnically Chinese co-emperors: planet China. Chinese civilization dominates everywhere, having subjugated or eradicated all other world civilizations, including the European and American cultures. Wingrove's fiction is not immune from exoticizing Orientalism, and there are certainly traces in it of the kind of paranoid fantasies that characterized the "Japan-bashing" episode of the early nineties, but redirected toward China. Nevertheless, Wingrove's sympathies seem evenly divided between the Chinese overlords, struggling to maintain order in a world on the verge of chaotic breakdown, and the submerged populations, some of whom are beginning to resist the Chinese world order.

A kind of capstone to the development of alternative world orders in the nineties is Kim Stanley Robinson's alternative-history novel, *The Years of Rice and Salt* (2002), where Robinson imagines an alternative past in which the fourteenth-century pandemic of bubonic plague destroyed, not a third of the population of Europe (as it did in real-world history), but 90 percent of it. World history, in this alternative reality, develops without the Europeans or the Euro-Americans. Thus, it falls to the Chinese to discover the New World; Renaissance science emerges first in the cities of the Silk Road, where the Islamic and Chinese cultural spheres overlap; the nineteenth-century Industrial Revolution begins in South India instead of Great Britain; the Great War of the early twentieth century is fought not among the European powers, but between China and Islam; and so on.

Robinson's thought experiment about a world without Europe reflects the interregnum sensibility, but arrives belatedly in 2002, after the events of September 11, 2001, which effectively put an end to the interregnum period. In the aftermath of 9/11, the depolarized world of the post–Cold War interregnum was rapidly *repolarized* – to the manifest relief of some, who welcomed a return to the manichaean certainties of a new (or renewed) "clash of civilizations," albeit one differently oriented than the old one. *The Years of Rice and Salt* stands as a monument to the monstrous and sublime experience of alternativity and multidirectionality of the in-between years, foreclosed by the twenty-first century's War on Terror.

ANGELS IN AMERICA

1. Angels Everywhere

"There are no angels in America," says Louis Ironson, a character in Tony Kushner's two-part epic drama *Angels in America* (*Millennium Approaches* [1990]; *Perestroika* [1992]) (Kushner, 1995, 98). A religious skeptic and political progressive who has just abandoned Prior, his AIDS-stricken lover, Louis is wrong about angels (among other things). In the world of the play itself, Prior will soon be visited by an angel, while in the real world of 1990–91, when the play premiered, angels were proliferating throughout popular culture.

On December 27, 1993, *Time* magazine featured a cover story on the ubiquity of angels, and of course *Time*'s imprimatur meant that angels had definitely "arrived." Scores of popular angel books were already in print by then, with titles like *Touched by Angels, An Angel to Watch Over Me, Brush of an Angel's Wing, Where Angels Walk, Angels: An Endangered Species* (a misleading title), and, from the Reverend Billy Graham himself, one simply entitled *Angels*. Harold Bloom dates the onset of the publishing boom in angel books to 1990, when Sophy Burnham's *A Book of Angels* became a surprise bestseller (Bloom, 2007, 4). The dating is symbolically appropriate, since the pop-cultural fascination with angels seems to be a nineties phenomenon.

And not just a publishing phenomenon, but a mass-media one. Rex Hauck's book *Angels: The Mysterious Messengers* (1994) was advertised as the "basis of the NBC television special." The CBS television series *Touched by an Angel* debuted that same year. Angels also thrived at the movies: *Angels in the Outfield* (1994) remade a popular 1951 film by the same name; *Michael,* released in time for the Christmas season of 1996, featured John Travolta as an earth-bound angel; *City of Angels,* a Hollywood remake of Wim Wenders' *Der Himmel über Berlin* (*Wings of Desire*), starring Nicholas Cage and Meg Ryan, appeared in 1998; and so on.

"Angels Everywhere," ran the headline of a *New York Times* editorial published on Sunday, September 4, 1994. Back in the nineties, angels used to be everywhere – if not everywhere in reality, then at least everywhere in popular culture, especially in the United States. In a daily comic strip dated March 16, 1995, Calvin says to his tiger playmate, Hobbes, "I think angels are everywhere." Hobbes replies, "You do?" Calvin says, "They're on calendars, books, greeting cards ... almost every product imaginable," and Hobbes, ever ready with an ironic last word, says, "What a spiritual age we live in." As if to confirm Hobbes's insight, the retailer Victoria's Secret in the summer of 1997 introduced a new line of "Angel" undergarments, and the winged runway model in skimpy lingerie remains a major marketing device for the company. What a spiritual age, indeed.

Popular culture's obsession with angels might be said symbolically to have culminated midway through the decade, on or about February 7, 1995. On that date, Judge Lance Ito, presiding over O. J. Simpson's intensively televised trial for murder – advertised at the time as "the trial of the century" – reprimanded prosecutor Marcia Clark for wearing an angel pin similar to one worn by the relatives of the victim, Nicole Brown Simpson. Prosecutor Clark removed the pin, but she might have argued, with some justice, that *everybody* was wearing such pins nowadays. In an editorial cartoon published later that month, the cartoonist Jeff Stahler depicts one angel admiring a fellow angel's jewelry: "Ooh a Marcia Clark pin," she coos.

So closely were angels associated with popular culture in the nineties that they came to serve as a sort of shorthand in debates about popular culture itself. The *Times* editorial writer of 1994 called them "a sweet antidote to the nastiness of most popular culture." A colleague, the *Times* reviewer Michiko Kakutani, writing in the *New York Times Magazine* for September 22, 1996, took the opposite view, complaining that angels were symptomatic of the progressive dilution and commercialization of high culture: "The fierce, awe-inspiring cherubim of the Old Testament," she writes,

> gave way to the beautiful angels of Renaissance painting, which gave way to the somewhat-less-dignified angels of [the eighteenth-century painter] Poussin, which gave way to the bumbling angels of 1940's movies, which gave way to Michael Landon in [the television series] *Highway to Heaven* [1984–89]. If that were not enough, we now have cute, plump cherubs adorning everything from pillows to earrings.

And pins like Marcia Clark's, one might add.

But it would be a mistake to assume that angels were restricted to popular culture in the nineties, as these sorts of comments seem to imply. In fact, angels in the nineties were thoroughly postmodern in their capacity to *cross over* between low and high cultural spheres (see Chapter 3). For one thing, angels "enjoyed a special ubiquity" in serious poetry of the decade (Gilbert, 2001, 240). By way of confirmation, Roger Gilbert lists no fewer than twenty-five books of American poetry published in the nineties with "angel" in their titles. Angels also came to be associated with the discourse surrounding the AIDS epidemic, a phenomenon that Kushner's *Angels in America* reflects and reinforces (Lather and Smithies, 1997). The angel vogue yielded at least one bona fide masterpiece of public art, in Antony Gormley's "Angel of the North" (1998), a monumental steel sculpture of an angel, wings extended horizontally, overlooking Gateshead in northeast England (Jones, 2010, 29, 30; Smith, 2011, 56).

The angel of the nineties is a thoroughly ambiguous figure, simultaneously high and low, avant-garde and pop, sublime and sentimental. This ambiguity is captured by Don DeLillo's short story "The Angel Esmeralda" (1994), about a collective vision (or delusion) of transfiguraton, in which an entire community sees (or thinks it sees) the face of a murdered girl in a billboard advertisement for orange juice. The story would later be incorporated in DeLillo's major postmodern megafiction of the late nineties, *Underworld* (1997) (see Chapter 3). The same ambiguity colors Kushner's *Angels in America,* which mingles campy pop-culture allusions – "*Very* Steven Spielberg," exclaims Prior at the special lighting effects that herald the angel's entrance (Kushner, 1995, 124) – with a sublime serious-ness appropriate to a public-health crisis of catastrophic proportions. If the angel is a crossover figure, and in that sense a signifier of postmodernism, then *Angels in America*, as canonically a postmodern work as *Gravity's Rainbow,* is one of the crossing points where the angel passes back and forth between cultural realms – and between worlds.

2. Gravity's Angels

The angels of postmodernism are hardly uniform. In some varieties of postmo-dernism, the angel has been subjected to ironic deflation and an iconoclastic impulse. This is the case in Gabriel García Márquez's story "A Very Old Man with Enormous Wings" (1972), whose exhausted and debased angel figure recurs, fifteen years later, in Patrick McGrath's gothic-horror angel story, "The Angel" (1987), then in a music video by the indie-rock band R.E.M. for their aptly titled song, "Losing My Religion" (1991). Donald Barthelme's angels, in his mock essay "On Angels" (1970), are sadly disoriented, having been "left ... in a strange position" by the death of God:

> They were overtaken suddenly by a fundamental question. One can attempt to imagine that moment. How did they *look* at the instant the question invaded them, flooding the angelic consciousness, taking hold with terrifying force. The question was, "What are angels?"
> New to questioning, unaccustomed to terror, unskilled in aloneness, the angels (we assume) fell into despair. (Barthelme, 1982, 135)

This ironic and iconoclastic strand in postmodern angel fiction persists right down to the eighties and beyond, in novels such as Milan Kundera's *The Book of Laughter and Forgetting* (1978) and Stanley Elkin's *The Living End* (1980), and in the surfictionist Steve Katz's short story "Mongolian Whiskey" (1984), where the pearly gates of heaven are guarded by winged angel-dogs.

It is, however, not irony, or not irony alone, but mainly *sublimity* that charac-terizes postmodernist representations of angels during the major phase, 1973–90, in landmark works such as Thomas Pynchon's *Gravity's Rainbow* (1973), James Merrill's long poem *The Changing Light at Sandover* (1976–1982), Joseph McElroy's novel *Women and Men* (1987), Wim Wenders' and Peter Handke's film *Der Himmel über Berlin* (*Wings of Desire*, 1987), Salman Rushdie's *The Satanic Verses* (1988), the Dutch novelist Harry Mulisch's *De ontdekking van de hemel* (*The Discovery of Heaven*, 1992), and Kushner's *Angels in America*. None of these texts is devoid of irony, it goes without saying; *The Satanic Verses* in particular seems, on balance, more ironic than sublime in its treatment of angels. However, all of them, despite or indeed because of their irony, display that peculiarly postmodern sublimity that Lyotard characterized as the aspiration to invoke the unpresentable (Lyotard, 1993, 12–6).

In Merrill's verse trilogy, for example, the poet and his partner David Jackson receive communications from otherworldy beings by means of a Ouija board (see Chapter 3). The world that the angels and spirits of the dead reveal to Merrill and Jackson is organized in successively higher levels, at each level of which Merrill and Jackson receive instruction from a different mentor, only to be "handed off" to a being of a still higher order for initiation into the secrets of the next level (McHale, 2004b, 23–32). However high they ascend, however, they never actually gain direct access to these higher realms, which remain out of reach, evoked only by the words picked out on the Ouija board. In McElroy's *Women and Men* (1987), by contrast, angels seem to hover above the characters, monitoring them from outside, slipping from one to another in defiance of time and space, and sometimes *dipping into* their minds. They behave, in other words, much like the omniscient narrators of nineteenth-century fiction (McHale, 1992, 203–5).

Gravity's Rainbow, perhaps surprisingly for so technologically oriented a novel, is profoundly preoccupied with the occult and otherworldly, including angels. The sublime here is technological, in something like Jameson's sense (see Chapter 3), embodied in the V-2 rocket and its associated technologies, but it is also angelic; one type of sublimity mirrors the other. Just as the wartime world of *Gravity's Rainbow* is dominated by military, governmental, and corporate bureaucracies, so too there appear to be "bureaucracies of the other side" (Pynchon, 1973, 411) that govern the adjoining spirit world. Inhabited by spirits of the dead, Pynchon's other world is also the realm of angels, and their incursions into our own world, sometimes violent, are always terrifying. Typical of these manifestations is the miles-high angel glimpsed by British pilots over Lübeck during a bombing raid, harbinger of the subsequent V-2 rocket blitz of London (Pynchon, 1973, 150–1, 214–5). (See Hohmann, 1986; Hume, 1987; McLaughlin, 1988; Eddins,1990.)

The performance artist Laurie Anderson, a crossover star of the eighties (see Chapter 3), seized on this angel motif in Pynchon and made it into a major motif of her own music and performances, notably in a song called "Gravity's Angel" (1984), which she dedicated to Pynchon (see McHale, 1998):

> Last night I woke up. Saw this angel. He flew in my window.
> And he said: Girl, pretty proud of yourself, huh?
> And I looked around and said: Who me?
> And he said: The higher you fly, the faster you fall. He said:
> Send it up. Watch it rise. See it fall. Gravity's rainbow.
> Send it up. Watch it rise. See it fall. Gravity's angel.

Figure 5. Robert Yarber, *The Tender and the Damned* (1985). Oil and
acrylic on canvas 72 in. × 132 in. (183 cm × 335 cm).
Courtesy of Sonnabend Gallery, New York. Photo: Jon Abbott.

"Gravity's rainbow" is the parabolic trajectory traced by a ballistic missile; "gravity's angel" is the rocket's sublime Other. Subsequently Anderson would contribute atmospheric music, under the title "Angel Fragments," to the soundtrack of Wim Wenders' *Wings of Desire*, going on to produce a CD of songs entitled *Strange Angels* (1989) and an angel-filled touring show, *Empty Places* (1989–90).

At around the same time, angels begin appearing in some of the most characteristic visual art of the eighties, including that of the graffiti-artist Keith Haring, the photographers Duane Michaels and Joyce Tenneson, the German Neoexpressionist Anselm Kiefer, and the American painter Robert Yarber, among others (see Chapter 3). Yarber's characteristic images of flight and free-fall (see section 5) include the mock-religious painting "Announcement" (1992), in which a transparent, miniature angel hovers over a restaurant patio. Both more ambitious and more ambiguous is his painting "The Tender and the Damned" (1985) (see Figure 5), showing a woman throwing herself from a hotel balcony – or taking flight? The suicide's nightgown, billowing around her, appears in the mirror's reflection to take the shape of a pair of angel wings. Is this an ironic image, or a sublime one?

By the time of Kushner's *Angels in America*, then, sublimity was already well established as a viable stance for postmodern representations of angels, whether colored by irony or not. Given its subject matter – gay life in America in the face of the AIDS epidemic – *Angels in America* could hardly avoid a certain sobriety, mingled with its camp gestures. Kushner evokes the unpresentable – death itself, the "final frontier" – by figuring it in the violent manifestation of an angel to Prior, a gay man afflicted with AIDS. Prior eventually discovers that the angels are merely bureaucrats and administrators, like the ones in *Gravity's Rainbow*, and that their mission has been thrown into confusion by the departure of God. They blame God's abandonment of them on the human race, for it is from observing human beings that God learned how to change. Visiting heaven, Prior witnesses the angels' disorganization and demoralization.

Nevertheless, *Angels in America* is not, like Barthelme's "On Angels" twenty years earlier, an ironic text in which the angel figure is drained of its meaning and power. Rather, as Kushner insists in his stage directions to Part Two, *Perestroika* (premiered 1992), "the Angel is immensely august, serious, and dangerously powerful *always*" (Kushner 1995, 142) and never to be played for laughs: a sublime angel, after all.

At the end of the Part One, *Millennium Approaches* (1991), when the angel, long anticipated and long delayed, finally does manifest itself, it literally blasts through the ceiling of Prior's room, scattering debris everywhere, administering a ferocious ontological shock. "A membrane has broken," Kushner writes; "there is disarray and debris" (Kushner, 1995, 142). This violent moment, apparently echoing a dream that Franz Kafka recorded in his diary for June 25, 1914 (Hobson, 2007, 498), also evokes the ontological shock of that moment in November 1989 when sledge hammers broke through the Berlin Wall, and Cold War dualism gave way, if only temporarily, to the possibility of plurality.

3. Close Encounters

Postmodern angels are everywhere by the beginning of nineties, but what do they signify? Hypotheses abound: maybe they compensate for what is perceived to be a loss of spirituality in contemporary culture, or they offer an alternative to religious orthodoxy more palatable to New Age sensibilities; maybe they reflect anxiety about the approaching millennium, only a few years away, or conversely maybe they capture the longing for apocalyptic change and renewal. All of these factors, no doubt, have something to do with the proliferation of angels in the nineties. However, I want to highlight two particular meanings of nineties angels that seem to underwrite all the other possibilities. The first of these is captured in that image from *Angels in America* when the angel bursts through the ceiling of the room: the experience of ontological shock.

Ontological shock is explored in a remarkable but little-known novella from the mid-eighties by Harold Brodkey, entitled simply "Angel" (1985). It reports the apparition of an angel to a few dozen assorted persons in Harvard Yard on October 25, 1951, "a little after 3 o'clock." Reflecting on the significance of his angelic encounter, the unnamed narrator resorts to negative characterizations: the angel was not "a policeman of any kind, or a messenger exactly," nor did it "exemplify or ratify any human dream in the sense of what one dreams for oneself except in being not like us and closer to The Great Power or The Great Illumination" (Brodkey, 1988, 575–6). He continues:

> I could not see myself in It or imagine It as related to me in any way but that of superior power or perhaps of Its Hiddenness as a Personal Reality on the other side of a metamorphosis that was not occurring at this instant, that was not bringing me any closer to the possible thing of It and me embracing each other at least partly by *my* will. Just as being a man had been hidden from me on the other side of the sharp ridge of puberty when I was still ten years old, so The Angel existed on the far side of a metamorphosis involving Beauty and Goodness, strength and knowledge. . . . (Brodkey, 1985, 578)

The only positive characterization the narrator can offer is that the Angel was "a marker" (Brodkey, 1985, 575), standing for the very *existence* of a hidden world on the "far side" of metamorphosis (see Cacciari, 1994, 2, 4). The Angel represents ontological plurality, the fact of their being more worlds than this one, and its apparition imparts a shock of a particular kind – what I called ontological shock.

What we glimpse in Brodkey's novella is the cultural logic of angels. Angels are figures for what Jameson once memorably called the "reality-pluralism" of postmodernism, "a coexistence not even of multiple and alternate worlds so much as of fuzzy sets and semiautonomous subsystems whose overlap is perceptually maintained like hallucinogenic depth planes in a space of many dimensions" (Jameson 1991, 372). Angels signify the existence, or at least the possibility, of alternative worlds, in an extended sense – alternative subcultures, life styles, values systems, enclaves of meaning, and psychological realities (see Chapter 2). The shock that they induce is identical with the experience identified by the controversial Harvard psychologist John E. Mack, who coined the term "ontological shock" to characterize the testimony of people who claimed to have been abducted by unidentified flying objects (UFOs). Whether the encounter is with angels or aliens, the experience is apparently similar: what one undergoes is the shock of recognizing that there are other worlds besides this one, other orders of being beyond our own (Mack, 1994, 26, 44; see Damon, 1997, 207).

Reports of alien abduction, such as those Mack investigated, are a postmodern phenomenon, dating mainly from the eighties and nineties. During the first wave of UFO sightings in late forties and fifties, some enthusiasts claimed to have been contacted, either physically or by telepathy, by aliens who invariably bore messages about world peace, the dangers of nuclear power, and the like. This messenger function of aliens faded somewhat from the popular imagination during the sixties and seventies, when it was supplanted by a perception of aliens as threatening, and by an obsession with government conspiracies to withhold information about UFOs. Next came abductions, and the claims by abductees to have been examined, experimented upon, or even impregnated by aliens (see Mack, 1994; Peebles, 1994).

The language that the "contactees" of the fifties and the "abductees" of the eighties and nineties used to describe their "close encounters" often resembled the language of angelic encounters, and the interchangeability of angels and aliens has become a commonplace of the postmodern era (see Thompson, 1991). The association of angels with aliens dates at least from Eric Van Däniken's eccentric claims, in the early seventies, about evidence of alien visitations in the Bible (Jones, 2010, 89–91). Popular culture, however, had recognized the angelic dimension of alien encounters all along, as reflected in Hollywood movies such as *The Day the Earth Stood Still* (1951), Kubrick's *2001: A Space Odyssey* (1968), Spielberg's *Close Encounters of the Third Kind* (1977) and *E.T.* (1982), and even (in an undersea variation) James Cameron's and Gale Ann Hurd's *The Abyss* (1989). It is revealing that in the course of a single year, 1996, the actor John Travolta starred in a pair of films, one about a man who has experienced an alien encounter (*Phenomenon*), the other about an archangel on a mission to our world (*Michael*). From Hollywood's point of view, evidently, the two types of encounter, alien and angelic, amount to variations on a theme. It is hardly surprising that one of the popular angel books of the nineties is subtitled (what else?) *Close Encounters of the Celestial Kind*.

Subtler is the association implied by the MTV video for David Bowie's song "Day-In, Day-Out" (1987), in which angels are shown videotaping the everyday struggles of a young Chicano couple, while Bowie himself sings from the sidelines. The knowledgeable viewer automatically connects Bowie with the figure of the alien, for throughout the seventies he had been associated with extraterrestrials, as reflected in various ways by his alter egos Major Tom, Ziggy Stardust, and above all *The Man Who Fell to Earth* in Nicholas Roeg's 1976 film by that title. The "man" of Roeg's film, played by Bowie, is a visitor from another star system, but he behaves in many respects like angels do in angel narratives. A misfit among earthlings, he intervenes in the lives of various individuals; he is a kind of messenger, bearing disturbing knowledge; his coming threatens to disrupt the social order; and, like many angel of the nineties and before, he succumbs to earthly and fleshly temptations.

What generally remains subtextual in Hollywood films and MTV videos emerges explicitly in literary science fictions such as C. S. Lewis's *Out of the Silent Planet* (1938), Doris Lessing's *Shikasta* (1979), Joanna Russ's novella "Souls" (1984), John Fowles' *A Maggot* (1985), and Pat Cadigan's short story "Angel" (1987). In all these texts, angelic apparitions are rationalized in terms of alien "close encounters" – or vice versa, in Lewis's case, where aliens are "supernaturalized" as angels.

Angels *are* aliens – or at least, angels and aliens are functionally equivalent in popular culture (Bloom, 2007, 59). The ontological shock induced by close encounters with either of these figures of Otherness is sometimes traumatic, at other times reassuring or even redemptive. The full range of "close encounter" experiences can be found in popular culture of the nineties from, at one pole, the euphoric encounters reported in many popular angel books to, at the other, the dysphoric alien encounters that were the hallmark of one of the decade's most characteristic TV series, *The X-Files* (1993–2002). With its weekly narratives of monsters, supernatural manifestations, and alien abductions, what experience did *The X-Files* reflect, over and over again, if not that of ontological shock?

4. Annunciations

One other thing that *The X-Files* captured was the experience of postmodern *communication* – the exhilaration, but also the frustrations, of *being connected* all the time, everywhere. Week after week in the middle and late nineties, the FBI agent Fox Mulder and his partner, Dana Scully, communicated using the then-cutting-edge technology of mobile telephones, enabling the scene of their investigation to be, in effect, in two places at once but also often *separating* them at a moment when, had they been together, a mystery might have been solved. This preoccupation with electronic communication is appropriate in the context of close encounters of alien or angelic kinds, because both aliens and angels are often *bearers of messages*. After all, it was the angel Gabriel, who, according to scripture, delivered the most consequential of all messages when he announced to Mary that she would bear Jesus (in the scene parodied in the Yarber painting I mentioned earlier), and it was the same angel who dictated the *Koran* to the Prophet Mohammed. It is only fitting, then, that Gabriel, the angel of the Annunciation, is also the patron saint of messengers, postal workers, and telecommunications professionals (Jones, 2010, 62).

Angels, according to the French theorist Michel Serres, are figures of communication and information flow (Serres, 1995). "Figures of mediation," they travel "between distinct spheres while allowing each to communicate with the others" (Gilbert, 2001, 245). Throughout the postmodern decades, they are associated with *media*, especially electronic media, since it is the flow of electrons that most closely mimics the speed traditionally attributed to angels: "The ethereal bodies of angels traveled at the speed of thought," writes Serres; "their [media] successors travel at the speed of light" (Serres, 1995, 154). Only rarely are angels associated with "old media" such as film, though Robert Coover does allow the lonesome projectionist in his story, "The Phantom of the Movie Palace" (1987), to imagine that he glimpses angels up on the big screen:

> as the footage rolls by, music swelling, guns blazing, and reels rattling, he seems to see angels up there, or something like angels, . . . aglow with an eerie light not of this world. (Coover, 1988, 17–18)

However, this association is somewhat misleading, since the projectionist's medium is actually more like TV than film; in his abundant downtime, he manipulates the films he projects, cutting, pasting, and layering them in ways more akin to channel surfing with a TV remote than to anything that could actually be done with film. Moreover, the reason he is alone in the movie palace, and free to do what he pleases with the movies, is because audiences have abandoned moviegoing for the pleasures of staying home to watch TV. In other words, the angels glimpsed up there on the screen are really affiliated with television more than they are with the movies.

Television and videotape are the media with which postmodern angels are most intimately associated. Angels are televisual; in a sense, television is their natural habitat. The narrator of Barthelme's "On Angels" reports seeing a "famous angel" interviewed on a television talk show: "his garments glistened as if with light" (Barthelme, 1982, 137). Serres associates TV news with the angelus bell of traditional Catholic Europe, which commemorates the Annunciation three times a day; after all, he observes, news anchors, too, are "announcers," just like the angel of the Annunciation was (Serres, 1995, 154). Don DeLillo's *White Noise* (1985), a novel saturated with television from start to finish, has nothing to do with angels until, in an abrupt swerve just before the end, its protagonist, a college professor who up until now has never shown the slightest interest in otherworldly matters, inexplicably insists on discussing angels with a skeptical nun. Salman Rushdie, in an interview from 1989 (before the Ayatollah's *fatwah* against him), similarly juxtaposes angels and TV. When his interviewer remarks pertinently that "the late twentieth century [is] a world where TV is a medium as much as an angel is," Rushdie responds in the affirmative: "the television in the corner is a kind of miraculous being, bringing a kind of revelation ... television is what we now have for archangels" (Rushdie, 1989, 18). It is surely no coincidence that angelhood and television are juxtaposed and equated in Rushdie's *The Satanic Verses* (1988), where one of the major characters, a Bollywood movie star, is transformed into the angel Gibreel, while his friend and antagonist, once a voiceover actor for British radio and TV but now transformed into a demon, becomes a TV addict. "They say that heaven is like TV," Laurie Anderson sings in "Strange Angels" (1989):

> A perfect little world
> That doesn't really need you.
> And everything there is made of light.

The chorus goes: "Strange angels. Singin just for me."

We have already seen how eager commercial television was to capitalize on the angel craze, from *Angels: The Mysterious Messengers* on NBC and *Touched by an Angel* on CBS to the angel-pin controversy during O. J.'s televised "trial of the century," and beyond. Also symptomatic is the proliferation of angel imagery in MTV videos of the eighties and nineties, including some of the most memorable of that era, such as R.E.M.'s "Losing My Religion" and David Bowie's "Day-In, Day-Out," both mentioned earlier. The association of angels with video is a feature even of an art film such as Sally Potter's *Orlando* (1992), based on Virginia Woolf's novel. At the end of Potter's film, an angel, played by the gay pop-star Jimmy Sommerville, serenades Orlando from a treetop and is captured by Orlando's daughter on a video camera; the singer's performance is relayed to us as a video image – in effect, a music-video angel inserted into an art-house movie. The art world's embrace of angels on video reaches a kind of climax in the first years of the new century, with a large-scale, multi-screen museum installation by the video artist Bill Viola, called *Five Angels of the Millennium* (2001).

Angels as message bearers are figures of mediation, but this also means that they are *intermediaries*, passing *between* spheres. Consequently, their messenger function also entails an overrunning or violation of ontological boundaries – border violations of the sort that occurs when the Angel bursts through Prior's ceiling. Angels, writes Peter Lamborn Wilson, are "inhabitants of an intermediate world, and the function of messenger is *par excellence* that of intermediary.... They move between earth and heaven, like the figures in Jacob's vision of the ladder [in *Genesis,* Chapter 28]" (Wilson, 1980, 37). Serres concurs: "*Between* designates precisely the space in which angels operate." He continues:

> As beings with a double nature, pedagogues, guides and cherubims enable us to see the differences between worlds, and in doing so they stitch together the unity of the universe. (Serres, 1995, 165–6)

So messenger-angels are also figures of ontological difference, and in this respect, too, they are compatible with television. For, like angels, TV, in its own way, also contributes to the experience of plurality of worlds, the reality-pluralism that is one of the symptoms of postmodernism (McHale, 1992, 130–1). Television opens windows onto other spaces, other realities, so that any space we share with a TV screen is already "otherworldly." Commercial TV, characterized by its "flow" of programming and advertising spots (see Williams, 1974), is essentially plural in structure, projecting from moment to moment worlds radically different in kind, inhabited by beings of differing ontological status, governed by different sociological and psychological norms and even, in some cases, by different physical laws. Television's built-in ontological plurality can be heightened still further by multiplying the number of screens in a room – like Nam June Paik in his video installations or the alien in Roeg's *The Man Who Fell to Earth* (Jameson, 1991, 31), or for that matter like your neighborhood sports bars – or by using the remote to skip from channel to channel, world to world; channel surfing is surfing among worlds. Television, then, like angels and aliens, is a figure of ontological plurality – of the plurality of worlds (McHale, 1992, 126). Angels, aliens, and television all belong together, and in the eighties and nineties they are regularly found in each other's company.

By the end of the nineties, angels had begun to migrate from television onto the Internet. Angel-oriented sites have proliferated on the Web, to the point that, by 2010, Jones could cite a figure of 287,000,000 hits for an Internet search using the search term "angel" (Jones, 2010, xii). Inevitably, given the association of angels with telecommunication, at least one science-fiction novel projects a future in which angels take up residence in cyberspace: *Archangel Protocol* (2001), the first of a quartet of novels by Lyda Morehouse, a second-generation cyberpunk novelist. Morehouse's online angels are ultimately exposed as constructs, software programs installed by a renegade hacker to terrorize and manipulate Internet users – a sort of updated malware. However, as if to compensate for her debunking of the cyberspace angels, Morehouse also populates her world with a number of *real* angels, whose mission is to counter the false online ones. Her protagonist even has an affair with one of them – not the first time, and undoubtedly not the last, when a close encounter of an angelic kind has taken a carnal turn.

5. The Last of the Angels?

Having debuted in 1994, near the height of the angel craze, the once-popular CBS television series *Touched by an Angel* went off the air in April 2003, indicating, perhaps, that the era of the angels was drawing to a close. Only a few months later, however, the angels returned when, in December 2003, the cable network HBO (Home Box Office) screened a television version of Tony Kushner's play *Angels in America* in two 3-hour installments, to great popular and critical acclaim. *Angels in America* earned its writer (Kushner), director (Mike Nichols), and cast (including Al Pacino and Meryl Streep) no fewer than eleven Emmy Awards. Nevertheless, what the belated success of *Angels in America* on HBO actually demonstrated was not so much the continuing relevance of angels as their obsolescence. Though set, like the play itself, in the mid-eighties, the show's reflection on the AIDS epidemic still felt relevant and compelling; what did *not* seem so relevant any longer, however, was its angel material, which by the beginning of the new millennium had come to seem dated, a relic of a vanished era of popular taste, now consigned to the historical past.

Have we seen the last of the angels? Hardly. Neither orthodox Catholicism, Mormonism nor Islam, nor New Age belief for that matter, seem at all disposed to relinquish their belief in angels, or their angel iconography, and the figure of the angel can still be counted on to succeed in the commercial marketplace – though perhaps not so often or so resoundingly as in the nineties. Danielle Trussoni's bestselling novel, *Angelology* (2010), is a case in point. The first volume of a trilogy – the second, *Angelopolis*, appeared in 2013; a third is promised – *Angelology* capitalizes not only on the angel craze but on a whole range of successful genre formulas, including the fantasy novel of education (in the vein of J. K. Rowlings' "Harry Potter" series), the gothic "dark romance" (in the mold of the *Twilight* series of vampire novels), and theological conspiracy fiction (as popularized by Dan Brown's *Da Vinci Code*). As far as its angel motif is concerned, the novel is an encyclopedic compendium of angel lore – literally so, incorporating encyclopedia entries, lectures by learnéd angelologists, and other thinly veiled opportunities for conveying large quantities of background information about angels. It is the volume of this information, and its weak integration with the foreground events of the novel, that suggests how derivative *Angelology* is, and how belatedly it appears in the history of angels in postmodern culture. As with *Angels in America* on HBO, what Trussoni's novel mainly demonstrates is the exhaustion of the angel motif, not its continuing viability.

For, despite such belated returns of the nineties angel vogue, angels have been much less conspicuous since 2001, in popular culture and the avant-garde alike. In the new millennium, the figure of the angel has increasingly been displaced in popular culture by that of the *vampire* and the *zombie* – both of which, of course, were already present during the postmodern decades (e.g., Anne Rice's vampires, *Buffy the Vampire Slayer* on television, George Romero's zombie movies). When the population of angels begins to wane, or they lapse into relative inconspicuousness, as they seem to have done since 2001, then perhaps we are passing out of postmodernism into whatever comes after it (see Chapter 5).

The presence of angels in the last decades of the twentieth century served as something like a litmus test of postmodernism: where there was an abundance of angel, there was postmodernism; now that the angelic presence is waning, perhaps so is postmodernism. Maybe we are experiencing the waning of contemporary culture's openness to, or perhaps of its *need* for, the kind of ontological shock that angels were the agents of – the disruptive revelation of the plurality of worlds. Perhaps we have become acclimated to postmodern reality-pluralism, to the fact of plurality of worlds; perhaps we have learned to live with that fact and no longer need to be shocked into the recognition of it. On the other hand, it might be that the retreat of the angels from popular culture reflects the reinstatement of a dualistic world-view, dating from the events of September 11, 2001. Does the end of the angels mean the end of pluralism and the return of the "clash of civilizations"? In that case, the latest angel era in popular culture corresponds almost perfectly to that brief window between the end of one episode of polarized Cold War politics in 1989 and the onset of a new polarization in the aftermath of September 2001.

If I had to identify a symbolic "last" angel, my candidate would not be any of the ones in HBO's *Angels in America* or Trussoni's *Angelology*, but rather the angel that is conspicuously *absent* from *The Man Without a Past*, a postmodern Finnish film by Aki Kaurismäki, from 2002. Nominated for an Academy Award for best foreign film, Kaurismäki's movie lacks obvious angels – it has no winged beings – but that does not prevent it from evoking angels intertextually. Or, rather, it evokes one specific angel: the angel that the early-twentieth-century Finnish painter, Hugo Simberg, painted around 1903 and entitled "The Wounded Angel" (see Figure 6). This enigmatic image, a Finnish national icon, has attracted all kinds of interpretations over the years – as a figure of national consciousness, as a reflection of the painter's supposed sympathy with the industrial working class, as related somehow to the painter's recovery from a life-threatening illness, and so on. (See Levanto, 1993.)

Like his other films, Kaurismäki's *The Man Without a Past* ironically reworks a familiar cinematic formula – in this case, the cliché of the amnesiac who, cut off from his own past by his memory loss, makes a new life for himself. An unnamed man, arriving in Helsinki from the provinces, is assaulted by thugs and left for dead. He wanders out to the port where, unconscious, he is discovered by a pair of young brothers who live nearby with their parents in an abandoned shipping container. It is in the scene of the nameless stranger's rescue that Kaurismäki evokes the elements of "The Wounded Angel": a setting at the water's edge, a victim with a conspicuous head wound (though lacking the angel's wings), two boys carrying a burden between them (a jerry can of water, however, not the

Figure 6. Hugo Simberg, *The Wounded Angel* (1903). Oil on canvas. 50 in. × 61 in. (127 cm × 154 cm). Ateneum, Helsinki.

wounded angel itself). Wingless though he may be, it is this nameless stranger, the "man without a past," who stands in for the angel in Kaurismäki's revision of Simberg's image. Degraded and vulnerable, like García Márquez's "Very Old Man with Enormous Wings," a nonperson who, lacking documents, has no official identity, the man without a past intervenes in the lives of the outcasts living on the margins of Finnish society, transforming various people with whom he comes in contact. He surely fits the profile of many of the angels who flit in and out of literary, cinematic, and popular-culture works of the last decades of the twentieth century.

But what kind of angel is he? An everyday angel; one of us, not Other; not a visitor from another world, not an alien – not a being of a different order who has "fallen to earth." He delivers no ontological shock. If he is an angel at all, he is one who has faded into the light of common day. Here, then, in a nutshell, is a shorthand narrative of the era of angels – and maybe of postmodernism itself. Its trajectory stretches from, let's say, the mid-seventies to a few years after the turn of the millennium; from David Bowie to Aki Kaurismäki; from *The Man Who Fell to Earth* to *The Man Without a Past*.

Chapter 5

After Postmodernism

1. Millennium Approaches ... and Recedes

When did postmodernism end? It *ought* to have ended when the calendar rolled over from December 31, 1999 to January 1, 2000. Though not technically the beginning of the new millennium (which really occurred on January 2, 2001), this was the date that postmodern culture and popular imagination had identified as the apocalyptic threshold when everything would change. When the pop star known as Prince (Prince Rogers Nelson) wanted in 1982 to evoke the ultimate party, he urged his listeners to "Party like it's 1999" – in other words, like it's the eve of the apocalypse. Nineteen ninety-nine is also the date of the nuclear incident that disrupts global civilization in Wim Wenders's 1991 film *Until the End of the World* (see Chapter 4). It is the date when the entire human species uploads itself into its virtual-reality entertainment systems and physically vanishes from the face of the earth, according to J. G. Ballard's story "Report from an Obscure Planet" (1992). It is the date of the apocalyptic civil unrest in Kathryn Bigelow's updated cyberpunk film *Strange Days* (1995), an important link in the cinematic genealogy that runs from *Blade Runner* (1982) to *The Matrix* (1999). Not coincidentally, the interrupted New Year's Eve party at the climax of Bigelow's film is set in the Westin Bonaventure Hotel, revisiting the site that Fredric Jameson made iconic for postmodern architecture (see Chapter 3).

The Year 2000, in short, was the millennium whose approach is heralded, with equal parts anxiety and anticipation, in Kushner's *Angels in America* (see Chapter 4) and almost everywhere else in postmodern culture. The apocalyptic resonances of the date in the popular imagination were reinforced and amplified by hard-headed computer engineers and IT personnel, who predicted that computer systems would crash worldwide on New Year's Eve 1999 because they had not been programmed to roll over to dates beginning with "2000." The so-called "millennium bug" threatened to bring vital computer-dependent systems, including air traffic control, power stations, telecommunications, and banking, to a grinding halt, and with them the postmodern world as we knew it.

Of course, "Y2K," as everyone learned to call it, came and went without mishap. Either the millennium bug's effects had been averted by the heroic combined efforts of computer engineers around the world or the risks had been exaggerated in the first place – it was impossible to know which (Oxoby, 2003, 22–3). When the global banking system really did crash, in the fall of 2008, it was not buggy computers that were to blame but irresponsibly risky financial practices and a failure of regulation.

In any case, the world woke up on New Year's Day 2000 and carried on much as usual, like the characters in *Until the End of the World* and *Strange Days*, for whom the world didn't end after all. Then, nearly two years later, on September 11, 2001, the world as we knew it really did seem to come to an end, live on television, when two hijacked airliners were deliberately crashed into the World Trade Center towers in Manhattan and another into the Pentagon in Washington, D.C., while a fourth came down in a field in Pennsylvania. The events of 9/11 and the other terrorist attacks on Western capitals that followed it – notably in Madrid in 2003 and London in 2005 – were everything that Y2K was not: media spectacles, where Y2K was an invisible nonevent; horrific, where Y2K was anticlimactic and bathetic; shockingly unexpected, where Y2K had been tediously anticipated. Postmodern culture, it appeared, had been right to anticipate an apocalyptic break but wrong about the date.

September 11, too, had been anticipated, but its anticipations could only be identified retrospectively, after the fact (just as, in Borges's paradoxical genealogy-in-reverse, Kafka's precursors could only be identified retrospectively; see Chapter 1). Phillip Wegner writes of films and novels that

> seem to prefigure, in essence repeating before the fact what occurs on September 11, 2001. We see this in the images of falling twin towers in the conclusion of [David Fincher's film] *Fight Club* [1999] and in the smoldering ruins of the World Trade Center in [Roland Emmerich's film] *Independence Day* [1996], in the unanticipated terrorist attacks on the United States in *Independence Day* and in [Joe Haldeman's science-fiction novel] *Forever Peace* [1997], and in the haunting cover image of [Don DeLillo's] *Underworld* [1997] (this last becoming the topic of much Internet conversation in the weeks following September 11). . . . the true significance of these images emerges only through their repetition. (Wegner, 2009, 37)

DeLillo's anticipations of 9/11 seem particularly uncanny – not only the image of the Twin Towers on the cover of *Underworld* that Wegner mentions, but the fixation on the World Trade Center in his preceding novel, *Mao II* (1991), as well as his preoccupation with terrorism in that novel and in earlier ones such as *Players* (1977) and *The Names* (1982) (Knight, 2008, 205–5; Nealon, 2012, 155). Uncanniest of all, however, is the passage from *White Noise* (1985), in which Jack Gladney's wife Babette reads aloud a tabloid psychic's prediction that "members of an air-crash cult will hijack a jumbo jet and crash it into the White House in an act of blind devotion to their mysterious and reclusive leader. . . ." (DeLillo, 1985, 146).

DeLillo is a special case, and an especially uncanny one, but other works of the preceding decade also appear in a different light when seen from the perspective of 9/11, with previously inconspicuous details rendered salient in retrospect. Zadie Smith's novel *White Teeth* (2000), for instance, in which disaffected immigrant youth in London gravitate to a violent Islamist organization, reads in retrospect like a pre-9/11 novel, or a pre-7/7 one (7/7/2005 being the date of the London Tube bombings). Similarly, Sarah Kane's play *Blasted* (1995), revived on the London stage in spring 2001, marking the beginning of Kane's posthumous rediscovery, reads now like an anticipation of 9/11, despite its unmistakable reference to the mid-nineties civil war in the former Yugoslavia (see Chapter 4).

In the aftermath of 9/11, it did not take long for the events of that day to become a *topos*, a commonplace, in representations of all kinds, across a range of media and genres (Keniston and Quinn, 2008; Gray, 2009; Morgan, 2009). Some of these post-9/11 texts positioned their events in the period leading up to 9/11, exploiting the ironic potential of our retrospective knowledge, unavailable to people at the time; David Foster Wallace's novella "The Suffering Channel" (2004) is an example. Other texts, such as Art Spiegelman's graphic narrative *In the Shadow of No Towers* (2004), DeLillo's *Falling Man* (2007), and Pynchon's *Bleeding Edge* (2013), sought to do justice to the 9/11 events themselves. Still others, including Ian McEwan's *Saturday* (2003), Ballard's *Millennium People* (2003), and Jonathan Safran Foer's *Extremely Loud and Incredibly Close* (2005), addressed the experience of living on after 9/11, in changed circumstances. Among those changed circumstances, of course, were the U.S.-led wars in Afghanistan, Iraq, and around the world, which also became narrative *topoi*. For instance, in the aftermath of 9/11, Kathryn Bigelow abandoned the near-future science fiction of *Strange Days* for films about the wars of the new millennium: the Iraq War in *The Hurt Locker* (2008) and Afghanistan and the War on Terror in *Zero Dark Thirty* (2012).

Most intriguing and revealing of all are those works in progress whose composition in effect *straddles* the events of that morning, September 11, 2001. There are a number of these, and they register 9/11 as a kind of rupture or crack running right through their own fabric. In one sense, the Hollywood action-movie *Collateral Damage* is an example. An Arnold Schwarzenegger vehicle, ready for release in October 2011, its scenario of a terrorist attack was felt to be too close to reality and likely to alienate audiences still reeling from the television images of 9/11; its release was postponed until February 2002 (Morgan, 2008, 1). Similarly, the fall 2001 premiere of the Fox TV series *24* (2001–10), which would in time become the definitive popular representation of the shadowy "War on Terror," was postponed for a week because its first hour climaxed with the midair explosion of a passenger airliner – again, too close to 9/11 reality.

More interesting is William Gibson's novel *Pattern Recognition* (2003), whose composition was interrupted by the events of 9/11 and whose plot literally *changes direction* midway through in order to accommodate those events (see below). The same mid-course correction happens in *Last Fall* (2005), the final, posthumously published novel by Ronald Sukenick, author of the *Tempest* remake *Blown Away* (see "Prospero's Books"), who was hard at work on his novel in an apartment adjacent to the World Trade Center when the 9/11 attacks occurred and he had to be evacuated. In other cases, even where the 9/11 events are not mentioned by name, the fracture corresponding to the irruption of those events into the composition process can nevertheless be detected. This is the case, for instance, with Alexis Rockman's "great picture," *Manifest Destiny* (see "Ruins"), commissioned before 9/11 though not actually executed until 2003–04. It is also arguably the case with DeLillo's *Cosmopolis* (2003), set in the year 2000, pre-9/11, but full of intimations of apocalypse, and Pynchon's *Against the Day* (2006), a historical novel that displaces the 9/11 experience to the early decades of the twentieth century (see section 4).

When did postmodernism end? Certainly not on September 11, 2001, any more than it did on January 1, 2000. Nevertheless, the sense of a cultural threshold of some kind having been crossed on 9/11 is strong and widespread. If on or about November 1989 human relations changed, with the abrupt end of the Cold War, then perhaps on or about September 2001 they changed back again. The Cold War had been hospitable to postmodern culture, and for many the disorienting interregnum after the Soviet bloc's collapse felt like the end of something – the end of history, Francis Fukuyama said, but of course, as we have seen (Chapter 4), he used the wrong metaphor for the experience of being *in-between*. Other influential commentators at the time, such as the political scientist Samuel Huntington, anticipated not the end of history but a historic "clash of civilizations," in particular between the secular West and the Muslim world, and the events of 9/11 (corroborated by a whole series of precursor and successor events of a similarly violent kind) seemed to confirm that this view, not Fukuyama's, had been more prescient (Rodgers, 2011, 259). There were many, President George W. Bush among them, who seemed to welcome the return to a polarized world-view, albeit one polarized differently than in the days of the Cold War. "Either you are with us," the U.S. president said in a special address to a joint session of Congress on September 20, 2001, "or you are with the terrorists" (quoted in Crowley, 2009, 39; see Wiegand, 2009, 55–60). For or against, us or them: the bipolar world returned, and the interregnum was over.

When did postmodernism end? If the postmodern world as we know it didn't end punctually on the morning of September 11, its end was certainly in progress on or about that date. Whether everything *really* changed on 9/11 or not, that date can serve better than most the purpose of marking a cultural boundary, even if it is a more or less transparently *fabricated* boundary. "September 11" is a convenient shorthand for postmodernism's endgame, a way of telling the end of the story, no more fictitious (but no less so) than selecting 1966 as its starting point. After all, nothing appears more fabulously fictitious than the plain statement of certain historical facts, such as these: Minoru Yamasaki, the prize-winning architect of the Pruitt-Igoe housing project, the demolition of which inaugurated the postmodern era, according to Charles Jencks (see Chapter 3), was also the architect of the World Trade Center, the destruction of which arguably marked that era's ending. By a terrible and barely credible irony, the explosive destruction of Yamasaki's buildings bookended the postmodern era. What novelist (postmodern or otherwise) would dare to invent such a coincidence?

2. Post-Postmodernism, at Last?

Assuming, for the sake of argument, that postmodernism really did end on or about September 11, 2001, then what took its place? Nothing is certain, except that it is surely still too early for definitive characterization of whatever cultural phase is in the process of succeeding postmodernism. If it took us, arguably, until the new millennium to be in a position to see postmodernism whole, how can we expect to grasp its successor, still unfolding around us, with the hindsight of barely a decade or so at most?

Needless to say, our lack of hindsight has not prevented speculation about the nature of the new cultural phase. In particular, it has not prevented the proliferation of proposals for *naming* it. Trivial in itself, the act of naming is nevertheless crucial to the *branding* of a cultural development, which in turn helps set the agenda for further development and reflection. Something like a *name-that-period* sweepstakes has sprung up, mainly involving the affixing of an appropriate prefix to the term *modernism: neo-, meta-, pseudo-, semi-, alter-*, and so on. As early as the eighties, Charles Jencks had identified a *late-modernist* style of architecture – what others might call *neo-*modernism – that offered stiff competition to the postmodernism that he himself championed. (In the latest, updated iteration of his history of contemporary architecture, he seems confident that postmodernism has prevailed after all in the twenty-first century; see Jencks, 2011.) The acerbic British critic Owen Hatherley, a sort of anti-Jencks, has characterized the architecture of the "New Labour" era of U.K. politics (1997–2010) as *pseudo-*modernism (Hatherley, 2011, xiii). Christian Moraru, as we have already seen (Chapter 4), proposes to call the dialogic, interactive, hyper-networked phase of global culture that, according to him, emerged in the post-1989 period *cosmodernism*. Akin to Moraru's cosmodernism is the influential curator Nicolas Bourriaud's *alter-*modernism, that is, *other-*modernism. Applied first to the visual artworks, installations and text-based works that Bourriaud assembled for the Fourth Triennial exhibition of contemporary art at the Tate Britain gallery in London in 2009, the term has since been extended to other globally minded texts such as W. G. Sebald's *The Rings of Saturn* (see "Ruins"), Orhan Pamuk's *Istanbul* (2005), Mark Z. Danielewski's *Only Revolutions* (2006), and Jennifer Egan's *A Visit from the Goon Squad* (2010) (Gibbons, 2012). David James and Urmilla Seshagiri have proposed the term *meta-*modernism for twenty-first-century writing that self-consciously reverts to the dissident, defamiliarizing strain in early twentieth-century modernism, in works such as Ian McEwan's *Atonement* (2001), Tom McCarthy's *C* (2010), Zadie Smith's *NW* (2012), and novels by Kazuo Ishiguro, Michael Ondaatje, and others (James and Seshagiri, 2014). A similar argument for the renewed relevance of early twentieth-century modernism in the twenty-first century has been mounted by Marjorie Perloff with respect to poetry (Perloff, 2002).

Examples could be multiplied. Each proposed name carves out a particular area of contemporary cultural practice and identifies it as *typical* or *representative* of the whole. Each seems compelling enough, but none seems definitive or complete, and all of them are undoubtedly premature.

For the time being, the most useful and least inadequate term may be the ugliest coinage of them all, one that we've seen before (in Chapter 4): *post-postmodernism*. Its very ugliness has some strategic value, as Jeffrey Nealon observes (2012, ix), since it prevents us from seeing the phenomenon it refers to as some shiny new cultural artifact, and forces us to recognize the ways in which post-postmodernism *repeats,* albeit with a difference, the postmodernism that came before. As we have seen, post-postmodernism was first associated with writers in the nineties, such as David Foster Wallace, who sought to differentiate themselves from postmodern writers of the preceding generation (Barth, Pynchon, and others), but only ended up succumbing to their own "anxiety of influence" about their cultural belatedness. Their claim to have broken through to something *beyond* postmodernism – to the *post-post* condition – seems to have been premature. Why should a similar claim be any less premature in the 2010s?

What immunizes (to some extent) the "new" post-postmodernism from the kind of wishful thinking associated with the term's use in the nineties is the frank acknowledgement of the new phase's continuity with postmodernism. Nealon, whose views I am adapting here, sees twenty-first-century post-postmodernism not as any kind of clean break or reversal of direction, but rather as "an intensification and mutation within postmodernism" (2012, ix). "Intensification" suggests change of *degree* rather than *kind*, but of course at a certain point change in degree *becomes* change in kind, and so the first *post* of post-postmodernism serves to indicate "postmodernism's having mutated, passed beyond a certain tipping point to become something recognizably different in its contours and workings," yet without becoming "absolutely foreign to whatever it was before" (2012, ix).

Seeking the "mutations" that postmodernism is undergoing in the twenty-first century, Nealon revisits some of the canonical sites and classic moments of twentieth-century postmodernism. He revisits and updates Fredric Jameson, writing through, around and over Jameson's canonical account of postmodernism as the "cultural logic of late capitalism" (see Chapter 3). He *literally* revisits Las Vegas, site of Venturi's and ScottBrown's discoveries about architectural semiotics and populism (see Chapter 3), seeking to learn whatever the "new" Vegas might teach about post-postmodernism. He revisits Jameson's famously disoriented experience of postmodern hyperspace in the Westin Bonaventure Hotel, comparing it to his own experience of Caesar's Palace Casino and Hotel on the Las Vegas Strip, "an unapologetic overlap of hotel, casino, restaurant, theme park, and shopping mall – all done up in some hyper-postmodern version of the ancient past" (2012, 29).

He applies what he learned from Las Vegas to a reading of Ridley Scott's blockbuster sword-and-sandal movie *Gladiator* (2000), which Nealon sees as, in effect, an allegory of the situation of global capitalism at the beginning of the twenty-first century (2012, 32–8). In Roman history according to *Gladiator,* the empire, having attained the outer limits of its expansion, with no "outside" left to conquer, turns inward to stage simulacral spectacles of imperial conquest in intense gladiatorial contests. This, says Nealson, exactly mirrors the post-1989 condition of global capitalism: having expanded to encompass the whole world, leaving no region "outside" its sphere, it is compelled to turn inward to enhance the *intensity* of consumption. It is this enhancement of consumption that one glimpses in Las Vegas, the "empire of intensities":

> the economic force that's deployed in Last Vegas functions *not* by conquering or assimilating new territory but rather by intensifying new versions of familiar things . . . . In such settings, you don't so much *consume goods* as you *have experiences* where your subjectivity can be intensified, bent, and retooled . . . . The force of the new globalized economic empire – the empire one spies from Caesar's Palace – doesn't primarily turn outward in an expansive, colonialist, or consumerist assimilation. Now it turns inward toward intensification of existing biopolitical resources. The final product, in the end, is you and me. (Nealon, 2012, 30–31)

One might extend Nealon's allegorical reading of *Gladiator* by tracing the film's progeny on television, in the BBC/HBO series *Rome* (2005–2007) and the Starz series *Spartacus* (2010–13). Both of them, *Spartacus* especially, are heavy with computer-generated imagery, foregrounding their simulacral quality, and making CGI *itself* an object of consumption, quite apart from any illusionistic functions it might have. We watch these series, in part, in order to appreciate and take pleasure in the lavishness of their computer-generated effects. *Rome* and *Spartacus* further intensify what in *Gladiator* and at Caesar's Palace – and in the globalized economy generally – had already been subject to intensification. Is this what Nealon means by *hyper*-postmodernism?

3. Intensities and Mutations

Luckily, the term *hyper*-postmodernism is not really a contender in the *name-that-period* sweepstakes. But *post*-postmodernism is not only in the running for the sweepstakes, it is the clear front-runner, as long as it is understood not in the nineties sense of getting *beyond* postmodernism, but in Nealon's sense of the intensification and mutation of features and tendencies already present *within* postmodernism.

It is tempting to try using Nealon's return visits to the canonical sites of postmodernism as a template for further exploration of post-postmodernism's intensifications and mutations. So, for instance, just as Caesar's Palace intensifies the Westin Bonaventure, or Las Vegas ca. 2012 intensifies Las Vegas ca. 1972, so Ridley Scott's *Gladiator* can be seen as a mutation of his *Blade Runner* (1982), Frank Gehry's iconic Guggenheim Museum in Bilbao (1992–97) as a mutation of his deconstructed house in Santa Monica (1978) (see Chapter 3), DeLillo's *Cosmopolis* (2003) as a mutation of Ballard's *Crash* (1973), David Mitchell's *Cloud Atlas* (2004) as the intensification of Italo Calvino's *If on a Winter's Night a Traveler* (1979), and so on. Rather than proceeding in this piecemeal fashion, however, leafing through the pages of this *Introduction* for other cases of a postmodern something-or-other that undergoes intensification or mutation in the twenty-first century, let me briefly focus on just four areas that seem to display clear symptoms of an emergent post-postmodernism.

Uncreative Writing. Nealon himself can help us get started. He identifies the Conceptual Writing practiced by Kenneth Goldsmith and other writers of the new millennium as something like the post-postmodern intensification and mutation of postmodern L=A=N=G=U=A=G=E writing, such as that of Bruce Andrews (Nealon, 2012, 163–7). Andrews collects separate phrases and sentences – some "found" (or "sampled"), others newly composed – and then assembles them into longer, radically disjunctive blocks of text (see Chapter 3). Goldsmith goes further, beyond sampling to unrepentant *plagiarizing*. For instance, he retypes every word in the *New York Times* for September 1, 2000 (*Day*, 2003; see Chapter 4). He transcribes verbatim a year's worth of New York City weather reports (*The Weather*, 2005), a full day of radio traffic reports (*Traffic*, 2007), and the running commentary accompanying a televised baseball game (*Sports*, 2008) (Perloff, 2010, 146–65; Goldsmith, 2011; Epstein 2012, 315–8). The resulting texts are not disjunctive, at least not in the way the Andrews' are, except insofar as displacing them from one context (a newspaper page, a television broadcast) to another creates accidental disjunctions, as it were. Andrews' practice of sampling and assemblage is a rebuke to literary ideologies of originality and self-expression; Goldsmith's practice *intensifies* that rebuke. Though there are precedents for this sort of refusal to express oneself – more in the visual arts (e.g., Andy Warhol) than literature (Goldsmith, 2011, 139–49) – Goldsmith's refusal is more intense than his predecessors'; he is *intensely* "uncreative."

Other Conceptual Writers of Goldsmith's post-postmodern generation include Caroline Bergvall, Christian Bök, Craig Dworkin, Robert Fitterman, and Tan Lin (the brother, as it happens, of Maya Lin, the designer of the Vietnam War Memorial; see "Ruins") (see Dworkin and Goldsmith, 2011). Related to the "uncreative" practices of Goldsmith and his circle, but technologically driven in ways that theirs typically are not, are the search-engine poetics of the *Flarf* poets, including Gary Sullivan, K. Silem Muhammad, Jordan Davis, Drew Gardner, Nada Gordon, Michael Magee, and others (Goldsmith, 2011, 185–7; Bernstein, 2012, 292–3; Epstein, 2012, 318–9). Also dedicated, like the Conceptual Writers and the L=A=N=G=U=A=G=E poets before them, to the exploitation of "found" language, the Flarf poets use online Google searches to comb through the Internet for literally unimaginable (and often dissident, inflammatory or grossly offensive) word combinations, patching them together into collages. They are, in other words, proceduralists, in the tradition of OuLiPo and the New York School, and appropriators of language, in the tradition of Kathy Acker and others (see Chapter 3), with the difference that, in Flarf practice, proceduralism and appropriation are technologically mediated and enhanced – *intensified*.

All That Is Solid, Still Melting. Flarf, in other words, is a sort of *cyborg* poetics, involving a collaboration between flesh-and-blood poets and digital technologies. It is a zone where the real world in which poets live overlaps with cyberspace, or dovetails with it.

If on or about November 1989 human relations changed, then so did, in a parallel development, our relation to cyberspace and the virtual realities it sustains. The years 1989–90, when the Cold War ended and the interregnum began, are also the years when the Internet was launched, enormously expanding our access to virtual realities (see Chapter 4). By the turn of the millennia, most of the technological vehicles of expanded virtual experience – personal computers, video-game technology, the World Wide Web, wireless Internet access, smartphones and other handheld devices, and so on – were already in general use, and social media (blogs, Facebook, YouTube, Twitter, etc.) were under development or on the horizon. If no new threshold of virtuality was crossed in the first decades of the millennium, nevertheless virtual reality continued to *mutate*.

Virtual experience, of course, is a constant of human culture across time and space. Narratives, pictures, performances, representations, and enactments of all kinds – they all give access to virtual realities (see Cohen and Taylor, 1978). However, the technological power of the new digital media has made virtual realities more pervasive than ever before in human history, engrossing more and more of our time and attention, supplementing and even displacing what Berger and Luckman called "paramount reality" (see Chapter 2). We project ourselves into cyberspace, adopting the identities of game-world avatars, citizens of Second Life©, and other online selves (Elias, 2012). Conversely, virtuality infiltrates our real world through such portals as "reality television," a phenomenon that has been with us since at least 1973 (see Chapter 3) but that has exploded in the new millennium, threatening to engulf the entire mediascape (or so it sometimes seems). The erosion of ontological stability and the toppling of paramount reality, staples of the postmodern imagination since at least Borges, are becoming sober facts.

Symptoms of virtuality's ongoing mutation are all around us. One symptom, out of many that could be mentioned, is the emergence of the so-called "Truman Show" delusion, named after a 1998 movie directed by Peter Weir and starring Jim Carey. Sufferers of this delusion believe that, like Truman Burbank in the movie, they are starring in a reality TV show, a long-running film of their everyday lives, staged for others' entertainment (Marantz, 2013). A more benign development, but equally symptomatic of the contemporary mingling of reality and virtuality, is the introduction of Google Glass, the first hands-free, wearable computer, which makes it possible (among other things) to access the Internet while at the same time continuing to interact normally with one's immediate environment – to operate in cyberspace and the real world simultaneously (Shteyngart, 2013). Still being beta tested as of this writing, Google Glass may or may not represent the direction in which wearable computing ultimately develops, but in any case it marks another step toward the cyborg condition of machine/human integration imagined by science-fiction writers and theorized by Donna Haraway (see Chapter 3).

Consider, finally, the phenomenon of *fantasy sports leagues*. As long ago as the early sixties, the historian and cultural critic Daniel Boorstin presciently observed that reality was rapidly being preempted by the mass-mediated image. Whole categories of people ("celebrities") and events ("pseudo-events" such as press conferences, presidential debates, opinion polls, etc.) existed only as a function of the communications media that supposedly reported but actually generated them. Boorstin exempted from the pseudo-event category such "spontaneous events" as crime or sports (Boorstin, 1985 [1962]). Since then, of course, crime, too, has become image-based, *spectacular* and *simulacral*. What is terrorism if not crime designed to be consumed as spectacle? What were the 9/11 hijackers seeking, if not their reality-TV moment (though they would never have called it that)?

One wonders what Boorstin would say about twenty-first-century *fantasy sports*, where virtual teams are assembled from the profiles of real players (of American football, ice hockey, etc.), and compete virtually, based on the statistics of players' real-world performances. While fantasy sports predate the Internet – they really only require pencil, paper, and a steady supply of sports statistics – their popularity expanded with the introduction of Web-based games in the mid-nineties, and (after a brief hiatus when the dot-com bubble burst in 1999–2001; see Chapter 4) exploded in the new millennium. Fantasy sports has become a highly profitable industry, and an engrossing pastime that competes for attention (if anecdotal evidence is to be believed) with the real-world "spontaneous events" (ballgames, hockey games, etc.) on which they depend.

Robert Coover, in his postmodernist novel *The Universal Baseball Association, J. Henry Waugh, Proprietor* (1968) imagines a fantasy baseball league – a board game, since Web-based games did not yet exist – that obsesses its "proprietor," J. Henry Waugh, to the point that he apparently suffers a breakdown. Having lost its creator, Waugh's game achieves ontological independence, becoming a freestanding world of its own, with its own history and rituals (McHale, 1987, 20). In the world of the Universal Baseball Association, Waugh himself becomes a remote deity, inaccessible to the ballplayers who were once tokens in his game. One wonders whether the ontological hazards imagined by Coover might not apply to twenty-first-century fantasy sports. Are real-world sports in danger of being displaced by virtual sports and game players of being absorbed into their own game worlds?

The End of the Future. In William Gibson's novel *Pattern Recognition* (see "Alice"), the heroine suffers jet lag, uses e-mail and Photoshop, consults on the design of a corporate logo, goes "cool-hunting" for street fashions, encounters post-Soviet oligarchs, and becomes obsessed with an online video clip. In Neal Stephenson's *REAMDE*, some people make fortunes by designing a massively multiplayer online game, while others play – and hack – that same game in order to accumulate virtual currency. The two novelists, Gibson and Stephenson, belong to the first and second waves of cyberpunk, respectively, and if their novels had been published in the early eighties or even the early nineties, they would be regarded as science fictions. However, they were published in the twenty-first century, Gibson's in 2003, Stephenson's in 2011, and all of the components of their worlds mentioned previously, while they *once* would have appeared futuristic, are now commonplace features of everyday reality.

Whatever happened to cyberpunk? Beginning as a strain of science fiction in the eighties – a niche subgenre of a niche genre – it crossed over to mainstream popularity in the course of the nineties, climaxing with the blockbuster success of the Wachowski siblings' film *The Matrix* (1999; see Chapter 3). In the twenty-first century, cyberpunk motifs and style have become ubiquitous in popular culture, but they have also lost their speculative edge. In short, technological development has caught up with cyberpunk, which no longer projects a future reality but only mirrors a *present* one (Jameson, 2005; Tomberg, 2013). From the outset, cyberpunk had only ever aspired to imagine a world "twenty minutes into the future," as the short-lived cyberpunk TV series, *Max Headroom* (1987–88) put it, but in the post-postmodern era that twenty minutes has shrunk to nothing. The feedback loop between cyberpunk speculation and sober reality, inaugurated when Gibson imagined cyberspace and then real-world software engineers went ahead and actually *built* it (see Chapter 3), has tightened over the years, until now in the twenty-first century Gibson depends on contemporary techno-culture for fresh ideas at least as much as techno-culture ever depended on him back in cyberpunk's heyday.

Gibson's twenty-first-century trilogy of novels – *Pattern Recognition, Spook Country* (2007), and *Zero History* (2010) – unlike his trilogies of the eighties and nineties, are indistinguishable from contemporary thrillers from the point of view of their plots and worlds, and the same could be said for Stephenson's *Cryptonomicon* (1999) and *REAMDE*. However, at the level of their *sentences* – bristling with brand names, technical jargon, specialized knowledge, and calculatedly strange juxtapositions – they continue to *read like* science fiction, testifying to the fact that our *everyday reality* in the new millennium actually seems to have the texture of science fiction (Tomberg, 2013). In effect, we now experience real life *as though it were* science fiction. "We have annexed the future into our own present, as merely one of the manifold alternatives open to us" (Ballard, 1985b, 4), wrote J. G. Ballard, an important influence on the cyberpunks, in an introduction to his 1973 novel *Crash*. This could be the motto for many twenty-first-century cyberpunk novels.

The present that these novels inhabit is pointedly the *post-9/11* present. *Pattern Recognition*, one of those texts whose composition actually straddled the morning of September 11, retains the imprint of the 9/11 events in its heroine's double quest, split between searching for the source of a mysteriously compelling online video and trying to ascertain what happened to her father at Ground Zero on the morning of the attacks. The first quest reflects Gibson's original conception of the novel; the second, his changed conception after 9/11. *Pattern Recognition*'s two sequels, *Spook Country* and *Zero History*, are both unmistakably novels of the "War on Terror" era; so, too, is Stephenson's *REAMDE*, and so, for that matter, are Ballard's late novels, especially *Millennium People* (2003).

The lapse of cyberpunk's futurism into "mere" presentism can be regretted or even mourned, as a symptom of science fiction's loss of its utopian promise; this is Fredric Jameson's view, for instance (Jameson, 2005). Certainly, it is hard to identify anything very utopian in Gibson's *Pattern Recognition*, which hinges, after all, on the search for something as mundane as a YouTube video. Nothing very futuristic there – except that, as it turns out, *Pattern Recognition*'s publication in 2003 actually *predates* the launch of YouTube in 2004. So Gibson *does* predict the technological future after all, if only by a year. While this may not seem very impressive as predictions go, it gains stature when we take into account the intensity of response that this video clip seems to elicit from Gibson's characters, and the powerful aura of significance that they attribute to it. What, we may wonder, is all the fuss about?

What's at stake here is the *aesthetic* potential of social media. Gibson isn't so much predicting YouTube as such – a trivial prediction, after all – as he is imagining something that YouTube has yet to produce, something that it may never produce, that it may even be constitutionally incapable of producing: an aesthetic masterpiece. He is inviting us to join him in imagining what a YouTube masterpiece would be like, and in doing so he is carrying over into this novel of "mere" contemporary realism a trace of utopian speculation.

Postmagical Realism. Assuming that the cyberpunks really have more or less abandoned futurism and utopia, then perhaps they have ceded it to another genre, an *emergent* one. We can glimpse the cloudy outlines of that emergent genre in two celebrated U.S. ethnic novels of the turn-of-the-millennium years. Published on the eve of the millennium, Colson Whitehead's *The Intuitionist* (1999) seems to be some kind of *alternate-history* novel. It imagines a version of our present (though the era is unclear) in which the *horizontal* orientation of our urban infrastructure has been displaced into the *vertical* axis. Instead of a world of superhighways and interchanges, Whitehead imagines an alternative one of high-speed elevators, serviced by a guild of inspectors whose prestige and mystique, in this alternative reality, far exceed anything that real elevator inspectors enjoy in our world. Coupled with this counterfactual premise is a serious reflection on race in real-world America, addressing, among other things, white privilege, black upward mobility, workplace discrimination, the persistence of racial segregation, and the psychological toll of racial "passing." What holds these two disparate aspects of the storyworld together is an implicit pun on *uplift*: literal uplift in the case of elevators, racial uplift in the case of African Americans like the ambitious young female elevator inspector whose story this is.

The other exemplary ethnic novel is Junot Díaz's *The Brief Wondrous Life of Oscar Wao* (2007), an immigrant family saga and historical novel of the Dominican Republic, grittily realistic yet also saturated with the fantastic and the romantic – inherited curses and spells meant to counter them, faceless demonic pursuers, love stronger than death, and so on. It is also saturated with late-twentieth-century popular culture – the nerd culture of fantasy and science fiction, superhero comics, movie posters, and video games, of *The Lord of the Rings*, *Star Wars*, *X-Men*, and *The Matrix*.

Our skepticism aroused, we might ask, what's so novel here? Isn't *The Intuitionist* just another example of second-generation postmodernism, a novel written in the long shadow of Pynchon (see Chapter 4)? Jonathan Lethem, himself a second-generation postmodern, writes in a dustjacket blurb, "This splendid novel reads as though a stray line in Pynchon ... had been meticulously unfolded to reveal an entire world ...." That "stray line" might actually come from an episode in *Gravity's Rainbow* set on an enormous elevator in an imagined or hallucinated city of the future:

> By now the City is grown so tall that elevators are long-haul affairs, with lounges inside .... For those with faint hearts who first thing on entering seek out the Certificate of Inspection on the elevator wall, there are young women ... who've been well-tutored in all kinds of elevator lore, and whose job it is to set you at ease. (Pynchon, 1973, 735)

As for *Oscar Wao*, doesn't it just recycle magical realism, a postmodern formula that has been around since the sixties (see Chapter 3)? Like other magic realists before him, Díaz straddles a cultural divide, in this case between the Caribbean world of the Dominican Republic and the immigrant world of Dominicans displaced to New Jersey, and he builds the doubleness of this divide into the very ontological structure of his novel: magic vs. realism, nerd-boy escapism vs. fantastic Dominican reality. How is Díaz's family saga not just another iteration of Márquez's or Rushdie's or Zadie Smith's, merely updated and transplanted to New Jersey?

Ramon Saldívar, who has been tracking the emergence of this genre of U.S. ethnic writing, pushes back against such skepticism, arguing that these novels do more than merely recycle magical realism and that they have more in common with each other (and with other novels like them) than they do with precursors like Pynchon or Márquez. Novels by Whitehead and Díaz – as well as others by African Americans like Percival Everett and Dexter Palmer, Latinos such as Salvador Plascencia, Asian Americans like Karen Tei Yamashita, Sesshu Foster, Charles Yu, and Chang-rae Lee, even younger Jewish-American writers like Michael Chabon, Gary Shteyngart, and Jonathan Safran Foer – share several traits in common. They engage in critical dialogue with postmodern aesthetics and ransack the resources of genre history, mixing genres and mashing them up (e.g., alternate history, *noir* detective, and protest novel in *The Intuitionist*; historical fiction, family saga, and a swarm of pop-culture genres in *Oscar Wao*). They explore the thematics of race, and they all express, sometimes in veiled or displaced ways, a utopian impulse toward social justice, the aspiration for a better world (Saldívar, 2013, 4–6). Resisting "the picturesque and magical stereotypes the publishing world has come to demand of [ethnic] writers" (Saldívar, 2011, 589), they all exemplify what Saldívar calls *postmagical realism*.

Naming a tendency or movement – or, in this case, a genre – though trivial in itself, has powerful consequences, as we have seen. "Postmagical realism" is just one of the tentative solutions that Saldívar has proposed as he struggles to capture the specificity of this emergent genre. He also associates it with *Afrofuturism* (Saldívar, 2013, 7), a coinage attributed to Mark Dery (1994), which identifies a speculative or science-fictional strain in African-American creativity, spanning a range of art forms and genres, from the extraterrestrial jazz of Sun Ra, the UFO-themed funk of George Clinton and the dystopian hiphop of Public Enemy, to the science fiction of Samuel Delany and Octavia Butler, as well as the visual and mixed-media art showcased in "The Shadows Took Shape," an exhibition of the Studio Museum Harlem (November 2013 to March 2014). However, "Afrofuturism," though a relevant analogue, lacks the multi-ethnic scope of the genre that Saldívar envisages. Other proposals of Saldívar's include *historical fantasy, speculative realism*, and *sur*-realismo, a witty coinage meant to evoke the special brand of "fantasy-shaped realism" that emerges from the "global south" (or *sur* in Spanish; Saldívar, 2011, 593).

The most capacious of all of Saldívar's proposed names for this emergent genre, however, is also the one most susceptible of misunderstanding: *postrace aesthetic*. Saldívar's use of the term "postrace" does *not* imply that race has been *overcome* or *superseded* in the twenty-first century, as some contemporary ideologues would like to pretend. Rather, the *post-* of postrace identifies, first of all, the generation of writers who came of age *since* the Civil Rights movement. Like the *post-* of postcolonial, it designates "not a chronological but a conceptual frame, one that refers to the logic of something having been 'shaped as a consequence of' imperialism and racism" (Saldívar, 2011, 575). It is also akin to the first *post-* of post-postmodernism – another of the names that Saldívar associates with this genre. Postrace, says Saldívar, is a term to be used "under erasure and with full ironic force" (Saldívar, 2013, 2).

Whatever we ultimately decide to call this genre, we can trace the trajectory of its development in Whitehead's career, in the evolution from *The Intuitionist*, his first novel, to *Zone One* (2011), his fourth. His dialogue with postmodernism deepens and darkens in the later novel. No longer merely shadowing Pynchon, Whitehead in *Zone One* engages with the whole range of postmodern popular culture, daring to commandeer for his own uses one of the dominant popular genres of the turn-of-the-millennium – *zombie apocalypse*. If in the nineties the most typical figure of ontological otherness was the angel (see "Angels in America"), in the new millennium that role has passed to other figures: the *vampire*, as in the popular *Twilight* series of young adult novels and films and the *clone* as in Kazuo Ishiguro's novel *Never Let Me Go* (2005) and its 2010 film adaptation, as well as the BBC television series *Orphan Black* (premiered 2013), and above all the *zombie,* as in the TV series *The Walking Dead* (premiered 2010) and a myriad of zombie-apocalypse movies. Whitehead takes the popular motif of the zombie apocalypse and turns it into a multivalent metaphor for life in the new millennium. What do Whitehead's rampaging zombies stand for? The numbing effects of habit, the overwhelming pressure of consumerism, the immersion of the self in mass culture, the predatory nature of capitalism – all themes discernible in popular versions of the zombie genre, but nowhere exploited more fully or pointedly than here.

Whitehead also turns the zombie apocalypse into a metaphor for 9/11. *Zone One* is a post-9/11 novel, and the futile last stand against the zombies that it depicts is staged in a deserted and dilapidated Lower Manhattan – the Lower Manhattan of 9/11's aftermath, extrapolated here into a permanent condition of urban ruin and an interminable (and unwinnable) "War on Terror," conducted from building to building, from room to room. Finally, this is a postrace novel in precisely Saldívar's sense of the term, "under erasure and with full ironic force." Here at the end of the world, race has finally been rendered irrelevant. The hero, ironically nicknamed "Mark Spitz" after the Jewish-American swimming champion of the 1968 and 1972 Olympic Games, is belatedly revealed, on p. 231 of a 259-page novel, to be black – a measure of how little his blackness matters now. The complex joke in his nickname refers to an episode in which the hero refuses to escape danger by jumping into a river, supposedly because he can't swim (although he can, as it turns out), but it also hinges on a stereotype about African Americans, "the black-people-can't-swim thing" (Whitehead, 2011, 231). The stereotype no longer has any teeth, but only because there are (almost) no African Americans left alive to apply it to. Race has finally been overcome and superseded, just as the world of the living is being snuffed out, and only *because* that world is ending (Saldívar, 2013, 12–3). The irony is almost unbearable, and *Zone One* is terminally dystopian. But of course, every dystopia implies a utopia, its flipside, the negation of its negation (Jameson, 2005, 198–202). In this sense *Zone One,* dark as it is, is ultimately an expression of utopian optimism, turned inside out.

4. The End of the World as We Know It (and I Feel Fine)

No literary career, perhaps no career of any kind, is more intimately involved with the trajectory of postmodernism, from beginning to end, and even *beyond* the end, than Thomas Pynchon's. Pynchon's novels bookend post-modernism and keep pace with all of its successively unfolding phases, from its onset (*The Crying of Lot 49*, 1966) through its rebranding and peak phase (*Gravity's Rainbow*, 1973), to the post-1989 interregnum (*Vineland*, 1990), all the way down to the new millennium and the emergence of post-postmodernism. The threshold events of September 11, 2001 figure in two of Pynchon's novels, explicitly in *Bleeding Edge* (2013), implicitly in *Against the Day* (2006).

Against the Day is presumably one of those texts, like Gibson's *Pattern Recognition* (2003) and Sukenick's *Last Fall* (2005), whose composition was bisected by the 9/11 events. Pynchon had already been a resident of New York City for a number of years by the time of September 2001, and whether or not he was actually at home in Manhattan on that morning, his life was surely directly affected by what happened. A historical novel, *Against the Day* is set in the years between 1893 and the Great War of 1914–18, with a brief postwar coda, so its approach to 9/11 is necessarily oblique and coded. For instance, in one strange episode (Pynchon, 2006, 149–55), an indistinct, nameless monster rampages through New York, recalling both King Kong (frequently evoked in *Gravity's Rainbow*) and Godzilla (who figured in *Vineland*).

If the monster in the streets is one oblique strategy for capturing the 9/11 experience, another is the recurrent motif of *aftermath* – of living on after the end. On more than one occasion, Pynchon has his characters refer to the Great War, the cataclysm that looms over the book, as the end of their world, making the whole postwar twentieth century a kind of aftermath, or even *afterlife*. On one such occasion, midway through this very long novel, a time traveler from the future (or so he claims), visiting the year 1904, predicts the coming war:

> You have no idea what you're heading into. The world you take to be "the" world will die, and descend into Hell, and all history after that will belong properly to the history of Hell . . . Flanders will be the mass grave of History. (Pynchon, 2006, 554)

Another version of this conversation occurs almost 500 pages later, a few pages before the novel's end. The view is retrospective this time: an American woman, Dally Rideout, living in Paris in twenties, has a conversation with an old friend about the war that they have just come through:

> She bought him a cognac. They sat and watched the lighted boulevard. Policarpe worked for a Socialist newspaper. Death had not taken up residence in his eyes but had visited often enough.
> "We're in Hell, you know," he said conversationally.
> "Everybody thinks we're finally out of there," she said.

A shrug. "The world came to an end in 1914. Like the mindless dead, who don't know they're dead, we are as little aware as they of having been in Hell ever since that terrible August."

"But this" – gesturing round at the blossoming city – "how could this –"

"Illusion. When peace and plenty are once again taken for granted, at your most languorous moment of maximum surrender, the true state of affairs will be borne in upon you. Swiftly and without mercy." (Pynchon, 2006, 1077)

I take these to be conversations, not about the Great War, or not *only* about it, but about what it feels like to live on after 9/11, amid the "ruins of the future" (DeLillo, 2001). It feels like dystopia – like living in Hell – or like becoming a zombie ("the mindless dead, who don't know they're dead"). In this sense, these passages echo Cormac McCarthy's *The Road* (2006; see "Ruins"), or for that matter Whitehead's *Zone One*: "The world wasn't ending: it had ended, and now they were in the new place" (Whitehead, 2011, 257–8).

These are dark visions, appropriate to dark times. Still, as dark as the times are, it does not seem out of the question that one could live on. It is possible, after all, to drink cognac and watch the lighted boulevard, and even Whitehead's nihilism is alleviated, if ever so slightly, by the glimpse of a "new place" that might not necessarily be unlivable. I'm disposed to think that these end-time visions, like Fukuyama's "end of history" thesis before them, actually reflect the experience of cultural change – a transition, let's say, from post-modernism to post-postmodernism, the end of another beginning.

Of course, genuinely apocalyptic possibilities loom ahead of us, especially global ecological disaster, so Policarpe's grim warning about the "true state of affairs" that will sweep illusion away and "Mark Spitz's" dark vision of zombies in America are not *just* metaphors for something more benign, like cultural change, but perhaps literal end-time prophecies as well. Nevertheless, the End of the World *as We Know It* (as in R.E.M's ironic hit single of 1987) isn't quite the same thing as the End of the World, and so far it has proven to be endurable: "I feel fine."

RUINS

1. "America Has No Ruins"

Postmoderns were both imaginatively prepared for the terrorist attacks on the United States on September 11, 2001 – even *over*prepared – and paradoxically *underprepared*. They were overprepared in the sense that they had viewed such scenes of mass destruction before, at the cinema and on television, in disaster movies (e.g., *The Towering Inferno*, 1974), alien-invasion movies (e.g., *Independence Day*, 1996), nuclear-holocaust movies (e.g., *The Day After*, 1983), and the like. However, they were underprepared to imagine the aftermath, the condition of living on "In the Ruins of the Future" (the title of Don DeLillo's essay of December 2001) or *In the Shadow of No Towers* (Art Spiegelman's graphic narrative, produced between November 2001 and August 2003). The impediment to imagining life amid the ruins was that, as the German art historian Horst Janson put it succinctly in 1935, "America has no ruins" (quoted in Puff, 2010, 253). This is not strictly true, as we shall shortly see, but the fact that the United States was, by consensus, assumed to be ruin-free contributed to the shock of seeing iconic American skyscrapers reduced to rubble in the middle of America's greatest metropolis on 9/11.

The very juxtaposition of "America" and "ruin" poses a problem for the imagination. "The term 'American ruin' might seem to contradict itself," wrote the Chilean-born photographer Camilo José Vergara on the eve of the new millennium, "for the United States is a nation conventionally synonymous with innovation and resilience, modernity and progress" (Vergara, 1999, 12). America was largely spared the ruin that so many other parts of the world suffered in the course of the disastrous twentieth century. The iconic image of America threatened with destruction, but also preserved from it, is the missile poised just above the theater's roof on the last page of Pynchon's *Gravity's Rainbow*. In the real world, that missile actually fell elsewhere, on London and Antwerp, and later, in other incarnations, on places like Baghdad.

Europeans and Asians alike were compelled to live on amid the ruins of their cities, and to rebuild them (a challenge that colored the architectural thinking of Aldo Rossi, one of the fathers of postmodernism; see Chapter 2). They did their best to repress their memories of ruin, as the German-language novelist W. G. Sebald argued in his influential 1999 lectures on "Air War and Literature" (Sebald, 2003; Vidler, 2010), and not until the peak postmodern decades did those repressed memories begin to return, in displaced forms. It is from those decades that we find the representations of ruin in, for instance, Anselm Kiefer's paintings, Katsuhiro Otomo's manga series *Akira* (1982–90), adapted as an anime film in 1988, Wim Wenders' film *Wings of Desire* (1987), which hovers above still-ruinous parts of a divided Berlin, and Sebald's own *The Rings of Saturn* (1995), which features a visit to a ruined weapons-testing facility on England's Suffolk coast (Woodward, 2001, 221–6; Pressner, 2010, 202–9). J. G. Ballard, who made a career as a science-fiction writer imagining the "ruins of the future," belatedly acknowledged in an autobiographical novel, *Empire of the Sun* (1984), that the source of those imagined ruins lay in his childhood experience of war-ravaged Shanghai.

As for the United States, however, apart from Pearl Harbor, it was spared the large-scale ruin inflicted on other countries by two world wars and endless regional conflicts. Americans were typically observers of others' ruins, voyeurs of ruin: the ruins of Dresden, fire-bombed by the Allies, in Kurt Vonnegut, Jr.'s *Slaughterhouse-Five* (1969), of Berlin in *Gravity's Rainbow*, of Hiroshima in the writings of the fictitious poet "Araki Yasusada," supposedly a Japanese survivor of the atomic bombing (see Chapter 4; Freind, 2012).

Of course, the United States did have its own home-grown ruins, including literally indigenous ones, those of the Native Americans – the earthworks of the Ohio and Mississippi valleys, the ruined Anasazi pueblos of the Southwest – as well as the ruins of the Confederacy, whose memory was preserved regionally but only emerged sporadically into the national consciousness, as it did in the popular novel (1936) and film (1939) *Gone with the Wind*. "Because the United States is in many ways a country without a past," observes Rebecca Solnit,

> it seems, at first imagining, to be a country without ruins. But it is rich in ruins, though not always as imagined, for it is without a past only in the sense that does not own its past, or own up to it. It does not remember officially and in its media and mainstream, though many subsets of Americans remember passionately. (Solnit, 2011, 151–2)

The erasure of ruins from consciousness, she writes, "is the foundation of the amnesiac landscape that is the United States" (151). Collective amnesia about ruined America did not mitigate the shock of 9/11, but served to amplify it.

2. Sham Ruin

If amnesia is one dimension of the postmodern relation to ruins, another is *play*. Europeans have been playing with, and *in*, ruins since the eighteenth century, when a taste for ruins swept through the more aesthetically advanced circles of the Continent's privileged classes. The Europe-wide collective fascination with ruins manifested itself in literature – the gothic novel, Romantic poetry – as well as in the visual arts, from Giovanni Battista Piranesi's etchings of Roman ruins and imaginary prisons to the paintings of Caspar David Friedrich and beyond. Most extraordinarily of all, it also manifested itself in the fabrication of artificial or sham ruins, custom-made sites of melancholic reflection, conveniently erected on one's own property – ruins built to order, playgrounds of the ruin sensibility (see Zucker, 1961; Harbison, 1991, 99–130; Woodward, 2001, 126–76).

The ruin aesthetic, and the European vogue for sham ruins in particular, seems uncannily to anticipate postmodern simulation and pastiche (Holly, 1993). Outliving the era of the propertied gentlemen of taste, it persists into the twentieth century, turning up in such unlikely places as surrealist paintings (by Giorgio Di Chirico and Paul Delvaux, for instance) and even in one real garden, Ian Hamilton Finlay's garden at Stonypath, Scotland, which combines concrete poetry, installation art, and sham ruin (Abrioux, 1992). Here a revived ruin aesthetic converges with postmodernism, as it does in a different way in Rachel Whiteread's "House" 1(993–94; see Chapter 4), the concrete cast of the interior spaces of a London house slated for demolition (Sinclair, 2011).

As for the Americans, lacking ruins of their own, or at least failing to acknowledge the ones they *did* have, those who wished to experience the ruin aesthetic first-hand had to travel to Europe to sample it, as nineteenth-century figures such as Nathaniel Hawthorne and Henry James did (Woodward, 2001, 20–3). Against all the odds, however, the ruin aesthetic did come to the United States, through intermediaries such as the painter Thomas Cole. Born in England and apprenticed as a portrait painter in Ohio, Cole came into his own as a painter of Hudson Valley landscapes and founder of the Hudson River School. In the mid-1830s he completed a cycle of five paintings tracing *The Course of Empire*, beginning with *The Savage State* and *The Pastoral State* and continuing through *The Consummation of Empire* and *Destruction*, and ending in an image of *Desolation* – the ruins of an imperial city (see Perry, 1988, 131–87; Woodward, 2001, 196–9; Barringer, 2002, 51–3; Wilton, 2002, 21–4). Cole's empire may be a generically Mediterranean one, but his landscape is unmistakably North American, so that his cycle is both decorously historical and pointedly topical at a moment, that of Jacksonian expansionism, when America's imperial destiny was coming under troubled scrutiny and critique. Cole's cycle reflects on the course of American empire, America's so-called "Manifest Destiny"; his ruins are, in one sense, the ruins of the future – American ruins – and, in another sense, sham ruins.

After lying dormant for over a century, the taste for sham ruins revived in the United States in the second half of the twentieth century, expressing itself in new postmodernist forms. The revived aesthetics of ruin manifests itself in a range of conceptual, installation, and earth-art works: in the projects of Robert Smithson, such as his "Non-site" installations, or his "Buried Shed" at Kent State University (1970); in the split houses and sliced-up office buildings of the "anarchitect" Gordon Matta-Clark (Diserens, 1993); or in Michael Heizer's work-in-progress, his "City" in the Nevada desert, a sham ruin on a brobdingnagian scale. Traces of the ruin aesthetic can even be discerned in Maya Lin's Vietnam War Memorial on the National Mall in Washington, D.C., perhaps the most profound public artwork of the postmodern era, which evokes (among other things) an archaeological trench or the ruined foundations of a lost building.

Late-twentieth-century architecture, too, reflected a taste for the sham-ruinous. It manifested itself first in the New Brutalism of architects such as Louis Kahn, whose exposure to the classical ruins of Europe evidently left a lasting imprint on his own severe architecture style. Ruins serve even more decisively as a model for architects associated with the deconstructivist tendency, including Peter Eisenman, Frank Gehry (before he discovered titanium and turned populist), and Daniel Libeskind (who returned from Europe to design buildings for the Ground Zero site, which in the end remain unbuilt; Johnson and Wigley, 1988; Wigley,1993; Derrida and Eisenman, 1997; Woodward, 2001, 221).

Sham-ruinous though they may be, there is nothing particularly playful about most of these buildings, except some of Gehry's. Closer in spirit to the playfulness of the sham ruin aesthetic is the "de-architecture" of James Wines, including, during the peak postmodern decade of the mid-seventies to the mid-eighties, his collaborations on a series of mock-ruined façades for the Best Product store chain (Wines, 1987). This same sham-ruin aesthetic also animates Charles Moore's signature project, his giddily postmodern Piazza d'Italia in New Orleans (1976–79), which simulates a Roman ruin, but one tarted up with neon lighting and modern materials (see Figure 7). Tellingly, it is Moore's Piazza d'Italia that Charles

Figure 7. Charles Moore, *Piazza d'Italia*, New Orleans (1976–79). Photo credit: Norman McGrath.

Jencks regularly cited – along with Michael Graves's Portland Building (1982) and the British architect James Stirling's Neue Staatsgalerie in Stuttgart (1977–84) – as a paradigm of postmodern architecture. Certainly, if anything is double-coded in Jenck's sense (see Chapter 3), it is the Piazza d'Italia, which couples the populist pleasures of a theme-park aesthetic with a knowing in-joke for architects and other cognoscenti.

Pleasurable play with the idea and imagery of ruins runs throughout postwar science fiction and SF film, to the point of constituting a *topos* – that of the post-apocalypse. Memorable examples, among the dozens, perhaps hundreds of novels making use of the *topos*, are Walter M. Miller's classic *A Canticle for Leibowitz* (1959), Russell Hoban's *Riddley Walker* (1980), Kim Stanley Robinson's *The Wild Shore* (1984), and Dennis Johnson's *Fiskadoro* (1985), and, on the big screen, *Planet of the Apes* (1968), where Charlton Heston, as an astronaut returned to Earth from deep space, discovers the ruins of the Statue of Liberty, half-buried in the sand (Woodward, 2001, 1, 196) – a perfect icon of post-apocalypticism. The *topos* is hardly an American monopoly, of course; Hoban's *Riddley Walker*, though written by an American-born author, is set in a post-apocalyptic England, and one can readily think of many examples from outside the States – including Angela Carter's *Heroes and Villains* (1969), Maggie Gee's *The Burning Book* (1983), and almost anything by J. G. Ballard – not to mention movies such as the Australian director George Miller's *Mad Max* trilogy (1979, 1981, 1985).

Weightier than most of these examples – though playful, too, in the sense that all thought experiments are ultimately playful – are the chilling images of nuclear aftermath that the science-fiction illustrator Chesley Bonestell painted at the height of the Cold War, in 1950 and 1951. Illustrating articles in the mass-circulation magazine *Collier's*, these aerial views of Manhattan and Washington

D.C. ruined and ablaze clearly evoke what we might call the iconography of Hiroshima. Making exactly that connection, one of the *Collier's* articles that Bonestell illustrated was actually entitled "Hiroshima U.S.A." Though over half a century old, Bonestell's disturbing images of ruin are *not* obsolete – not relics of an outmoded Cold War sensibility. On the contrary, they have never seemed more topical than they do now, in the aftermath of the 9/11 events, which they seem almost to anticipate, and it takes very little updating to accommodate Bonestell's imagery to a twenty-first-century ruin sensibility. It is with images such as Bonestell's that pleasurable play with ruin imagery begins to give way to the return of the repressed.

3. Ruin Porn

Robert Smithson, fabricator of sham ruins, is also a crucial precursor for another tendency of the postmodern ruin sensibility, what some have mordantly labeled "ruin porn." Photographic documentation, for aesthetic purposes, of modern industrial sites in ruin arguably begins with Smithson's deadpan photographs of modern industrial wastelands in his conceptual-art project *A Tour of the Monuments of Passaic, New Jersey* (1967; Perloff, 1986, 217–24). In recent decades, the model of Smithson's photographic "tour" has proliferated into an abundant photographic record of urban decay and ruin in the wake of the de-industrialization of North American "Rust Belt" cities. No foreign enemy did this to the Americans, as with the ruined European and Asian cities or the ruins of 9/11. Rather, these ruins are self-inflicted: Americans did it to themselves by tolerating the gutting of their country's industrial base and the urban life that depended on it

"America leads the world in urban ruins," writes Camilo José Vergara (1995, 201), whom I have quoted before. Vergara's own photographs are exemplary of the ruin porn genre, especially the ones in his melancholy collection *American Ruins* (1999), where he captures images of a derelict sugar refinery in North Philadelphia; a warehouse in Detroit; Union Station in Gary, Indiana; the Pullman Palace Car factory near Chicago; the Camden, New Jersey, Public Library; and other ruined sites. A recurrent object of ruin photography, and even of "ruin tourism," is the bankrupt and underpopulated city of Detroit, once an industrial powerhouse and home of the automobile industry, but now attracting exactly the kind of voyeuristic fascination for which the term ruin porn was coined in the first place. Vergara himself has even proposed – how seriously or otherwise is hard to say – repurposing downtown Detroit's abandoned skyscrapers as a kind of open-air museum, an American Acropolis or "an urban Monument Valley" (1995, 220).

Apart from Vergara's own photographic projects, other manifestations of Detroit ruin porn include the Canadian photographer and videographer Stan Douglas's installation *Le Detroit* (1999; see Watten, 2003, 320–48), and the documentary film *Detroit: Ruin of a City* (2005) by Michael Chanan and George Steinmetz, with an appropriately stark soundtrack by the minimalist composer

Michael Nyman (Steinmetz, 2010). Ruin photography is not restricted to the United States, however, let alone to Detroit. Bernd and Hilla Becher's photographs of industrial structures in the Ruhr Valley and elsewhere – most of which fell into ruin not long after they were photographed (Barndt, 2010; Lingwood, 2011) – certainly qualify, as do the French artist Cyprien Gaillard's "Cairns" series of still photos of the mountains of debris left after the demolition of residential tower blocks. There is an analogous genre in contemporary Chinese photographic practice (e.g., Chen Jiagang), documenting the industrial wastelands of the Mao era.

A subgenre of ruin porn is what might be called "implosion porn," video or still photography of abandoned buildings being dynamited, images even more transient than ruin porn generally, capturing literally the split seconds of a building's collapse. In a sense, the implosion subgenre dates all the way back to the very onset of postmodernism in the dynamiting of the Pruitt-Igoe housing project, celebrated by Charles Jencks (see Chapter 2) and set to Philip Glass's minimalist music in Godfrey Reggio's film *Koyanisqaatsi* (1982), and it persists all the way down to the televised spectacle of the catastrophic collapse of the World Trade Center Towers, and beyond. Cyprien Gaillard, for instance, incorporates footage of a tower block being imploded at night in his video installation "Desniansky Raion" (2007).

Just as Detroit is a favored site of ruin porn generally, so Las Vegas is the favored site for implosion porn, as obsolete resort hotels and casinos are spectacularly demolished to make way for updated and upgraded replacements (Chaplin, 2000). The signage that once typified the Las Vegas cityscape has been replaced by LED signage, and many of the original signs have been deposited – decommissioned, decontextualized, and stripped of purpose – in the Neon Museum (formerly called the Neon Boneyard Park), an open-air museum of Las Vegas signage, curated and available for guided tours (Warhol, 2013). These are precisely the signs that once instructed Robert Venturi and Denise Scott-Brown about what could be learned from Las Vegas (see Chapter 3). Literally the ruins of postmodernism, the Neon Boneyard is the repository of everything that created the hyper-semiotic streetscape of the Strip that Venturi and his collaborators studied and canonized.

Ridley Scott exploits the appeal of ruin porn when he uses the ruinous interior of Los Angeles's Bradbury Building (which, in the real world, is not ruined at all) as the location for the climactic confrontation in *Blade Runner* (1982). Ruin porn figures also in literary representations, ranging from Paul Auster's *In the Country of Last Things* (1987) and Kathy Ackers' *Empire of the Senseless* (1988) to Octavia Butler's *Parable of the Sower* (1993), to the ruinous South Bronx of Don DeLillo's story "The Angel Esmeralda" (1994), subsequently incorporated into his novel *Underworld* (1997).

Perhaps surprisingly, not all of this literature of urban ruin is negative; some texts offer positive visions of the ruined city as utopia, or at least heterotopia. Positive ruins include Bellona, the ambiguously utopian city in Samuel R. Delany's *Dhalgren* (1974); the ruined Golden Gate Bridge of William Gibson's "Bridge" trilogy of the nineties, shaken to pieces by an earthquake but reclaimed and

resourcefully colonized by urban squatters; and Belize's vision of an urban afterlife in Part Two of Tony Kushner's *Angels in America*. Asked by Roy Cohn, a
Republican political operative (and a real historical figure), dying of AIDS, what
the afterlife is like, Belize answers, "Like San Francisco":

> Big city, overgrown with weeds, but flowering weeds. On every corner a
> wrecking crew and something new and crooked going up catty-corner to
> that. Windows missing in every edifice like broken teeth, fierce gusts of
> gritty wind, and a gray high sky full of ravens . . . . Piles of trash, but lapidary
> like rubies and obsidian, and diamond-colored cowspit streamers in the
> wind. And voting booths . . . . And everyone in Balenciaga gowns with red
> corsages, and big dance palaces full of music and lights and racial impurity
> and gender confusion. (Kushner, 1995, 209)

The afterlife of Belize's vision is a city in which we live on amid the ruins – or, in
other words, Downtown, the capital of postmodernism (see Chapter 3).

4. Manifest Destiny

All these manifestations of postmodern ruin sensibility, including sham ruins and
photographic ruin porn, seem to converge on the imagery of 9/11, or vice versa,
the imagery of 9/11 converges with the postmodern ruin sensibility. It is as if
postmodernism had secretly been anticipating 9/11 after all, and covertly preparing for it all along – and not just the shocking event itself, but life amid its
ruins. This seems to be true not only of postmodern texts that directly reflect the
9/11 events, such as William Gibson's *Pattern Recognition* (2003), Art
Spiegelman's *In the Shadow of No Towers* (2004), Jonathan Safran Foer's
Extremely Loud and Incredibly Close (2005), or Don DeLillo's *Falling Man* (2007)
(see Chapter 5), but even, or especially, of artworks that do not explicitly refer to
9/11 at all.

A case in point is Moore's Piazza d'Italia, Charles Jencks's favorite example of
postmodernism, which of course predates the 9/11 events by twenty-five years.
Designed to be the focal point for redevelopment of a downtown New Orleans
neighborhood with a historical connection to the Italian community, Moore's
sham-ruinous Piazza suffered years of neglect when the original redevelopment
scheme was abandoned. Reduced to a haunt for the city's homeless, the sham
ruin decayed into a *real* ruin, then underwent restoration in the new millennium –
just in time for Hurricane Katrina to ruin whole neighborhoods of New Orleans in
August 2005. The latest update is that the Piazza d'Italia has been restored once
again. Its strange history as a serially restored ruined ruin seems uncannily to
capture in miniature, as in a scale-model, the entire experience of postmodern
ruin that culminates in 9/11 and its aftermath.

A case of a different sort is Cormac McCarthy's post-apocalyptic novel *The
Road* (2006), and its 2009 film adaptation. A narrative about a nameless father
and son, survivors of an obscure global catastrophe (nuclear winter? asteroid
impact? ecological disaster?), who traverse an almost lifeless American landscape
of abandoned farmhouses and ruined towns, *The Road* couples familiar genre

conventions (last-man-on-earth, zombie-apocalypse, road movie) with high-art seriousness and an austere style. If the scenario recalls Ballard's stories of living on amid the ruins, the style evokes Samuel Beckett's severe minimalism or that of Ernest Hemingway. *The Road*, in other words, is double-coded, high art and pop culture simultaneously.

The disaster that puts McCarthy's protagonists on the road and sets them in motion, precisely because it is unspecified, opens the novel to a general allusiveness to the full range of postmodern catastrophes and their aftermaths, whether manmade or natural. This breadth of allusion is confirmed by the movie version, in which the director, John Hillcoat, makes sparing use of CGI (see Chapter 4), instead opting to film at genuinely ruinous locations, including post-industrial ruin-porn sites in the Pittsburgh area, post-Katrina landscapes in rural Louisiana, and locations around Mt. Saint Helens, ash-covered since the1980 volcanic eruption. Thus, the film realizes McCarthy's imagination of ruin by sampling all the types of postmodern ruin, leaving out only 9/11's Ground Zero itself, which is nevertheless present everywhere by implication and connotation.

A final example is a painting, Alexis Rockman's ironically titled *Manifest Destiny* (Figure 8). Commissioned by the Brooklyn Museum, executed in 2003–04, and now part of the American art collection of the Smithsonian Institution in Washington, D.C., this is a "great picture" (as nineteenth-century landscapes used to be called), measuring 8 feet by 24 feet (2.40 meters by 7.30 meters). A visionary image of the far future, it shows Brooklyn, viewed from Manhattan, several thousand years from now, after rising sea levels have drowned the city. The foreground is filled with creatures from southern seas that have migrated to northern waters as the oceans warmed. On the right are the ruins of the Brooklyn

Figure 8. Alexis Rockman, *Manifest Destiny* (2003–04). Oil and acrylic on wood. 96 in. × 288 in. (243.8 cm × 731.5 cm). Smithsonian American Art Museum, Washington, D.C. Museum purchase through the Lusita L. and Franz H. Denghausen Endowment.
© 2014 Alexis Rockman/Artists Rights Society (ARS), New York. Photo credit: Smithsonian American Art Museum, Washington, D.C./Art Resource, NY.

Bridge; in the background, the ruins of Brooklyn itself. The style of the painting is easily recognizable as that of popular-science illustrations, such as one might find in *National Geographic* magazine, or in the murals and dioramas of museums of natural history. Rockman's picture fuses cutting-edge fine art with popular illustration; it is double-coded.

Manifest Destiny is a narrative picture, or at any rate a *narrativizable* one (see "Alice"), depending, as traditional historical and mythological paintings also do, on a verbal narrative that is known in advance or available elsewhere, outside the painting itself. In this case, the relevant narrative – the one about warming oceans and rising sea levels, summarized in the preceding paragraph – is supplied either in an accompanying catalogue, or as a wall caption in the gallery, or both. Prompted by this supplementary text, the viewer readily fills in the earlier episodes in the narrative sequence, the series of "stills" of which *Manifest Destiny* itself is the last, like *Desolation* in Thomas Coles' cycle, *The Course of Empire* (from which *Manifest Destiny* is clearly descended). The implied story is one of phased ecological disaster: first complacency and denial, then heroic but futile effort (glimpsed in the ruined seawalls in the picture's middle distance, evidently meant to stem the rising waters), then gradual withdrawal to higher ground, and finally the abandonment of the city and its deterioration into ruin.

Like *The Road*, Rockman's painting evokes the full range of disaster and ruin imagery, high and low, from the sham ruins of deconstructivist architecture and Bonestell's Cold War illustrations, to the ruin porn of Smithson, Vergara and Ridley Scott, to big-screen disaster movies and post-apocalyptic science-fiction films like *Escape from New York* (1979). Looking at Rockman's image of the Brooklyn Bridge in ruins, it is impossible not to be reminded of the ruins of the Statue of Liberty at the end of *Planet of the Apes*. In other words, Rockman's great picture taps into what Susan Sontag (1965) once called the "imagination of disaster" in American popular culture.

However, if it is hard not to think of *Planet of the Apes* when looking at *Manifest Destiny*, it is even harder not to think of the ruins of September 11, 2001. Yet the destruction of the World Trade Center could *not* have been one of Rockman's intended references, at least not initially. Though the painting wasn't actually executed until 2003–04, it had already been commissioned, researched, and planned *before* 9/11. In the same way that catastrophic history, in the form of the failure of urban redevelopment, and then the failure of the levees, caught up with Moore's Piazza d'Italia, so history in the form of the attacks of 9/11 caught up with *Manifest Destiny*.

These are not cheap ironies, but painful and revealing ones. What they tell us is that all along, long before the actual catastrophes of 9/11 and Hurricane Katrina – or for that matter, of Chernobyl (1986), Fukushima (2011), and all the others – we postmoderns have been storing up images of such catastrophes and their aftermaths, staging them, rehearsing them in our imaginations and in our artworks, in apocalyptic movies, in paintings, even in works of architecture. We have been composing scenarios of the end of civilization, and life amid its ruins, not only in popular science-fiction novels and movies but also in demanding literary novels like *Gravity's Rainbow*, where the London of the V-2 blitz and the war-ruined cities of Germany obviously and self-consciously refer to the projected future ruins to which contemporary cities could so easily be reduced by catastrophes manmade or natural. Much more than the actual 9/11 memorial at the World Trade Center site, these artworks are what we have instead of monuments: they are our *countermonuments* (Young, 1993), commemorating the future and, maybe, the world that once sustained a postmodern culture.

References

Aarseth, Espen J. (1997) *Cybertext: Perspectives on Ergodic Literature.* Baltimore, MD: The Johns Hopkins University Press.

Abrioux, Yves (1992) *Ian Hamilton Finlay: A Visual Primer.* Cambridge, MA: MIT Press.

Acker, Kathy (1988) *Empire of the Senseless.* New York: Grove Weidenfeld.

Agar, Jon (2003) *Constant Touch: A Global History of the Mobile Phone.* Cambridge, UK: Icon Books.

Aldama, Frederick Luis (2003) *Postethnic Narrative Criticism: Magicorealism in Oscar "Zeta" Acosta, Ana Castillo, Julie Dash, Hanif Kureishi, and Salman Rushdie.* Nashville, TN: Vanderbilt University Press.

Aldridge, Alan, ed. (1991) *The Beatles Illustrated Lyrics.* Boston, MA: Houghton Mifflin.

Anderson, Laurie (1984) "Gravity's Angel." *Mister Heartbreak.* CD. Warner Brothers.

(1989) "The Dream Before." *Strange Angels.* CD. Warner Brothers.

(1991) *Empty Places: A Performance.* New York: Harper Collins.

Andrews, Bruce (1987) "Confidence Trick." In *Give 'Em Enough Rope.* Los Angeles: Sun & Moon Press. 142–86.

Andrews, Julia F. (2008) "Post-Mao, Postmodern." In Julia M. White, ed., *Mahjong: Art, Film and Change in China.* Berkeley, CA: University of California, Berkeley Art Museum and Pacific Film Archive. 29–36.

Antin, David (1972) "Modernism and Postmodernism: Approaching the Present in American Poetry," *Boundary 2* 1:1, 98–133.

Appignanesi, Lisa and Sarah Maitland, eds. (1989) *The Rushdie File.* London: Fourth Estate.

Bakhtin, Mikhail (1984) *Problems of Dostoevsky's Poetics.* Trans. Caryl Emerson. Minneapolis, MN: University of Minnesota Press. 1929, 1963.

Baldick, Chris (1996) "Literary Theory and Textual Politics: Since 1968." In *Criticism and Literary Theory, 1890 to the Present.* London and New York: Longman. 161–208.

Ballard, J.G. (1985a) *Concrete Island.* New York: Vintage.

(1985b) "Introduction to the French Edition." In *Crash.* New York: Random House. 1974.

(1990) *The Atrocity Exhibition.* Revised, expanded, annotated, illustrated edition. San Francisco, CA: V/Search.

Banes, Sally (1993) *Greenwich Village, 1963: Avant-Garde Performance and the Effervescent Body*. Durham, NC: Duke University Press.

Barker, Francis and Peter Hulme (1985) "'Nymphs and reapers heavily vanish': The discursive contexts of *The Tempest*." In John Drakakis, ed., *Alternative Shakespeares*. London: Methuen. 191–205.

Barndt, Kerstin (2010) "'Memory Traces of an Abandoned Set of Futures': Industrial Ruins in the Postindustrial Landscapes of Germany. "In Julia Hell and Andreas Schönle, eds., *Ruins of Modernity*. Durham, NC: Duke University Press. 270–93.

Barringer, Tim (2002) "The Course of Empires: Landscape and Identity in America and Britain, 1820–1880." In Andrew Wilton and Tim Barringer, eds., *American Sublime: Landscape Painting in the United States, 1820–1880*. Princeton, NJ: Princeton University Press. 38–65.

Barth, John (1966) *Giles Goat-Boy or, The Revised New Syllabus*. Greenwich, CT: Fawcett.

(1984) *The Friday Book: Essays and Other Nonfiction*. New York: Putnam.

(1995) "Postmodernism Revisited: A Professional Novelist's Amateur Review." In *Further Fridays: Essays, Lectures, and Other Nonfiction 1984-94*. Boston, MA: Little, Brown. 291–310. 1991.

Barthelme, Donald (1982) "On Angels." In *Sixty Stories*. New York: Dutton. 135–37.

The Beatles Anthology (2000) San Francisco, CA: Chronicle Books.

Becker, Daniel Levin (2012) *Many Subtle Channels: In Praise of Potential Literature*. Cambridge, MA: Harvard University Press.

Belgrad, Daniel (1998) *The Culture of Spontaneity: Improvisation and the Arts in Postwar America*. Chicago, IL: University of Chicago Press.

Bell, Alice (2010) *The Possible Worlds of Hypertext Fiction*. Basingstoke, UK: Palgrave Macmillan.

Benedickt, Michael, ed. (1991) *Cyberspace: First Steps*. Cambridge, MA: MIT Press.

Berger, Peter L. and Thomas Luckmann (1966) *The Social Construction of Reality: A Treatise in the Sociology of Knowledge*. Garden City, NY: Doubleday.

Berman, Marshall (1982) *All That Is Solid Melts into Air: The Experience of Modernity*. New York: Simon and Schuster.

(2007) "Introduction." In Marshall Berman and Brian Berger, eds., *New York Calling: From Blackout to Bloomberg*. London: Reaktion Books. 9–38.

Bernstein, Charles (2012) "The Expanded Field of L=A=N=G=U=A=G=E." In Joe Bray, Alison Gibbons and Brian McHale, eds., *The Routledge Companion to Experimental Literature*. Abingdon, VA: Routledge. 281–97.

Berry, R.M. (2012) "Metafiction." In Joe Bray, Alison Gibbons and Brian McHale, eds., *The Routledge Companion to Experimental Literature*. London: Routledge. 128–40.

Bertens, Han (1995) *The Idea of the Postmodern: A History*. London: Routledge.

(1997) "The Detective." In Hans Bertens and Douwe Fokkema, eds., *International Postmodernism: Theory and Literary Practice.* Amsterdam: John Benjamins. 195–202.

Bloom, Harold (2007) *Fallen Angels.* New Haven, CT: Yale University Press.

Bolter, J. David (1991) *Writing Space: The Computer, Hypertext, and the History of Writing.* Hillsdale, NJ: Erlbaum.

Boorstin, Daniel J. (1985) *The Image: A Guide to Pseudo-Events in America.* New York: Atheneum. 1962.

Borges, Jorge Luis (1952) "Magias parciales del Quijote." In *Otras inquisiciones (1937–1952).* Buenos Aires: Sur.

(1964) "Kafka and His Precursors." In *Other Inquisitions 1937–1952.* Trans. Ruth L.C. Simms. Austin, TX: University of Texas Press. 106–108. 1952.

Boswell, Marshall (2003) *Understanding David Foster Wallace.* Columbia, SC: University of South Carolina Press.

Bradbury, Malcolm (1993) "Postmodernism, the Novel, and the TV Medium." In Heide Ziegler, ed., *The End of Postmodernism: New Directions. Proceedings of the First Stuttgart Seminar in Cultural Studies 04.08–18.08.1991.* Stuttgart: M&P Verlag für Wissenschaft und Forschung. 81–100, 115–34.

Bray, Joe (2012) "Concrete Poetry and Prose." In Joe Bray, Alison Gibbons and Brian McHale, eds., *The Routledge Companion to Experimental Literature.* Abingdon, VA: Routledge. 298–309.

Brodkey, Harold (1988) "Angel." In *Stories in an Almost Classical Mode.* New York: Knopf. 553–93. 1985.

Brooker, Will (2004) *Alice's Adventures: Lewis Carroll in Popular Culture.* New York: Continuum.

Bruster, Douglas (2001) "Local *Tempest*: Shakespeare and the Work of the Early Modern Playhouse." In Patrick Murphy, ed., *The Tempest: Critical Essays.* New York: Routledge. 257–75.

Burn, Stephen (2008) *Jonathan Franzen at the End of Postmodernism.* London: Continuum.

Butler, Judith (1990) *Gender Trouble: Feminism and the Subversion of Identity.* New York: Routledge.

Cacciari, Massimo (1994) *The Necessary Angel.* Trans. Miguel E. Vatter. Albany, NY: SUNY Press. 1987.

Calinescu, Matei (1987) *Five Faces of Modernity: Modernism, Avant-Garde, Decadence, Kitsch, Postmodernism.* Durham, NC: Duke University Press.

(1997) "Rewriting." In Hans Bertens and Douwe Fokkema, eds., *International Postmodernism: Theory and Literary Practice.* Amsterdam: John Benjamins. 243–8.

Calle, Sophie (2007) *Double Game.* With the participation of Paul Auster. New York: Distributed Art Publishers. 1999.

Calvino, Italo (1988) "Lightness." In *Six Memos for the Millennium.* Trans. Patrick Creagh. Cambridge, MA: Harvard University Press. 3–29.

(1995) "How I Wrote One of My Books." Trans. Iain White. In *OuLiPo Laboratory: Texts from the Bibliothèque Oulipienne*. London: Atlas Press.

Carroll, Lewis (1971) *Alice in Wonderland: A Norton Critical Edition*. Ed. Donald J. Gray. New York: W.W. Norton.

Cartelli, Thomas (1999) *Repositioning Shakespeare: National Formations, Postcolonial Appropriations*. London: Routledge.

Chaplin, Sarah (2000) "Heterotopia deserta: Las Vegas and other spaces." In Iain Borden and Jane Rendell, eds., *Intersections: Architectural Histories and Critical Theories*. London: Routledge. 203–20.

Chollet, Derek and James Goldgeier (2008) *America between the Wars, from 11/9 to 9/11: The Misunderstood Years between the Fall of the Berlin Wall and the Start of the War on Terror*. New York: Council on Foreign Relations.

Chu, Seo-Young (2010) *Do Metaphors Dream of Literal Sleep? A Science-Fictional Theory of Representation*. Cambridge, MA: Harvard University Press.

Ciccoricco, David (2007) *Reading Network Fiction*. Tuscaloosa, AL: University of Alabama Press.

(2012) "Digital Fiction: Networked Fictions." In Joe Bray, Alison Gibbons and Brian McHale, eds., *The Routledge Companion to Experimental Literature*. Abingdon, VA: Routledge. 469–82.

Clover, Joshua (2009) *1989: Bob Dylan Didn't Have This to Sing About*. Berkeley, CA: University of California Press.

Coe, Jonathan (2004) *Like a Fiery Elephant: The Story of B.S. Johnson*. London: Picador.

Cohen, Samuel (2009) *After the End of History: American Fiction in the 1990s*. Iowa City: University of Iowa Press. E-book.

Cohen, Stanley and Laurie Taylor (1978) *Escape Attempts: The Theory and Practice of Resistance to Everyday Life*. Harmondsworth: Penguin.

Cohn-Sherbok, Dan, ed. (1990) *The Salman Rushdie Controversy in Interreligious Perspective*. Lewiston, NY: Edwin Mellen Press.

Conte, Joseph (2002) "American Oulipo: Proceduralism in the Novels of Gilbert Sorrentino." In *Design and Debris: A Chaotics of Postmodern American Fiction*. Tuscaloosa, AL: University of Alabama Press. 75–111.

Cooper, Martha and Henry Chalfant (1984) *Subway Art*. New York: Henry Holt.

Coover, Robert (1969) *Pricksongs & Descants*. New York: New American Library.

(1988) *A Night at the Movies, or, You Must Remember This*. New York: Macmillan.

(1992) "The End of Books," *The New York Times Book Review*, June 21. *Academic OneFile*. Web. Accessed 6 August, 2013.

(1992) "Hyperfiction: Novels for the Computer" and "And Now, Boot Up the Reviews," *The New York Times Book Review*, Aug. 29. *Academic OneFile*. Web. 6 August, 2013.

(2010) " One Hot Book: Richard Seaver and *The Public Burning's* Wild Ride." *The Humanist*, May/June. Web.

Crowley, P. J. (2009) "The Battle of Narratives: The Real Central Front against Al Qaeda." In Matthew J. Morgan, ed., *The Impact of 9/11 on the Media, Arts, and Entertainment: The Day That Changed Everything?* New York: Palgrave Macmillan. 37–50.

Crumb, Robert and Peter Poplaski (2005) *The R. Crumb Handbook*. London: MQ Publications.

Culler, Jonathan (1992) "Literary Theory." In Joseph Gibaldi, ed., *Introduction to Scholarship in Modern Languages and Literatures*. New York: Modern Language Association of America. 2nd ed. 201–35.

   (2007) *The Literary in Theory*. Stanford, CA: Stanford University Press.

Damon, Maria (1997) "Angelology: Things with Wings." In Peter Gibian, ed., *Mass Culture and Everyday Life*. New York: Routledge. 206–11.

Danto, Arthur C. (2007) "Things Fall Together: An Introduction to the Sculptural Achievement of Sarah Sze." In *Sarah Sze*. New York: Abrams. 6–7.

Delany, Samuel R. (1988) "Is Cyberpunk a Good Thing or a Bad Thing?" *Mississippi Review* 16, 2–3:28–35.

Derrida, Jacques and Peter Eisenman (1997) *Chora L Works*. Eds. Jeffrey Kipnis and Thomas Leeser. New York: The Monacelli Press.

Dery, Mark (1994) "Black to the Future: Interviews with Samuel R. Delany, Greg Tate and Tricia Rose." In Mark Dery, ed., *Flame Wars: The Discourse of Cyberculture*. Durham, NC: Duke University Press. 179–222.

D'haen, Theo (1995) "Magic Realism and Postmodernism: Decentering Privileged Centers." In Lois Parkinson Zamora and Wendy B. Faris, eds., *Magical Realism: Theory, History, Community*. Durham, NC: Duke University Press. 191–208.

   (1997) "Postmodernisms: From Fantastic to Magic Realist." In Hans Bertens and Douwe Fokkema, eds., *International Postmodernism: Theory and Literary Practice*. Amsterdam: John Benjamins. 283–93.

Diserens, Corinne (2003) "Gordon Matta-Clark." In Andrew Benjamin, ed., *Installation Art. Art and Design*. London: Academy Editions. 34–41.

DeKoven, Marianne (2004) *Utopia Limited: The Sixties and the Emergence of the Postmodern*. Durham, NC: Duke University Press.

Deutsche, Rosalyn and Cara Gendel Ryan, (1984) "The Fine Art of Gentrification," *October* 31: 91–111.

Dobson, Michael (2001) "'Remember/First to Possess His Books': The Appropriation of *The Tempest*, 1700–1800." In Patrick Murphy, ed., *The Tempest: Critical Essays*. New York: Routledge. 245–255.

Dusinberre, Juliet (1987) *Alice to the Lighthouse: Children's Books and Radical Experiments in Art*. Basingstoke: Macmillan.

Dworkin, Craig (2003) *Reading the Illegible*. Evanston, IL: Northwestern University Press.

Dworkin, Craig and Kenneth Goldsmith, eds. (2011) *Against Expression: An Anthology of Conceptual Writing*. Evanston, IL: Northwestern University Press.

Dylan, Bob (1974) *Writings and Drawings*. St. Albans: Panther.

Eco, Umberto (1983) *The Name of the Rose*, trans. William Weaver. San Diego: Harcourt Brace Jovanovich. 1980.

(1984) Postscript to *The Name of the Rose*, trans. William Weaver. San Diego: Harcourt Brace Jovanovich. 1983.

Eddins, Dwight (1990) *The Gnostic Pynchon*. Bloomington, IN: Indiana University Press.

Eklund, Douglas (2009) *The Pictures Generation, 1974–1984*. New York: Metropolitan Museum of Art/New Haven: Yale University Press.

Elias, Amy J. (2012) "Virtual Autobiography: Autographies, Interfaces and Avatars." In Joe Bray, Alison Gibbons and Brian McHale, eds., *The Routledge Companion to Experimental Literature*. Abingdon, VA: Routledge. 512–27.

Elliott, Kamilla (2003) *Rethinking the Novel/Film Debate*. Cambridge, UK: Cambridge University Press.

Ensslin, Astrid (2012) "Computer Gaming." In Joe Bray, Alison Gibbons and Brian McHale, eds., *The Routledge Companion to Experimental Literature*. Abingdon, VA: Routledge. 497–511.

Epstein, Andrew (2012) "Found Poetry, 'Uncreative Writing,' and the Art of Appropriation." In Joe Bray, Alison Gibbons and Brian McHale, eds., *The Routledge Companion to Experimental Literature*. Abingdon, VA: Routledge. 310–22.

Eskelinen, Markku (2012) *Cybertext Poetics: The Critical Landscape of New Media Literary Theory*. London: Continuum.

Everdell, William R. (1997) *The First Moderns: Profiles in the Origins of Twentieth-Century Thought*. Chicago, IL: University of Chicago Press.

Fariña, Richard (1969) "The Monterey Fair." In *Long Time Coming and a Long Time Gone*. New York: Random House. 135–54.

Faris, Wendy (1995) "Scheherazade's Children: Magical Realism and Postmodern Fiction." In Lois Parkinson Zamora and Wendy B. Faris, eds., *Magical Realism: Theory, History, Community*. Durham, NC: Duke University Press. 163–90.

(2004) *Ordinary Enchantments: Magical Realism and the Remystification of Narrative*. Nashville, TN: Vanderbilt University Press.

Fensch, Thomas (1970) *Alice in Acidland*. Cranbury, NJ: A.S. Barnes.

Federman, Raymond (1993) *Critifiction: Postmodern Essays*. Albany: SUNY Press.

(2001) *Aunt Rachel's Fur*. Normal, IL and Tallahassee, FL: Fiction Collective Two.

Fokkema, Douwe (2008) "Chinese Postmodernist Fiction," *Modern Language Quarterly* 69, 1: 141–65.

Foster, Hal (2009) "Questionnaire on 'The Contemporary,'" *October* 130: 3.

Foster, Hal, Rosalind Krauss, Yves-Alain Bois, Benjamin H. D. Buchloh, and David Joselit (2011) *Art Since 1900: Modernism, Antimodernism, Postmodernism*. Vol. 2, *1945–2010*. New York: Thomas & Hudson. 2nd ed.

Foucault, Michel (1984) "Des espaces autres," *Architecture, Mouvement, Continuité* 5: 46–9.

Freind, Bill, ed. (2012) *Scubadivers and Chrysanthemums: Essays on the Poetry of Araki Yasusada*. Bristol, UK: Shearsman Books.

Friedman, Ellen G. and Corinne Squire (1998) *Morality USA*. Minneapolis, MN: University of Minnesota Press.

Frow, John (1997) "What Was Postmodernism?" In *Time and Commodity Culture: Essays in Cultural Theory and Postmodernity*. Oxford: Clarendon Press. 13–63.

Gallup, Jane (1992) *Around 1981: Academic Feminist Literary Theory*. New York: Routledge.

Gass, William H. (1970) *Fiction and the Figures of Life*. New York: Knopf.

Gates, Henry Louis, Jr. (1988) *The Signifying Monkey: A Theory of Afro-American Literary Criticism*. New York: Oxford University Press.

Gavins, Joanna (2012) "The Literary Absurd." In Joe Bray, Alison Gibbons and Brian McHale, eds., *The Routledge Companion to Experimental Literature*. Abingdon, VA: Routledge. 62–74.

Gibbons, Allison (2012) "Altermodernist Fiction." In Joe Bray, Alison Gibbons and Brian McHale, eds., *The Routledge Companion to Experimental Literature*. Abingdon, VA: Routledge. 238–52.

Gibson, Andrew (1999) *Postmodernity, Ethics and the Novel: From Leavis to Levinas*. London: Routledge.

Gibson, William (1984) *Neuromancer*. New York: Ace.

(2003) *Pattern Recognition*. New York: Putnam.

Gilbert, Roger (2001) "Awash with Angels: The Religious Turn in Nineties Poetry," *Contemporary Literature* 42, 2: 238–69.

Gillies, James and Robert Cailliau (2000) *How the Web was Born: The Story of the World Wide Web*. Oxford: Oxford University Press.

Gitlin, Todd (1988) "Hip-Deep in Postmodernism," *New York Times Book Review*, 6 November, 35.

Goldberg, Jonathan (2004) *Tempest in the Caribbean*. Minneapolis, MN: University of Minnesota Press.

Goldsmith, Kenneth (2011) *Uncreative Writing: Managing Literature in the Digital Age*. New York: Columbia University Press.

Gray, Richard (2009) "Open Doors, Closed Minds: American Prose Writing at a Time of Crisis," *American Literary History* 21, 1: 128–51.

Green, Jeremy (2005) *Late Postmodernism: American Fiction at the Millennium*. New York: Palgrave Macmillan.

Greene, Roland (2000) "Island Logic." In Peter Hulme and William H. Sherman, eds., *"The Tempest" and Its Travels*. Philadelphia, PA: University of Pennsylvania Press. 138–45.

Hajdu, David (2001) *Positively 4th Street: The Lives and Times of Joan Baez, Bob Dylan, Mimi Baez Fariña, and Richard Fariña*. New York: Farrar, Straus and Giroux.

Haraway, Dona (1991) *Simians, Cyborgs, and Women: The Reinvention of Nature*. New York: Routledge.

Harbison, Robert (1991) *The Built, the Unbuilt, and the Unbuildable*. Cambridge, MA: MIT Press.

Harrison, Thomas (1996) *1910: The Emancipation of Dissonance*. Berkeley, CA: University of California Press.

Hartley, George (1989) *Textual Politics and the Language Poets*. Bloomington, IN: Indiana University Press.

Harvey, David (2005) *A Brief History of Neoliberalism*. New York: Oxford University Press.

Hatherley, Owen (2011) *A Guide to the New Ruins of Great Britain*. London: Verso.

Hayles, N. Katherine and Nick Montfort (2012) "Interactive Fiction." In Joe Bray, Alison Gibbons and Brian McHale, eds., *The Routledge Companion to Experimental Literature*. Abingdon, VA: Routledge. 452 66.

Hayot, Eric (2007) *Chinese Dreams: Pound, Brecht, and Tel Quel*. Ann Arbor, MI: University of Michigan Press.

Heise, Ursula (2006) "1970, Planet Earth: The Imagination of the Global." In Brian McHale and Randall Stevenson, eds., *The Edinburgh Companion to Twentieth-Century Literatures in English*. Edinburgh: Edinburgh University Press. 201–16.

(2008) *Sense of Place and Sense of Planet: The Environmental Imagination of the Global*. New York: Oxford University Press.

Hellmann, John (2006) "1967, Liverpool, London, San Francisco, Vietnam: 'We Hope You Will Enjoy the Show." In Brian McHale and Randall Stevenson, eds., *The Edinburgh Companion to Twentieth-Century Literatures in English*. Edinburgh: Edinburgh University Press. 189–200.

Herr, Michael (1978) *Dispatches*. New York: Avon.

Higgins, Dick (1978) *A Dialectic of Centuries: Notes towards a Theory of the New Arts*. New York and Barton, VT: Printed Editions.

(1987) *Pattern Poetry: Guide to an Unknown Literature*. Albany, NY: State University of New York Press.

Hoberek, Andrew (2007) "Introduction: After Postmodernism," *Twentieth Century Literature* 53, 3: 233–47.

Hobson, Suzanne (2007) "A New Angelology: Mapping the Angel through Twentieth-Century Literature," *Literature Compass* 42: 494–507.

Hofstadter, Douglas R. (1979) *Gödel Escher Bach: An Eternal Golden Braid*. Harmondsworth: Penguin.

Hohmann, Charles (1986) *Thomas Pynchon's* Gravity's *Rainbow: A Study of Its Conceptual Structure and of Rilke's Influence*. New York: Peter Lang.

Holly, Grant I. (1993) "The Ruins of Allegory and the Allegory of Ruins." In Bill Readings and Bennet Schaber, eds., *Postmodernism Across the Ages: Essays for a Postmodernity That Wasn't Born Yesterday*. Syracuse, NY: Syracuse University Press. 188–215.

Hughes, Jane Elizabeth and Scott B. MacDonald (2004) *Carnival on Wall Street: Global Financial Markets in the 1990s*. Hoboken, NJ: John Wiley and Sons.

Hulme, Peter and William H. Sherman, (2000) *"The Tempest" and Its Travels*. Philadelphia, PA: University of Pennsylvania Press.

Hume, Kathryn (1987) *Pynchon's Mythography: An Approach to Gravity's Rainbow*. Carbondale, IL: Southern Illinois University Press.

Huntsperger, David W. (2010) *Procedural Form in Postmodern American Poetry: Berrigan, Antin, Silliman, and Hejinian*. New York: Palgrave Macmillan.

Huyssen, Andreas (1986) *After the Great Divide: Modernism, Mass Culture, Postmodernism*. Bloomington, IN: Indiana University Press.

Israel, Kali (2000) "Asking Alice: Victorian and Other Alices in Contemporary Culture." In John Kucich and Dianne F. Sadoff, eds., *Victorian Afterlife: Postmodern Culture Rewrites the Nineteenth Century*. Minneapolis, MN: University of Minnesota Press. 252–87.

Jakobson, Roman (1960) "Closing Statement: Linguistics and Poetics." In Thomas A. Sebeok, ed., *Style in Language*. Cambridge, MA: MIT Press. 350–77.

(2002) "The Dominant." In Ladislav Matejka and Krystyna Pomorska, eds., *Readings in Russian Poetics: Formalist and Structuralist Views*. Normal, IL: Dalkey Archive Press. 82–7.

James, David and Urmila Seshagiri (2014) "Metamodernism: Narratives of Continuity and Revolution," *PMLA* 129, 1:87–100.

Jameson, Fredric (1988) "Periodizing the Sixties." In *The Syntax of History. The Ideologies of Theory: Essays, 1971 – 1986*, vol. 2. Minneapolis, MN: University of Minnesota Press. 178– 208. 1984.

(1991) *Postmodernism; or, The Cultural Logic of Late Capitalism*. Durham, NC: Duke University Press.

(2002) *A Singular Modernity: Essay on the Ontology of the Present*. London: Verso.

(2005) *Archaeologies of the Future: The Desire Called Utopia and Other Science Fictions*. London: Verso.

Jencks, Charles (1984) *The Language of Post-Modern Architecture*, 4th ed. London: Academy.

(1986) *What Is Post-Modernism?* London: Academy Editions/New York: St. Martin's Press.

(2011) *The Story of Post-Modernism: Five Decades of the Ironic, Iconic and Critical in Architecture*. Chichester: John Wiley.

Jenkins, Henry (2004) "Game Design as Narrative Architecture." In Noah Wardrip-Fruin and Patt Harrigan, eds., *First Person: New Media as Story, Performance, and Game*. Cambridge, MA: MIT Press. 118–30.

Johnson, Philip and Mark Wigley (1988) *Deconstructivist Architecture*. Boston, MA: Little, Brown/The Museum of Modern Art, New York.

Johnston, Ollie and Frank Thomas (1993) *The Disney Villains*. New York: Hyperion.

Jones, David Albert (2010) *Angels: A History*. Oxford: Oxford University Press.
Jones, Jo Elwyn and J. Francis Gladstone (1998) *The Alice Companion: A Guide to Lewis Carroll's Alice Books*. New York: NYU Press.
Junod, Tom (2003) "The Falling Man," *Esquire* 140, 3: 177+.
Kelly, James Patrick and John Kessel, eds. (2007) *Rewired: The Post-Cyberpunk Anthology*. San Francisco, CA: Tachyon Publications.
Keniston, Ann and Jeanne Follansbee Quinn (2008) *Literature after 9/11*. New York: Routledge.
Kern, Stephen (2011) *The Modernist Novel: A Critical Introduction*. Cambridge, UK: Cambridge University Press.
Killen, Andreas (2006) *1973 Nervous Breakdown: Watergate, Warhol, and the Birth of Post-Sixties America*. New York: Bloomsbury.
Kinnahan, Linda (2006) "1912, London, Chicago, Florence, New York: Modernist Moments, Feminist Mappings." In Brian McHale and Randall Stevenson, eds. *The Edinburgh Companion to Twentieth-Century Literatures in English*. Edinburgh: Edinburgh University Press. 23–34.
Knight, Peter (2008) "Beyond the Cold War in Don DeLillo's *Mao II* and *Underworld*." In Jay Prosser, ed., *American Fiction of the 1990s: Reflections of History and Culture*. New York: Routledge. 193–205.
Kolocotroni, Vassiliki (2006) "1899, Vienna and the Congo: The Art of Darkness." In Brian McHale and Randall Stevenson, eds., *The Edinburgh Companion to Twentieth-Century Literatures in English*. Edinburgh: Edinburgh University Press. 11–22.
Kosuth, Joseph (1999) "Art After Philosophy." In Alexander Alberro and Blake Stimson, eds., *Conceptual Art: A Critical Anthology*. Cambridge, MA: MIT Press. 158–77.
Kostelanetz, Richard (2003) *SoHo: The Rise and Fall of an Artists' Colony*. New York: Routledge.
Krafft, John M. (2012) "Biographical Note." In Inger H. Dalsgaard, Luc Herman and Brian McHale, eds., *The Cambridge Companion to Thomas Pynchon*. Cambridge: Cambridge University Press. 9–16.
Kurlansky, Mark (2004) *1968: The Year That Rocked the World*. New York: Ballantine.
Kushner, Tony (1995) *Angels in America: A Gay Fantasia on National Themes*. New York: Theatre Communications Group.
Landow, George P. (1992) *Hypertext*, Baltimore, MD: The Johns Hopkins University Press.
(1997) *Hypertext 2.0*, Baltimore, MD: The Johns Hopkins University Press.
Lather, Patti and Chris Smithies (1997) *Troubling the Angels: Women Living with HIV/AIDS*. Boulder, CO: Westview Press.
Laurence, Peter L. (2006) "Contradictions and Complexities: Jane Jacob's and Robert Venturi's Complexity Theories." In George Dodds and Kazys Varnelis, eds. *1966: Forty Years After*. Special issue, *Journal of Architectural Education* 59: 3, 49–60.

Lears, T. J. Jackson (1983) "From Salvation to Self-Realization: Advertising and the Therapeutic Roots of the Consumer Culture, 1880–1930." In Richard Wrightman and T. J. Jackson Lears, eds., *The Culture of Consumption: Critical Essays on American History, 1880–1980.* New York: Pantheon. 1–38.

LeBlanc, Jim (2002) "Premature Turns: Thematic Disruption in the American Version of Revolver." In Russell Reising, ed. *"Every Sound There Is": The Beatles' "Revolver" and the Transformation of Rock and Roll.* Aldershot: Ashgate. 194–205.

LeClair, Tom (1996) "The Prodigious Fiction of Richard Powers, William Vollmann, and David Foster Wallace," *Critique* 88, 1: 12–37.

Lee, Benjamin (2012) "Spontaneity and Improvisation in Postwar Experimental Poetry." In Joe Bray, Alison Gibbons and Brian McHale, eds., *The Routledge Companion to Experimental Literature.* Abingdon, VA: Routledge. 75–88.

Lehman, David (1998) *The Last Avant-Garde: The Making of the New York School of Poets.* New York: Doubleday.

Levanto, Marjatta (1993) *Hugo Simberg: The Wounded Angel.* Helsinki: The Finnish National Gallery.

Levin, Harry (1960) "What Was Modernism?" *The Massachusetts Review* 1, 4: 609–30.

Lie, Nadie and Theo D'Haen (1997) *Constellation Caliban: Figurations of a Character.* Amsterdam: Rodopi.

Ling, Rich and Jonathan Donner (2009) *Mobile Communication.* Cambridge, UK: Polity Press.

Lingwood, James (2011) "The Weight of Time" [2002]. In Brian Dillon, ed. *Ruins. Documents of Contemporary Art.* London: Whitechapel Gallery/ Cambridge, MA: MIT Press. 109–18.

Lippard, Lucy (1997) *Six Years: The Dematerialization of the Art Object from 1966 to 1972.* Berkeley: University of California Press..

LIU Kang (2004) *Globalization and Cultural Trends in China.* Honolulu: University of Hawai'i Press.

Lobsinger, Mary Louise (2006) "The New Urban Scale in Italy: On Aldo Rossi's *L'architettura della città.*" In George Dodds and Kazys Varnelis, eds. *1966: Forty Years After.* Special issue, *Journal of Architectural Education* 59:3, 28–38.

Lotringer, Sylvère (2003) "Better than life. (My '80s)," *Artforum International*, 41, 8:194.

Lowenstein, Roger (2004) *Origins of the Crash: The Great Bubble and Its Undoing.* New York: Penguin.

Lyotard, Jean-François (1984) *The Postmodern Condition: A Report on Knowledge.* Trans. by Geoff Bennington and Brian Massumi. Minneapolis, MN: University of Minnesota Press.

 (1993) "Answer to the Question, What Is the Postmodern?" In *The Postmodern Explained: Correspondence, 1982–1985.* Translation edited by Julian Pefanis and Morgan Thomas. Minneapolis, MN: University of Minnesota Press. 1–16.

Mack, John E. (1994) *Abduction: Human Encounters with Aliens*. New York: Scribner's.

Mackey, Louis (1997) *Fact, Fiction and Representation: Four Novels by Gilbert Sorrentino*. Columbia, SC: Camden House.

Macksey, Richard and Eugenio Donato, eds. (1972) *The Structuralist Controversy: The Languages of Criticism and the Sciences of Man*. Baltimore, MD: Johns Hopkins University Press.

Marantz, Andrew (2013) "Unreality Star," *The New Yorker Magazine*, 16 September. 32–7.

Marcus, Greil (1989) *Lipstick Traces: A Secret History of the Twentieth Century*. Cambridge, MA: Harvard University Press.

(1997) *Invisible Republic: Bob Dylan's Basement Tapes*. New York: Holt.

Marqusee, Mike (2003) *Chimes of Freedom: The Politics of Bob Dylan's Art*. New York: New Press.

Marx-Scouras, Danielle (2012) "The Nouveau Roman and Tel Quel." In Joe Bray, Alison Gibbons and Brian McHale, eds., *The Routledge Companion to Experimental Literature*. Abingdon, VA: Routledge. 89–100.

Mathews, Harry (1986) "Mathews's Algorithm." In Warren F. Motte, Jr., ed., *Oulipo: A Primer of Potential Literature*. Lincoln: University of Nebraska Press. 126–39.

Mathews, Harry and Alastair Brotchie, eds. (1998) *Oulipo Compendium*. London: Atlas Press.

McCaffery, Larry (1995) "Avant-Pop: Still Life After Yesterday's Crash." In Larry McCaffery, ed., *After Yesterday's Crash: The Avant-Pop Anthology*. New York: Penguin. xi–xxix.

McHale, Brian (1987) *Postmodernist Fiction*. London and New York: Methuen.

(1992) *Constructing Postmodernism*. London and New York: Routledge.

(1998) "Gravity's Angels in America, or, Pynchon's Angelology Revisited," *Pynchon Notes* 42–43: 303–16.

(2000a) "Mason & Dixon in the Zone, or, A Brief Poetics of Pynchon-Space." In Brooke Horvath and Irving Malin, eds., *Pynchon & Mason & Dixon*, Cranbury, NJ: Associated University Press/University of Delaware Press, 43–62.

(2000b) "Poetry as Prosthesis," *Poetics Today* 21, 1: 1–32.

(2000c) "Telling Stories Again: On the Replenishment of Narrative in the Postmodernist Long Poem," *The Yearbook of English Studies*, 30, 250–62.

(2001) "Weak Narrativity: The Case of Avant-Garde Narrative Poetry," *Narrative* 9:2, 161–67.

(2003) "'A Poet May Not Exist': Mock-Hoaxes and the Construction of National Identity." In Robert J. Griffin, ed. *The Faces of Anonymity: Anonymous and Pseudonymous Publication from the*

Sixteenth to the Twentieth Century. New York: Palgrave Macmillan. 233–52.

(2004a) "Mech/Shaper, or, Varieties of Prosthetic Fiction: Mathews, Sorrentino, Acker, and Others." In Peter Freese and Charles B. Harris, eds., *The Holodeck in the Garden: Science and Technology in Contemporary American Fiction*. Normal, IL: Dalkey Archive. 143–62.

(2004b) *The Obligation toward the Difficult Whole: Postmodernist Long Poems*. Tuscaloosa, AL: University of Alabama Press.

(2005) "Poetry under Erasure." In Eve Müller-Zettelman and Margarete Rubik, eds., *Theory into Poetry: New Approaches to the Lyric*. Amsterdam: Rodopi. 277–301.

(2007) "*En Abyme*: Internal models and cognitive mapping." In John Gibson, Wolfgang Huemer and Luca Pocci, eds., *A Sense of the World: Essays on Fiction, Narrative, and Knowledge*. New York: Routledge. 189–205.

(2008) "1966 Nervous Breakdown, or, When Did Postmodernism Begin?" *Modern Language Quarterly* 69, 3: 391–413.

(2011) "A Narrative Poetics of Raymond Federman." In Jeffrey Di Leo, ed., *Federman's Fictions: Innovation, Theory, and the Holocaust*. Albany: SUNY Press. 93–107.

(2012a) "Postmodernism and Experiment." In Joe Bray, Alison Gibbons and Brian McHale, eds., *The Routledge Companion to Experimental Literature*. London: Routledge. 141–53.

(2012b) "The Yasusada Notebooks and the Figure of the Ruined Text." In Bill Freind, ed., *Scubadivers and Chrysanthemums: Essays on the Poetry of Araki Yasusada*. Bristol, UK: Shearsman Books. 86–106.

McLaughlin, Robert McLaughlin, Robert J. (1988) "Pynchon's Angels and Supernatural Systems in *Gravity's Rainbow*," *Pynchon Notes* 22–23:25–33.

(2008) "Post-postmodern Discontent: Contemporary Fiction and the Social World." In R.M. Berry and Jeffrey R. Di Leo, eds., *Fiction's Present: Situating Contemporary Narrative Innovation*. Albany: SUNY Press. 101–17.

(2012) "Post-Postmodernism." In Joe Bray, Alison Gibbons and Brian McHale, eds., *The Routledge Companion to Experimental Literature*. Abingdon, VA Routledge. 141–53.

Melville, Stephen (2004) "Postmodernism and Art: Postmodernism Now and Again." In Steven Connor, ed., *The Cambridge Companion to Postmodernism*. Cambridge, UK: Cambridge University Press. 82–96.

Mepham, John (1991) "Narratives of Postmodernism." In Edmund J. Smyth, ed., *Postmodernism and Contemporary Fiction*. London: Batsford. 138–55.

Mercer, David (2006) *The Telephone: The Life Story of a Technology*. Westport, CT: Greenwood Press.

Merivale, Patricia and Susan Elizabeth Sweeney, eds (1999) *Detecting Texts: The Metaphysical Detective Story from Poe to Postmodernism*. Philadelphia, PA: University of Pennsylvania Press.

Miller, Tyrus (2009) *Singular Examples: Artistic Politics and the Neo-Avant-Garde*. Evanston, IL: Northwestern University Press.

(2012) "*Lettrism and Situationism.*" In Joe Bray, Alison Gibbons and Brian McHale, eds., *The Routledge Companion to Experimental Literature*. London: Routledge. 101–14.

Molesworth, Helen (2012) "This Will Have Been: Art, Love and Politics in the 1980s." In Helen Molesworth, ed., *This Will Have Been: Art, Love and Politics in the 1980s*. Chicago, IL: Museum of Contemporary Art/New Haven: Yale University Press. 14–46.

Montfort, Nick (2004) "Interactive Fiction as 'Story,' 'Game,' 'Storygame,' 'Novel,' 'World,' 'Literature,' 'Puzzle,' 'Problem,' 'Riddle,' and 'Machine.'" In Noah Wardrip-Fruin and Patt Harrigan, eds., *First Person: New Media as Story, Performance, and Game*. Cambridge, MA: MIT Press. 310–17.

Moore, Steven (1986) "Alexander Theroux's *Darconville's Cat* and the Tradition of Learnéd Wit," *Contemporary Literature* 27, 2: 233–45.

(2010) *The Novel: An Alternative History. Beginnings to 1600*. New York: Continuum.

(2013) *The Novel: An Alternative History. 1600–1800*. New York: Bloomsbury.

Moraru, Christian (2001) *Rewriting: Postmodern Narrative and Cultural Critique in the Age of Cloning*. Albany: SUNY Press.

(2011) *Cosmodernism: American Narrative, Late Globalization, and the New Cultural Imaginary*. Ann Arbor: University of Michigan Press.

Morgan, Matthew J., ed. (2009) *The Impact of 9/11 on the Media, Arts, and Entertainment: The Day That Changed Everything?* New York: Palgrave Macmillan. 2009.

Motte, Warren F., Jr., trans. and ed. (1986) *Oulipo: A Primer of Potential Literature*. Lincoln, NE: University of Nebraska Press.

Murphy, Graham J. and Sherryl Vint, eds. (2010) *Beyond Cyberpunk: New Critical Perspectives*. New York: Routledge.

Murphy, Patrick (2001) "Interpreting *The Tempest*." In Patrick Murphy, ed., *The Tempest: Critical Essays*. New York: Routledge. 3–11.

Nair, Supriya (1996) *Caliban's Curse: George Lamming and the Revisioning of History*. Ann Arbor, MI: University of Michigan Press.

Nealon, Jeffrey (2012) *Post-Postmodernism or, The Cultural Logic of Just-in-Time Capitalism*. Stanford, CA: Stanford University Press.

Newman, James (2008) *Playing with Videogames*. London: Routledge.

Newton, Adam Zachary (1995) *Narrative Ethics*. Cambridge, MA: Harvard University Press.

Nixon, Rob (1987) "Caribbean and African Appropriations of The Tempest." In Robert von Hallberg, ed., *Politics and Poetic Value*. Chicago, IL: University of Chicago Press. 185–206.

Norden, Linda (2007) "Show and Hide: Reading Sarah Sze." In *Sarah Sze*. New York: Abrams. 8–13.

Nussbaum, Martha (1990) *Love's Knowledge: Essays on Philosophy and Literature*. New York: Oxford University Press.

Orgel, Stephen (1987) "Introduction." In William Shakespeare, *The Tempest*, ed. Stephen Orgel. Oxford: Oxford University Press.

Ortega, Julio (1997) "Postmodernism in Spanish-American Writing." In Hans Bertens and Douwe Fokkema, eds., *International Postmodernism: Theory and Literary Practice*. Amsterdam: John Benjamins. 315–26.

O'Shea, Edward (2001) "Modernist Versions of *The Tempest*." In Patrick Murphy, ed., *The Tempest: Critical Essays*. New York: Routledge. 543–59.

Oxoby, Marc (2003) *The 1990s*. Westport, CT: Greenwood Press.

Paperny, Vladimir (2010) "Modernism and Destruction in Architecture." In Julia Hell and Andreas Schönle, eds., *Ruins of Modernity*. Durham, NC: Duke University Press. 41–57.

Pearce, Celia (2004) "Towards a Game Theory of Game." In Noah Wardrip-Fruin and Pat Harrigan, eds., *First Person: New Media as Story, Performance, and Game*. Cambridge, MA: MIT Press. 143–53.

Peebles, Curtis (1994) *Watch the Skies! A Chronicle of the Flying Saucer Myth*. Washington, DC: Smithsonian Institution Press.

Perelman, Bob (1981) *Primer*. Berkeley, CA: This Press.

(1996) *The Marginalization of Poetry: Language Writing and Literary History*. Princeton, NJ: Princeton University Press.

Perloff, Marjorie (1986) *The Futurist Moment: Avant-Garde, Avant Guerre, and the Language of Rupture*. Chicago, IL: University of Chicago Press.

(1991) "The Return of the (Numerical) Repressed: From Free Verse to Procedural Play." In *Radical Artifice: Writing Poetry in the Age of Media*. Chicago, IL: University of Chicago Press. 134–70.

(2002) *21st-Century Modernism: The "New" Poetics*. Malden, MA: Blackwell.

(2010) *Unoriginal Genius: Poetry by Other Means in the New Century*. Chicago, IL: University of Chicago Press.

Perry, Ellwood C., III (1988) *The Art of Thomas Cole: Ambition and Imagination*. Newark, DE: University of Delaware Press/London and Toronto: Associated University Presses.

Phelan, James (1996) *Narrative as Rhetoric: Technique, Audiences, Ethics, Ideology*. Columbus, OH: Ohio State University Press.

Pipes, Daniel (1990) *The Rushdie Affair: The Novel, the Ayatollah, and the West*. New York: Carol Publishing Group.

Poster, Mark (1999) "Theorizing Virtual Reality: Baudrillard and Derrida." In Marie-Laure Ryan, ed., *Cyberspace Textuality: Computer Technology and Literary Theory*. Bloomington, IN: Indiana University Press. 42–60.

Potter, Russell A. (1995) *Spectacular Vernaculars: Hip-Hop and the Politics of Postmodernism*. Albany, NY: SUNY Press.

Powers, Richard (2001) *Plowing the Dark*. New York: Picador USA.

Pressner, Todd Samuel (2010) "Hegel's Philosophy of World History via Sebald's Imaginary of Ruins: A Contrapuntal Critique of the 'New Space' of Modernity." In Julia Hell and Andreas Schönle, eds., *Ruins of Modernity*. Durham, NC: Duke University Press. 193–211.

Puff, Helmut (2010) "Ruins as Models: Displaying Destruction in Postwar Germany." In Julia Hell and Andreas Schönle, eds., *Ruins of Modernity*. Durham, NC: Duke University Press. 266–69.

Pynchon, Thomas (1967) *The Crying of Lot 49*. New York: Bantam. 1966.
(1973) *Gravity's Rainbow*. New York: Viking.
(2006) *Against the Day*. New York: Penguin.

Readings, Bill and Bennet Schaber, eds (1993) *Postmodernism Across the Ages: Essays for a Postmodernity That Wasn't Born Yesterday*. Syracuse, NY: Syracuse University Press.

Reising, Russell (2002) "'It Is Not Dying': *Revolver* and the Birth of Psychedelic Sound." In Russell Reising, ed., *"Every Sound There Is": The Beatles' "Revolver" and the Transformation of Rock and Roll*. Aldershot: Ashgate. 234–53.

Richter, David H. (1997) "The Mirrored World: Form and Ideology in Umberto Eco's The Name of the Rose." In Rocco Capozzi, ed., *Reading Eco: An Anthology* Bloomington, IN: Indiana University Press. 256–75.

Rodgers, Daniel T. (2011) *Age of Fracture*. Cambridge, MA: Harvard University Press.

Rohter, Larry (2010) "Drinking Blood: New Wonders of Alice's World," *New York Times*, 28 February, AR12+.

Rose, Barbara (2002) "The Return of Painting." In Paul F. Fabozzi, ed., *Artists, Critics, Context: Readings in and Around American Art since 1945*. Upper Saddle River, NJ: Prentice. 380–414. 1980.

Rose, Tricia (1994) *Black Noise: Rap Music and Black Culture in Contemporary America*. Hanover, NH: Wesleyan University Press/University Press of New England.

Rothberg, Michael (2012) "Progress, Progression, Procession: William Kentridge and the Narratology of Transitional Justice," *Narrative* 20, 1: 1–24.

Round, Julia (2013) "Anglo-American Graphic Narrative." In Daniel Stein and Jan-Noel Thon, eds., *From Comic Strips to Graphic Novels: Contributions to the Theory and History of Graphic Narrative*. Berlin: DeGruyter. 325–45.

Rushdie, Salman (1989) "An Interview with Catherine Bush," *Conjunctions* 14: 7–20.

Rushkoff, Douglas (2002) "Playing with Fractals." In *Sarah Sze*. Annandale-on-Hudson, NY: Center for Curatorial Studies, Bard College. 47–54.

Ryan, Marie-Laure (1999) "Cyberspace, Virtuality, and the Text." In Marie-Laure Ryan, ed., *Cyberspace Textuality: Computer Technology and Literary Theory*. Bloomington, IN: Indiana University Press. 78–107.

Sabin, Roger (1993) *Adult Comics: An Introduction*. London: Routledge.

Saldívar, Ramon (2011) "Historical Fantasy, Speculative Realism, and Postrace Aesthetics in Contemporary American Fiction," *American Literary History* 23, 3: 574–99.

(2013) "The Second Elevation of the Novel: Race, Form and the Postrace Aesthetic in Contemporary Narrative," *Narrative* 21, 1: 1–18.

Sandler, Irving (1996) *Art of the Postmodern Era: From the Late 1960s to the Early 1990s.* New York: Harper Collins.

Savran, David (1997) "Ambivalence, Utopia, and a Queer Sort of Materialism." In Deborah R. Geis and Steven F. Kruger, eds., *Approaching the Millennium: Essays on Angels in America.* Ann Arbor, MI: University of Michigan Press. 13–39.

Schor, Hilary M. (2013) *Curious Subjects: Women and the Trials of Realism.* New York: Oxford University Press.

Scott, A.O. (2000) "The Panic of Influence, *New York Review of Books* 47:2 (10 February). http://www.nybooks.com/articles/archives/2000/feb/10/the-panic-of-influence

Sebald, W.G. (2003) "Air War and Literature: Zürich Lectures." *In on the Natural History of Destruction.* Trans. Arthur Bell. New York: Random House. 1–104. 1999

Serres, Michel (1995) *Angels: A Modern Myth.* Trans. Francis Cowper. Paris: Flammarion. 1993.

Shaman, Sanford Sivitz (1989) *Robert Yarber Paintings: 1980–88.* University Park, PA: Palmer Museum of Art, The Pennsylvania State University.

Shklovsky, Viktor (1990) *Theory of Prose.* Trans. Benjamin Sher. Normal, IL: Dalkey Archive Press. 1929.

Showalter, Elaine (1991) "Miranda's Story." In *Sister's Choice: Tradition and Change in American Women's Writing.* Oxford: Oxford University Press.

Shteyngart, Gary (2013) "O.K., Glass," *The New Yorker Magazine,* 5 August. 32–7.

Siegle, Robert (1989) *Suburban Ambush: Downtown Writing and the Fiction of Insurgency.* Baltimore, MD: Johns Hopkins University Press.

Sigler, Carolyn, ed. (1997) *Alternative Alices: Visions and Revisions of Lewis Carroll's* Alice Books. Lexington, KY: University Press of Kentucky.

Silliman, Ron (2008) *The Alphabet.* Tuscaloosa, AL: University of Alabama Press.

Sinclair, Iain (2011) "Lights Out for the Territory." In Brian Dillon, ed. *Ruins. Documents of Contemporary Art.* London: Whitechapel Gallery/ Cambridge, MA: MIT Press. 156–58. 1997

Smith, Terry (2011) *Contemporary Art: World Currents.* Upper Saddle River, NJ: Prentice Hall.

(2009) *What Is Contemporary Art?* Chicago, IL: University of Chicago Press.

Solnit, Rebecca (2011) "The Ruins of Memory." In Brian Dillon, ed. *Ruins. Documents of Contemporary Art.* London: Whitechapel Gallery/ Cambridge, MA: MIT Press. 150–52. 2007.

Spector, Nancy (2003) "Only the Perverse Fantasy Can Still Save Us." In Nancy Spector, ed., *Matthew Barney: The Cremaster Cycle.* New York: Guggenheim Museum Publications. 3–91.

Spivak, Giyatri Chakravorty (2003) *Death of a Discipline*. New York: Columbia University Press.

Stallabrass, Julian (1999) *High Art Lite: British Art in the 1990s*. London: Verso.

Stansbaugh, John (2007) "From Wise Guys to Woo-Girls." In Marshall Berman and Brian Berger, eds., *New York Calling: From Blackout to Bloomberg*. London: Reaktion Books. 53–61.

Stansky, Peter (1996) *On or about December 1910: Early Bloomsbury and Its Intimate World*. Cambridge, MA: Harvard University Press.

Steiner, Hadas S. (2006) "Brutalism Exposed: Photography and the Zoom Wave." In George Dodds and Kazys Varnelis, eds, *1966: Forty Years After*. Special issue, *Journal of Architectural Education* 59:3, 15–27.

Steinmetz, George (2010) "Colonial Melancholy and Fordist Nostalgia: The ruinscapes of Namibia and Detroit." In Julia Hell and Andreas Schönle, eds., *Ruins of Modernity*. Durham, NC: Duke University Press. 294–320.

Sterling, Bruce (1996) "Twenty Evocations." In *Schismatrix Plus*. New York: Ace. 313–19.

Stevenson, Randall (2006) "1916, Flanders, London, Dublin: 'Everything Has Gone Well.'" In Brian McHale and Randall Stevenson, eds. *The Edinburgh Companion to Twentieth-Century Literatures in English*. Edinburgh: Edinburgh University Press. 35–47.

Stosuy, Brandon, ed. (2006) *Up Is Up but So Is Down: New York's Downtown Literary Scene, 1974–1992*. New York: NYU Press.

Strongman, Phil (2007) *Pretty Vacant: A History of Punk*. London: Orion Books.

Tatsumi, Takayuki (2006) *Full Metal Apache: Transactions between Cyberpunk Japan and Avant-Pop America*. Durham, NC: Duke University Press.

(2013) "Planet of the Frogs: Thoreau, Anderson, and Murakami," *Narrative* 21, 3: 346–56.

Thompson, Keith (1991) *Angels and Aliens: UFOs and the Mythic Imagination*. Reading, MA: Addison-Wesley.

Tomasula, Steve (2012) "Code Poetry and New-Media Literature." In Joe Bray, Alison Gibbons and Brian McHale, eds., *The Routledge Companion to Experimental Literature*. Abingdon, VA: Routledge. 483–96.

Tomberg, Jaak (2013) "On the 'Double Vision' of Realism and SF Estrangement in William Gibson's Bigend Trilogy," *Science Fiction Studies* 40, 2: 263–85.

Torpey, Maureen (2009) "Winterson's Wonderland: *The PowerBook* as a Postmodern Re-Vision of Lewis Carroll's Alice Books." In Susan Redington Bobby, ed., *Fairy Tales Reimagined: Essays on New Retellings*. Jefferson, NC: McFarland. 111–21.

Tynjanov, Jurij (2000). "The Literary Fact." In David Duff, ed. *Modern Genre Theory*. Harlow, UK: Longman. 29–49.

Venkatasawmy, Rama (2013) *The Digitization of Cinematic Visual Effects: Hollywood's Coming of Age*. Lanham, MD: Lexington Books. E-book.

Vergara, Camilo José (1995) *The New American Ghetto*. New Brunswick, NJ: Rutgers University Press.

Vergara, Camilo José (1999) *American Ruins*. New York: The Monacelli Press.

Varnedoe, Kirk and Adam Gopnik (1990) *High & Low: Modern Art & Popular Culture*. New York: Museum of Modern Art.

Vaughan, Alden T. (1998) "Caliban in the 'Third World': Shakespeare's Savage as Sociopolitical Symbol." In Virginia Mason Vaughan and Alden T. Vaughan, eds., *Critical Essays on Shakespeare's The Tempest*. New York: G.K. Hall. 247–66.

Venturi, Robert (1977) *Complexity and Contradiction in Architecture*, 2nd ed. New York: Museum of Modern Art.

Vidler, Anthony (2010) "Air War and Architecture." In Julia Hell and Andreas Schönle, eds., *Ruins of Modernity*. Durham: Duke University Press. 29–40.

Wallace, David Foster (1996) *Infinite Jest*. Boston, MA: Little, Brown.

(1997) "E Unibus Pluram." In *A Supposedly Fun Thing I'll Never Do Again: Essays and Arguments*. Boston, MA: Little, Brown. 21–82.1993

Wallace, Mark and Steven Marks, eds. (2002) *Telling It Slant: Avant-Garde Poetics of the 1990s*. Tuscaloosa, AL: University of Alabama Press.

WANG Ning (1997) "The Reception of Postmodernism in China: The Case of Avant-Garde Fiction." In Hans Bertens and Douwe Fokkema, eds., *International Postmodernism: Theory and Literary Practice*. Amsterdam: John Benjamins. 499–510.

(2010) *Translated Modernities: Literary and Cultural Perspectives on Globalization and China*. New York: LEGAS.

(2013) "A Reflection on Postmodernist Fiction in China: Avant-Garde Narrative Experiment," *Narrative* 21, 3: 296–308.

Ward, Geoff (1993) *Statutes of Liberty: The New York School of Poetry*. New York: St. Martin's Press.

Warhol, Andy and Pat Hackett (1990) *Popism: The Warhol '60s*, New York: Harcourt Brace Jovanovich.

Warhol, Robyn (2013) "Neon Bones." Unpublished conference paper. ASAP/5, Wayne State University, Detroit, MI: 5 October.

Watten, Barrett (2003) *The Constructivist Moment: From Material Text to Cultural Poetics*. Middletown, CT: Wesleyan University Press.

Wegner, Phillip E. (2009) *Life Between Two Deaths, 1989–2001: U.S. Culture in the Long Nineties*. Durham, NC: Duke University Press.

Weinstein, Philip (2005) *Unknowing: The Work of Modernist Fiction*. Ithaca, NY: Cornell University Press.

Whitehead, Colson (2011) *Zone One*. New York: Doubleday.

Wiegand, Krista E. (2009) "Islamic Terrorism: The Red Menace of the Twenty-First Century." In Matthew J. Morgan, ed., *The Impact of 9/11 on the Media, Arts, and Entertainment: The Day That Changed Everything?* New York: Palgrave Macmillan. 51–61.

Wigley, Mark (1993) *The Architecture of Deconstruction: Derrida's Haunt*. Cambridge, MA and London: MIT Press.

Williams, Gilda (2011) "It Was What It Was: Modern Ruins." In Brian Dillon, ed. *Ruins. Documents of Contemporary Art.* London: Whitechapel Gallery/ Cambridge, MA: MIT Press. 94–99.

Williams, Raymond (1974) *Television: Technology and Cultural Form.* New York: Schocken.

Wilson, Peter Lamborn (1980) *Angels.* New York: Pantheon Books.

Wilton, Andrew (2002) "The Sublime in the Old World and the New." In Andrew Wilton and Tim Barringer, eds., *American Sublime: Landscape Painting in the United States, 1820–1880.* Princeton, NJ: Princeton University Press. 10–37.

Wines, James (1987) *De-Architecture.* New York: Rizzoli.

Wolfe, Tom and E.W. Johnson, eds. (1973) *The New Journalism.* New York: Harper and Row.

Woodward, Christopher (2001) *In Ruins.* New York: Pantheon.

Young, James E. (1993) *The Texture of Memory: Holocaust Memorials and Meaning.* New Haven, CT: Yale University Press.

Zabus, Chantal (2002) *Tempests after Shakespeare.* New York: Palgrave.

Zucker, Paul (1961) "Ruins – An Aesthetic Hybrid," *Journal of Aesthetics and Art Criticism* 20, 2: 119–30.

Index

Cambridge Introductions to Literature

Authors

Margaret Atwood   Heidi Macpherson

Jane Austen   Janet Todd

Samuel Beckett   Ronan McDonald

Walter Benjamin   David Ferris

Lord Byron   Richard Lansdown

Chekhov   James N. Loehlin

J. M. Coetzee   Dominic Head

Samuel Taylor Coleridge   John Worthen

Joseph Conrad   John Peters

Jacques Derrida   Leslie Hill

Charles Dickens   Jon Mee

Emily Dickinson   Wendy Martin

George Eliot   Nancy Henry

T. S. Eliot   John Xiros Cooper

William Faulkner   Theresa M. Towner

F. Scott Fitzgerald   Kirk Curnutt

Michel Foucault   Lisa Downing

Robert Frost   Robert Faggen

Gabriel Garcia Marquez   Gerald Martin

Nathaniel Hawthorne   Leland S. Person

Zora Neale Hurston   Lovalerie King

James Joyce   Eric Bulson

Thomas Mann   Todd Kontje

Christopher Marlowe   Tom Rutter

Herman Melville   Kevin J. Hayes

Milton   Stephen B. Dobranski

Toni Morrison   Tessa Roynon

George Orwell   John Rodden and John Rossi

Sylvia Plath   Jo Gill

Edgar Allan Poe   Benjamin F. Fisher

Ezra Pound   Ira Nadel

Marcel Proust   Adam Watt

Jean Rhys   Elaine Savory

Edward Said   Conor McCarthy

Shakespeare   Emma Smith

Shakespeare's Comedies   Penny Gay

Shakespeare's History Plays   Warren Chernaik

Shakespeare's Poetry   Michael Schoenfeldt

Shakespeare's Tragedies   Janette Dillon

Harriet Beecher Stowe   Sarah Robbins

Mark Twain   Peter Messent

Edith Wharton   Pamela Knights

Walt Whitman   M. Jimmie Killingsworth

Virginia Woolf   Jane Goldman

William Wordsworth   Emma Mason

W. B. Yeats   David Holdeman

Topics

American Literary Realism   Phillip Barrish

The American Short Story   Martin Scofield

Anglo-Saxon Literature   Hugh Magennis

Comedy   Eric Weitz

Creative Writing   David Morley

Early English Theatre   Janette Dillon

The Eighteenth-Century Novel   April London

28294086R00151

Printed in Great Britain
by Amazon